to Dan & Carolyn
for your dreams
Michael &
Edi

Carefree on the European Canals

Michael Walsh

Carefree on the European Canals

Copyright © 2014 by Michael Walsh

Cover by Edi Gelin & Michael Walsh

ISBN: 978-0-9919556-4-0

Published by Zonder Zorg Press

www.zonderzorg.ca
michael@zonderzorg.ca

Printed in the United States of America
on Sustainable Forestry Initiative® (SFI®) Certified Sourcing papers

Contents

Acknowledgements

Most of the photos in this book were shot by the author and his mate Edi Gelin. Many of the maps in the book were prepared by the author using NASA satellite images. Older maps and images were found in the public domaine. The author is grateful for the following: The map of Chinese canals on page 3 created by Yug/Wikimedia Commons. Maps on pages 12, 13, 14, 132, 133 and 271 from the Voies Navigables de France (VNF) website. The map of the Belgian canals on page 14 from the Promotie Binnenvaart Vlaanderen website. The map of British waterways on page 15 from Canal & River Trust website. The bottom two photos on page 23 and the photos on pages 88, 89 and 90 were taken by the author of displays in the Fries Scheepvaart Museum, Sneek. The photo of the luxemotor on page 24 is taken of a model on display in Scheepvaartmuseum, Amsterdam. The photos of the Linssens on pages 26 and 29 are from the Linssen website. The photo at the top of page 30 is from the Aqualine website. The photo of Owlpen on page 31 is by Ad Meskens/Wikimedia Commons. The photo of La Cité on page 131 is by Jean-Pierre Lavoie/Wikimedia Commons. The maps on page 318 are by PinPin/Wikimedia Commons. The map on page 337 is from the City of Carcassonne website: www.carcassonne.org.

Throughout the book, screenshots of the TomTom© and Navionics© apps on the author's iPad are used to illustrate points in the narrative. They are meant as illustrations only and are not intended for navigation. Similarly, photos of selected portions of the Dutch ANWB charts, and the French Éditions de l'Écluse Fluviacarte and Éditions du Breil Guide Fluvial are used to illustrate the text and are not meant for navigation, but rather to illustrate their usefulness.

Introduction

This book begins with a brief outline of the history of inland navigation. The précis is more broadly international in its earlier overview, but it quickly narrows to focus on the waterways of Western Europe, and in particular those of France and the Netherlands, where most of the finest cruising is located. A section touches on some of the many types of boat that have used these waterways through the centuries and how they were used. There is a brief examination of the backgrounds of the most suitable ex-commercial barges for conversion to liveaboard cruising.

There is some discussion of other types of boat that are suitable for cruising the European waterways, such as modern motor cruisers and replicas of classic barge designs. Considerable hands-on detail and insights are given in the search, selection, survey, purchase and conversion of a classic Dutch barge.

The meat of the book; however, is in the sections dealing with the actual cruising through the Netherlands, Belgium and France. Here will be found both overviews and details on the broad variety of cruising waters. These sections often read like a log of selected portions of our travels to give the reader a flavour of what it is like cruising these waters. These are not intended as a definitive guides, but rather as sketches of some possibilities.

Michael Walsh
Vancouver, Canada
January 2014

Dedication

This book is for you, Edi. Your steady hand on the tiller,
both of Zonder Zorg and of our carefree course through life,
makes adventures like those described here not only possible,
but so much more enjoyable.

Chapter One

Some Historical Context

Across Europe there is a complex network of waterways. The ocean and seas surrounding the continent are interconnected by a web of canals linking rivers and lakes to each other, enabling navigation far inland. There are hundreds of canals and today it is possible to cross Europe by boat from the North Sea to the Mediterranean, from the Irish Sea to the Black Sea, from the Mediterranean to the Atlantic.

The use of oceans, seas, lakes and rivers to transport goods pre-dates recorded history. As civilization expanded, communities were established on the coasts and along rivers that were suitable for navigation. Settlements extended up the rivers to the first cataracts, which became barriers to further water transport, requiring goods to be offloaded and carried overland. The oldest known navigational canal is the one that was built approximately 2300 BC to bypass the First Cataract of the Nile at Aswan. Egypt then expanded up river.

In China, canals had been built to tame rivers for navigation during the era of the Warring States, 481-221 BC and during the following centuries, many more canals were built. In 609 AD the Grand Canal of China was completed, and with a total length of 1794 kilometres, it is still the longest in the world. It incorporated and linked several older works, the oldest of these dating back to 486 BC.

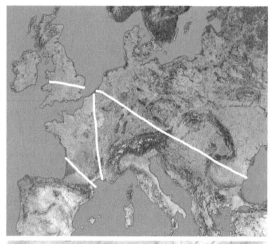

3

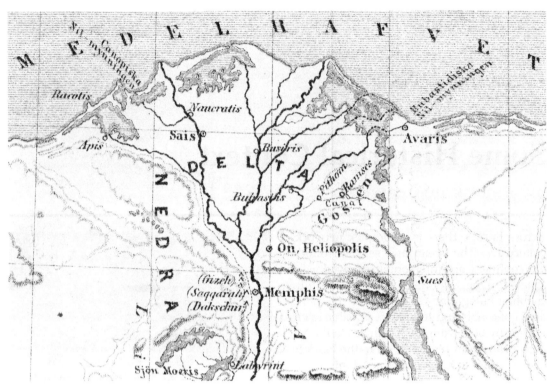

The first recorded use of canal locks was in the Canal of the Pharaohs, the first Suez Canal. The canal had been started in the late sixth century BC, linking the Red Sea to the Nile, but it is thought to have remained unfinished until the third century BC when Greek engineers under Ptolemy II devised flash locks to deal with the height differences between the sea and the river. With a flash lock, as the gates are opened, a barge flows through the gap in the weir with the current. Moving upstream against the current requires much more time and effort and spills much more water downstream.

The Romans built many canals, mainly for drainage, irrigation or water supply; however, several were for transportation. In the late first century BC, Fossa Augusta was built to link Ravenna to the Po estuary. Also in the first century BC, in Gaul they linked Narbonne to the Mediterranean and dug canals around Arles for military transport. In 12 BC, also for military purposes, they built Fossa Drusiana to link the Rijn to the Flevomeer, today's IJsselmeer in Friesland. In 47 AD Fossa Corbulonis, a 35-kilometre link was dug to join the Rijn and the Maas without having to go out into the Nordzee. In the early second century AD Trajan rerouted the Ancient Suez Canal and improved it.

The Foss Dyke in England is thought to have been built around 120 AD by the Romans to connect River Trent to Lincoln. It is likely the oldest canal in Europe that is still in use. It was refurbished in 1121 during the reign of Henry I.

During the Middle Ages the transport of goods inland by water cost a tiny fraction of transport overland. A pack horse or mule could carry an eighth of a ton over long distances and on a soft road it could pull a cart of little more than half a ton. The same animal could pull a load of thirty tons on a barge.

In Germany, the Fossa Carolina south of Nuremberg was begun in 793 under the orders of Charlemagne. He is said to have personally supervised the digging of a waterway between Treuchtlingen and Weißenburg, south of Nuremberg to cross the European Watershed and connect the basins of the Main/Rhine and the Danube. This was primarily to improve the transportation of goods between the Rhineland and Bavaria. Twelve hundred years later, after three re-routings, heavy ship traffic crosses this pass with huge cargos from the North Sea to the Black Sea.

Back in England, the Glastonbury Canal, built around the middle of the tenth century, is thought to be the first post-Roman canal in Britain. It was built to link the River Brue with Glastonbury Abbey, its initial purpose being to bring building stone for the abbey's construction. It later served for delivering produce from the abbey's outlying properties.

The first recorded use of a pound lock, or chamber lock was in 984 in China. To negotiate a steep decline, two flash locks were built within a short distance of each other. The engineer, Qiao Wei-yo realised he had just devised a system to allow boats to move upstream as easily as down. The pound lock is standard on all modern canals and uses gates at each end of the lock chamber to raise or lower the water taking boats to the level upstream or downstream.

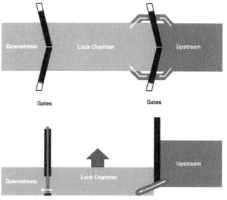

Leonardo da Vinci is credited with inventing miter gates in the late fifteenth century. This refinement uses the upstream water pressure to hold the gates tightly closed.

A Simple Pound Lock with Miter Gates

The first pound lock in Europe is believed to be the one built in 1373 in Vreeswijk, Netherlands where the Merwede Canal from Utrecht joins the River Lek. It was used to adjust for the different levels between the river and the canal. In the Netherlands, canal building was primarily done to drain the polders and create dry land, but in so doing, an extensive and efficient inland waterways network evolved and the ease of transportation spurred economic development.

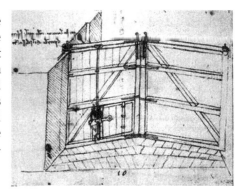

In more hilly topography than found in the Netherlands, navigation had been limited to the river valleys, either in the rivers themselves or in works constructed alongside to bypass steep sections. The first canal to break out of a river valley and head over a pass, in what is called a summit level canal, was the Grand Canal of China in the late sixth century AD. It used flash locks.

In Europe the first summit level canal was the Stecknitz Canal in Schleswig-Holstein, Germany in 1398. Using seventeen wooden-gated flash locks, it transited the thirteen-metre rise to the summit and back down the other side over a ninety-four kilometre length, connecting the watersheds of the Elbe and the Trave.

In the Netherlands, Amsterdam became increasingly prosperous and the Singel was completed in 1480 to encircle the medieval city. It served as transportation, and until 1585, as a protective moat. After 1585 the city expanded beyond it and the expansion soon came under the guidance of careful city planning. This called for four concentric semicircular canals with their ends leading to and from the IJ.

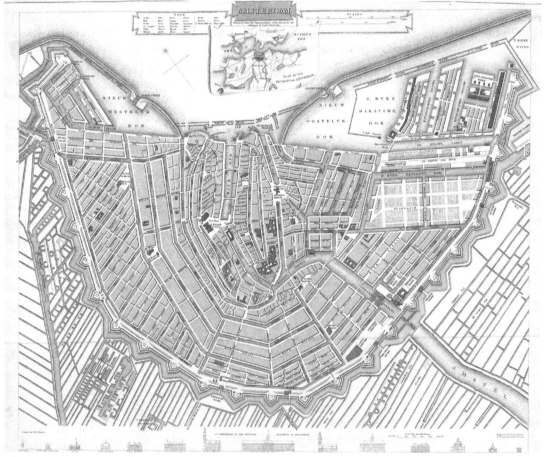

The urban plan was the largest and most homogeneous of its time; it became the model of large-scale town planning and served as a reference throughout the world for three centuries.

The planning was developed around the "grachtengordel", the canal girdle or belt. The three inner canals: Herengracht, Keizersgracht and Prinsengracht, were mostly for residential development and the outer canal, Singelgracht was for defence and water management. The plan also called for interconnecting canals along the radii, a set of parallel canals in one quarter mainly for transportation of goods, and the conversion of the existing moat, the Singel from defence to residential and commercial development. Construction was started in 1613 and today Amsterdam has more than 100 kilometres of canals and 1,281 bridges, making Venice with its mere 42 kilometres of canals and only 409 bridges, seem a poor imitation as the Amsterdam of Italy.

Much of the Netherlands lies on delta lands formed by two great rivers, the Rhine and the Meuse. The Rhine (Rhein, Rhin, Rijn in German, French and Dutch) flows over 1200 kilometres from the Swiss Alps to the North Sea. As it enters the Netherlands it splits into three main distributaries: the IJssel, the Nederrijn and the Waal and various other names that they are called as they flow toward the sea. The Meuse is 925 kilometres long and rises on le Plateau de Langres in France. It flows northward through France and Belgium into the Netherlands, where it follows a course very near the southern forks of the Rhine.

The slow currents in the various Rhine and Meuse branches provided excellent navigation and centuries of water management works by the Dutch have kept them as efficient and viable commercial waterways. With much of the Netherlands flat and less than a metre above sea level, canal building was easy and was greatly assisted by soft ground and an absence of bedrock. Canals were dug to expand commerce throughout the increasingly prosperous country.

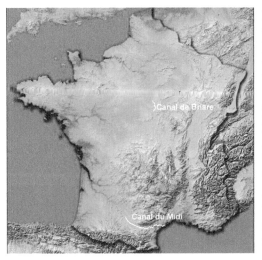

Elsewhere in Europe, the first summit canal to use pound locks was the Canal de Briare in France, completed in 1642 to connect the basins of the Loire and the Seine. In 1681 le canal royal du Languedoc was completed to connect Toulouse to the Mediterranean. It rises 189.4 metres through 74 locks over a distance of 183.5 kilometres to a 5 kilometre summit pound. From there it descends 57.18 metres through 17 locks in 51.6 kilometres to Toulouse and the junction with the River Garonne, which flows through Bordeaux to the Atlantic. Along its course it passes through the first canal tunnel in Europe and over three major aqueducts spanning river valleys. Canal construction had reached its maturity.

During the French Revolution in the late eighteenth century, the canal was renamed Canal du Midi. In listing it as a World Heritage Site, UNESCO called it: "one of the most remarkable feats of civil engineering in modern times".

The Industrial Revolution spurred a rapid expansion of canal networks across Europe. In Britain, the navigable waterways network grew to keep up with the increasing demand for industrial transportation. A system of large pack horse trains had developed, but few roads at the time could stand up to the heavy wheeled vehicles required to move large amounts of heavy materials. Canal boats were very much quicker, could carry large volumes, and were much safer for fragile items. As the canal network expanded, transportation of raw materials improved, prices fell and this continued to feed the rapid pace of the Industrial Revolution.

British inland navigations near their greatest extent in 1831

From the late eighteenth century, new designs and technology allowed canals to be improved. Where earlier canals had contoured around hills and valleys, later ones went straighter. Locks took canals up and down hills and longer and higher aqueducts spanned broader and deeper valleys. Longer and deeper tunnels pierced the ridges and passes. By the mid-nineteenth century, Britain had more than 7700 kilometres of inland waterways.

The first recorded canal in Belgium is one completed in 1270 between Gent and Damme. In the mid-sixteenth century there was a flurry of canal building in response to the closure of the Schelde downstream from Antwerp during the religious wars and after Netherlands independence. New canals had to be dug to move goods in and out of the Spanish Netherlands without going through the independent United Provinces. Major early projects were the Willebroek-Brussels canal, the Brugge-Oostende canal along the coast to France, and a new canal between Gent and Brugge. In the eighteenth and nineteenth centuries many new canals were built and old ones were upgraded.

In Germany, canal building progressed steadily during the seventeenth and eighteenth centuries. Three great rivers, the Elbe, the Oder and the Weser were linked by canals.

In the Netherlands the already huge canal infrastructure was improved and refined for transportation. The Bijlands Kanaal in Gelderland was dug between 1773 and 1776 as part of an extensive reconstruction works to better regulate water flow around the Rijn-Waal fork. It cut off a large bend in the Waal and today continues to be of enormous importance to Rhine navigation.

In France, canal building continued, with the Canal d'Orleans completed in 1692 to add another link between the Loire and Seine valleys. During the second half of the eighteenth century many canals were begun. In 1789 the Canal du Loing completed the link between the Loire and the Seine and in 1794 the Saône was linked to the Loire by completion of the Canal du Centre. The other works in progress were interrupted by the French Revolution and very little happened with them through the Napoleonic era.

With the Restoration after Napoleon's defeat, came a huge public works program. In 1820 François Becquey, Director of Bridges and Highways proposed an immense program of 126 canal and river improvement projects totalling over 25,000 kilometres. Many of these projects were discarded or postponed, but by 1822 Becquey had pushed bills through the French legislature authorizing the finance, construction and operation of ten new waterways. Another 2000 kilometres were built. By the time of the abdication of King Louis Philippe in 1848, France had more than 10,000 kilometres of navigable inland waterways. During the last third of the nineteenth century, another 3000 kilometres of canals were upgraded or completed and 4000 kilometres of rivers had improvements to navigation.

The Rivers of France

Among the major works: the Rhine and Saône were linked by a canal over the southern Vosges in 1834, the Seine and Saône were linked in 1842 by the Canal de Bourgogne, the Marne and Rhine were linked in 1853 over the northern Vosges, and in 1856 the Canal Lateral à la Garonne eased navigation from Toulouse to Bordeaux. Also constructed during the first half of the nineteenth century were canals leading northward into Germany, Belgium and the North Sea. A canal linking the Marne and the Saône was begun in 1870 and completed in 1907. At this point, the French network reached its greatest extent with 12,778 kilometres of navigable inland waterways.

From the mid-nineteenth century, the expanding railway network began replacing canals, especially the narrow ones in Britain. With their bridges and locks barely over two metres wide, their carrying capacity was severely restricted. As rail transportation became more advanced, land transportation became cheaper and faster than the narrow canal system. The improvement of road vehicles in the first third of the twentieth century dealt the final blow to the viability of the narrow canals. Many became unusable as they filled with weeds, silt and rubbish, or were filled-in and converted to railways or roads. Today about 3200 kilometres of the British canals remain navigable, just over 40% of total navigable length that existed in 1850.

In France, to deal with the decline in canal usage, the engineer, Charles-Louis Freycinet as Minister of Public Works in 1879 began a standardization of the waterway network that had been built over the previous three centuries. He saw that the large variety of lock dimensions was impeding efficient commerce, so he began a rebuilding project that by 1913 had refitted over 1500 kilometres of canals to standard dimensions. These have been called Gabarit Freycinet, the Freycinet Gauge and call for lock dimensions to handle barges with maximum dimensions of 38.50 meters length, 5.06 metres beam and 1.8 metres draft. Low bridges were rebuilt to allow for a minimum clearance of 3.5 metres.

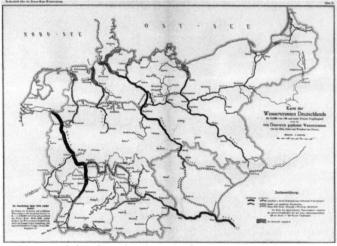

Inland navigations in Germany in 1903

Germany continued to build canals and improve river navigation. Between 1875 and 1914, the total length of navigable waterways in Germany doubled. The rapid industrialization and the dramatic economic growth in the last quarter of the nineteenth century brought an increased need for fast, dependable and inexpensive transportation. Improvements in their network of waterways allowed them to compete with the expanding railway network. Improvements such as the replacement of many small locks with fewer, but larger ones sped the traffic, as did the introduction of electric and steam power for towing rather than using horses. Unlike in Britain and France, in Germany the waterways and the railways worked together. At the turn of the twentieth century, 28 of the 41 larger ports on the Rhine were connected to railways.

Among the major works, were canals between the Rhine and the Dortmund-Ems Canal, between the Dortmund-Ems Canal and the Weser River, and between Berlin and Stettin. The Oder River was canalized between the Glatzer Neisse River and the city of Breslau. Canalization of the Moselle, the Lahn, and the Saar Rivers were commenced and the Württemberg government ordered the construction of a canal from the Rhine via the Neckar to the Danube so that goods could be transported from the Near East and the Black Sea to the North Sea at minimal cost.

After World War I the commercial transportation in much of Western Europe increasingly went to rail and road and the economic viability of many of the canals steadily declined. Their decreasing use meant reduced revenues for maintenance and they fell into disrepair. Many became non-navigable and were closed. Some were filled-in. In France between 1926 and 1957 nearly 5000 kilometres of navigable waterways were closed or abandoned.

The exception to this trend was in the Netherlands, where the already large and complex network continued to be expanded, upgraded and made even more efficient.

Chapter Two

Today's European Waterways Network

In 1992 continental Europe adopted a classification system for its inland waterways. It was created by the European Council of Ministers of Transport, which rated the canals ECMT Class I to Class VII. The classification was based on the dimensions of the waterway structures, such as lengths and widths of locks, clearance under bridges and the available depths.

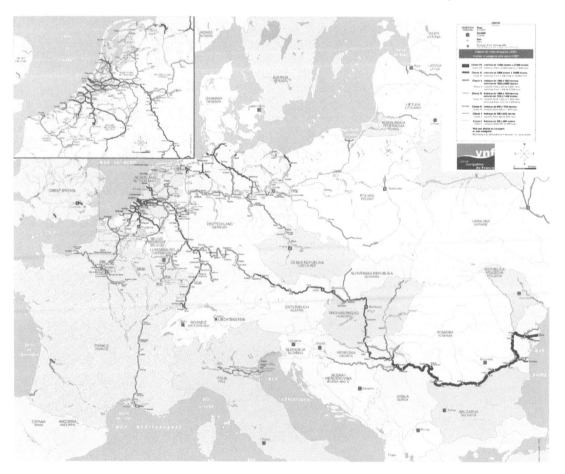

Class I corresponds to the historical Freycinet gauge of France dating to 1879. The larger river classification sizes focus on the waterway's ability to handle convoys of mulit-barge convoys propelled by pusher tugs. Britain didn't participate because most of its canals have smaller locks that are below the dimensions of the smallest classification. In 2004, the standards were extended with four smaller sizes RA, RB, RC and RD, covering recreational craft up to 15 metres in length.

In France today there remain 94 navigable rivers and canals with a total length of 8800 kilometres and 2165 locks. Most of these are interconnected waterways in the northeast and the southwest parts of the country and the remaining 500 kilometres are isolated waterways in western France. About twenty percent of the French waterways are Class IV and above, mainly the major rivers. Of the remainder, the vast majority are Class I and lower, ideally suited to pleasure cruising.

The inland network in the Netherlands extends about 6000 kilometres on 270 navigable public waterways that criss-cross a country that is only a sixteenth the area of France. Of these, 2200 kilometres are Class IV and higher and carry huge volumes of commercial traffic. In addition, there are many hundreds of private dead-end canals leading to homes, farms and commercial enterprises. Because of the flatness of much of the country, there are only 186 locks. Many of these are to step down from lakes and rivers into the recovered polders below sea level. In the Netherlands there are more canal boaters per capita than anywhere else in the world.

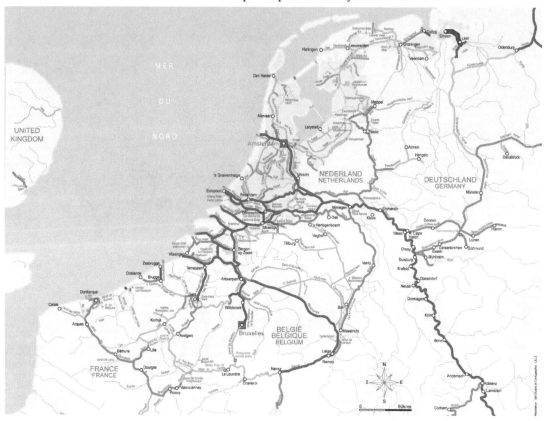

WATERWEGEN IN VLAANDEREN
(situatie april 2011) © Promotie Binnenvaart Vlaanderen

The network of canals that was built in Belgium filled most of the small nation, with exception of the rugged areas along the German and Luxembourg borders. As elsewhere in Europe, some of the original canals fell into disuse and have been abandoned. However, 1,580 kilometres of inland waterways are still navigable. Much of the remaining system is Class IV and above, having been upgraded in a massive project spanning the last half of the twentieth century.

In Flanders, the low lying northern part of the country, the terrain is similar to that of the Netherlands and the 33 canals there have a total of only 102 locks. In Wallonia, the hilly southern part of the country, the three navigable rivers and six canals have only 50 locks among them, most of them huge.

In Germany, the current network of inland waterways measures around 7350 kilometres. Of this, about 750 kilometres are tidal waters in river estuaries. About a third of the network length consists of free-flowing and regulated stretches of river, about a quarter of the length is canals and the remaining forty percent or so is canalised stretches of river. About seventy percent of the length of the German network is Class IV and above; traffic on these is very heavy and they are not particularly suited to pleasure cruising.

While many European countries progressively upgraded their canals to compete with or complement the railways, this did not happen in England and Wales. From a peak of 7700 kilometres in the 1840s, the system went into decline. Canal companies began to sell out to railway companies and many lines were built over filled-in canals.

After the Second World War, a slowly growing interest in pleasure boating spurred efforts to restore some of the neglected canals. Gradually the steady loss of navigations was slowed and then reversed. Today the network of canals and navigable rivers is up to about 3200 kilometres and restoration continues to add navigable sections.

Chapter Three

Canal Barges - France

The English word barge traces its origin to 1300 from the Old French, which had adopted it from colloquial Latin. The word originally referred to any small boat and the modern meaning didn't evolve until around 1480. The word bark, meaning a small ship, entered the English language around 1420 from the Old French word barque, which had come from the colloquial Latin barca at the beginning of the fifth century. By the seventeenth century, the word bark was being used to refer to a three-masted ship, and it often used the French spelling, barque to distinguish this meaning. Both colloquial Latin words had likely evolved from the classic Latin barica and from the Greek baris, meaning Egyptian boat. The Coptic word bari meant small boat. The Ancient Egyptian word ba-y-r, hieroglyphic ⟨image⟩ or ⟨image⟩ referred to a basket-shaped boat.

In the context used in this book, a barge is a flat-bottomed vessel of shallow draft that was designed for navigation along a river or canal. They evolved differently in each region, their designs dictated by local navigational conditions and the nature of the cargoes they carried.

Throughout the Middle Ages in France, most of the heavy inland transportation was along the courses of its many rivers. Shallow boats of simple design and construction drifted and sailed downstream with the current and were sailed, pulled or poled back up. Often, where the current was too strong for the upstream voyage, crude barges were cheaply built to last only the downstream trip. On arrival with their cargo, they were broken-up and sold as lumber or firewood.

Different regional uses spawned dozens of designs, such as: the marnois of the Marne, upper Seine and Yonne valleys; the chaland from the Loire; the sisselande from the Saône and Rhône; the courpet in the Dordogne; the chalibardon on the Adour; and the sapine of the Allier. Very few examples of these have survived, but in recent years enthusiasts have built working replicas of some of the old designs.

Two Chalands unloading at Orléans on the Loire

With the coming of the canals, barge designs quickly evolved to take advantage of the still waters made possible by the locks. The barges grew in length and width to match the dimensions of the locks and bridge cuts they needed to transit. Their draft increased to the maximum depth available on the canal. In many regions of France, cargo barges became rather boxy in appearance, but there were exceptions.

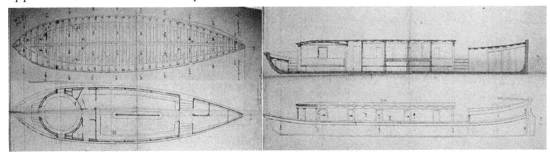

With the 1681 opening of le canal royal en Languedoc, (now called le Canal du Midi), the demand for fast passenger service was quickly met. Post boats were designed and built for the opening and they began providing a fast, efficient transportation system between Toulouse and Agde.

To save time spent in locks, a total of forty boats shuttled in the pounds between the locks and passengers changed boats at the ends of the pounds. Fresh horses at the trot hauled the post boats along at eight kilometres per hour in vessels that could accommodate fifty passengers, divided between the first class lounge in the front and the commu-

nal room in the centre. Passengers took their beds and meals ashore in the hostels along the canal, while the helmsman had accommodations in the vessel's stern.

The 240 kilometre journey from Toulouse to Agde took four days. Boat designs and management of the system evolved and by 1834 the boats were travelling at ten kilometres per hour and the trip was cut to three days.

With later canal construction, the service expanded to Beaucaire on the Rhône and Agen on the Garonne upstream from Bordeaux. At its peak, the passenger volume reached 100,000 per year. In 1858 the opening of the railway almost immediately killed the post boat service; it didn't quite make two centuries.

Sailing was one of the methods of propelling a barge along a river or canal, but in vessels with flat bottoms and little or no keel, this was limited to downwind sailing. In contrary winds, the barge had to either be poled or hauled. The current in the lower 400 kilometres of the Loire flows to the west and the prevailing wind blows upstream from the west. This enabled barges to run downstream with the current and sail back up in a following wind.

In canals and rivers with no current or gentle currents and few favourable winds, hauling was done by men. With family operated barges, often the women and children would do the hauling, while the man tended to more exacting tasks like relaxing, smoking and steering. It takes some effort to get the barge moving, but in calm conditions, little effort is required to keep it moving at two kilometres per hour.

More often in France, horses were used, and sometimes oxen. Moving along at six kilometres per hour through the placid waters of canal pound in this fashion was peaceful. Towpaths had been built alongside the canals and through the bridge cuts and the only complications were when meeting a barge coming in the opposite direction. Tow lines had to be detached from harnesses and reattached once the barges had drifted past each other.

On rivers with stronger currents, such as the Saône and the Rhône, barges like the sisselande were steered using long sweep oars. For better control when heading downstream in swift current, they often used steering sweeps both fore and aft.

To do the re-ascent against the current required very large teams of horses. Depending on the current, this could mean from twenty to as many as forty horses, and these required one driver per two or three horses.

Animal haulage on the faster sections of the Saône and the Rhône quickly diminished around 1840 with the expanding use of steam tugs. In a few hours these powerful machines could haul a string of barges upstream over a distance that would have required two hundred horses and seventy to a hundred men a day or more to accomplish. The Industrial Revolution was in full swing.

On the more gentle rivers and on many of the çanals, less powerful steam tugs began being used to pull long trains of barges. In much of Western Europe there was a ready adoption of these new methods, though an exception to this was in France, where the old ways, the gentle and quiet ways were maintained by many.

Motorized tractors began appearing on the towpaths to replace animals. Various versions were also devised of electric motors running suspended from overhead cables.

In some of areas, such as Cambrai, rail-mounted traction machines were introduced. Then in 1926 la Compagnie Générale de Traction sur les Voies Navigables (CGTVN) was established in the north and east of France. The company operated electric tractors running on rails on the towpaths. The transition to the mechanical haulage was resisted by bargemen, many of whom saw it as a disruption to their gentle ways.

However, the traditional barge operators were being challenged on another front. Since the turn of the century, engines had begun being installed in barges. Initially this was usually a retrofit to an existing wooden barge, but gradually new iron or steel barges, loosely called automoteurs, were designed specifically for power. However, unlike in other areas of Europe, the transition to motor barges in France was slow.

Verdun, le 190

La Meuse Canalisée

In 1935 there were still 1500 working bateaux-écurie, horse barges along the French canals. Most of these were built of wood and they were equipped with horse stables and a loading ramp to move the horses between the barge and the bank. By the late 1950s horse haulage was still common along the canals, but the horses were being gradually replaced by electric traction along the towpaths. The northern and eastern canals were the first to retire horses, but in the centre of France, horses stayed on despite the powered tractors and the convenience of powered barges. The last bateau-écurie docked in 1969. The self-powered barges gradually took over, and because of a lack of business, in 1972 la Compagnie Générale de Traction sur les Voies Navigables filed for bankruptcy.

The style of barge most common in France in the late nineteenth century and through the first half of the twentieth was the péniche, which was based on the Flemish Spits. This 1908 photo, taken during a chomage, when the canal was drained for maintenance, shows its boxy shape.

The standard péniche had evolved to take full advantage of the maximum space available in the canal locks. The new gauge for canals that was implemented in 1879 by the French Minister of Transport, Charles-Louis Freycinet, was based on the péniche dimensions.

At the end of the nineteenth century there were about 12,000 commercial canal boats in France. Of these, 8000 were the péniches in northern France that were employed with hauling coal to Paris.

The péniche was based on the Flemish spits, which the French called bélandre, It had evolved from the Dutch bijlander, whose name meaning *near land*, referred to its coastal use. Its gracefully curved ends, sweeping sheer and tumblehome bulwarks were the results of how wood could be bent in building the hull.

That such a graceful ship as the bijlander evolved in Belgium and France into the mundane, utilitarian péniche, is a major reason why modern canal boating enthusiasts gravitate to Dutch barges.

Chapter Four

Canal Barges - The Netherlands

The geography and conditions in the Netherlands caused inland boats to evolve very different-ly from those in France. The bijlander, from which the French bélandre and then the péniche descended, was a flat-bottomed vessel used for coastal trade. Variations of it are known back to about 1500.

From the bijlander the tjalk evolved in the seventeenth century. Tjalk is a rather ge-neric term used to designate a long, narrow and shallow barge shaped somewhat like a shoebox with round-ed corners. Most tjalks had a mast rigged with a gaff, they carried a bowsprit, and be-cause of the shallow waters of the Netherlands, they had flat bottoms and no keel. To counter the press of the wind when sailing, they were fitted with leeboards. Their grace-fully rounded ends and pro-nounced sheer lead to their being likened to Dutch wood-en shoes.

There were many different styles of tjalk, their variations being based on the particu-lar conditions and intended uses where they were built and sailed. They were broad-ly classified by style, such as paviljoentjalk, which had a raised after deck with accommodations below or a roefschip, which had a small cabin aft of the hold and a lower aft deck, or a dektjalk, which had neither cabin nor raised deck. They also were classified by the region where they were built, such as Groninger tjalk, IJsseltjalk, Friese tjalk or Hollandse tjalk. Tjalken were generally 20 to 30 metres in length with beams of 4 to 5 metres.

The skûtsje was a smaller tjalk, shorter and narrower to trade in the shallow lakes and narrow, winding canals in southwest Friesland. They were generally between 15 and 20 metres in length and had beams 3.4 to 4 metres. The skûtsje was developed between 1855 and 1860 and they were initially built of wood. Then in 1887 riveted iron was introduced, and during the first decade of the twentieth century, the yards gradually converted from iron to steel. A total of 870 iron and steel skûtsjes were built until the final one in 1933.

With the closing of the Zuiderzee in 1932, the commercial usefulness of the skûtsje dropped. Some had engines fitted, but even then, they could not compete with the purpose-built motor barges. During the ensuing years, many skûtsjes were scrapped, some were converted to homes and some to pleasure

or racing vessels. There are currently about 90 of these historic vessels restored to full sailing trim and competing in regular races in Friesland.

The larger tjalken also declined in usefulness as the new breed of motor barges took over the commerce. Like the skûtsje, many were scrapped, but hundreds of them have survived. Many live on as woonboten, houseboats permanently moored along the canals, while others have been converted for pleasure cruising. In most towns around the IJsselmeer there are restored sailing tjalken offering a variety of trips, tours and charters.

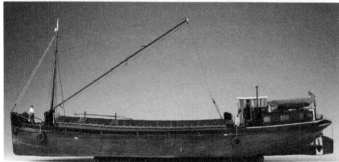

Other unpowered sailing barges included various versions of the aak, such as the Hasselteraak, Lemsteraak, boeieraak, and klipperaak. Like the tjalk, these had leeboards for sailing. With their hulls not designed for motor propulsion, they too became commercially obsolete and other uses were found for them. Unfortunately, for many, this meant the scrap heaps.

In the early 1920s the old non-motorized barges became uncompetitive after the introduction of the luxemotor, the modern classic of Dutch ship design. Its sharp, plumb entry and its stern designed for proper water flow to the propeller made it an efficient and fast barge. Adding to its attraction and giving the barge its name were the luxurious accommodations in the stern.

With their larger hold capacity, much better efficiency and greater comfort, luxemotors quickly became the standard on the canals of the Netherlands, rapidly replacing the older aak and tjalk hull styles. They were built in lengths from 18 to 30 metres, though many were lengthened in the 1950s in an attempt to compete with the falling price of truck freight. Even with lengthening, the design became increasingly commercially unviable in face of competition from more modern barges.

Other types of motor barge enjoyed some limited success during the reign of the luxemotor. The steilesteven, with a fatter stern and its wheelhouse all the way aft, provided an increased hold capacity. Another was the kitwijker, which like the steilsteven was designed originally without an engine. Neither ever achieved the popularity of the luxemotor, and they too were eclipsed by improved designs after the middle of the twentieth century.

Retired examples of the luxemotor, the stilesteven and the kitwijker are popular choices for makeover to liveaboard and cruising barges. With the tjalks and aaks, they form the most popular group of barges for conversion to pleasure cruising on the canals of Europe.

Chapter Five

Pleasure Cruising on French Canals

I first became aware of the European canals in 1966 when I was serving in France with the Royal Canadian Air Force. In the Lorraine, Champagne, Franche Compté and the Bourgogne I saw old brown péniches moving slowly along the canals, I watched some of the last horses on the towpaths and I frequently paused to watch barges passing through locks. I saw no pleasure boating.

After I resigned my commission from the navy in 1981, I set-up in the wine business. For two decades we made very frequent visits to Europe while searching for wines to import or later while conducting wine and food tours. During these trips we always spent a week or two or longer in France and never failed to search-out the canals and watch the activity along them.

In 1984 we rented our first canal boat in France from Blue Line in St-Jean-de-Losne in the Burgundy. It was mid-Spring and we had the Canal de Bourgogne, the Canal du Centre and the Saône almost completely to ourselves. There was minimal commercial traffic, it was off-season for the few hotel barges that existed at the time and we saw very few other rental boats and even fewer private cruisers during our three weeks. The lock houses on the canals all had resident lock keepers, with whom we paused to chat while assisting them with the gates and sluices. We bought fresh eggs and garden produce from them and learned of interesting places to visit and favourite dining spots. We were hooked.

I had not been able to find a travel agent in Canada with any knowledge of French canal boat rentals, so I had to write to Blake's in England to book our boat. Since then the number of companies offering canal boat rentals has dramatically increased. There are currently a dozen large companies and more than four dozen smaller companies with canal boat fleets in over a hundred locations throughout France. It is an important and growing tourism sector.

Voies Navigables de France (VNF) is the French inland waters authority. Its report on the 2011 season showed that there were 63 rental companies offering a total of 1568 boats from 113 rental bases throughout France. There were 33,550 rental contracts for a total of 144,376 guests, 74.5% of whom were foreigners. With the average weekly rental fee of €2000, this volume of rentals would have generated more than €67 million in revenue. With each guest spending an average of €100 in incidentals along the way, this adds another €14 million, meaning the rental boat industry generates over €80 million, €60 million of this from abroad.

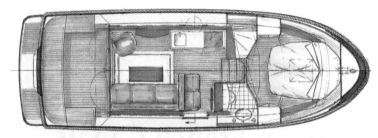

In 2013, a typical weekly rental fee for a boat for two people was €1300 in low season, around €1700 in shoulder season and close to €2000 in high season. This Dutch-built Linssen 28 Sedan is a fine example of a two-person rental boat.

Larger boats for four, six, eight, ten and more people cost more, but the small incremental increase per person makes multi-couple rentals very popular. A 14.9-metre boat like the Linssen Euroclassic 149 shown here, with four cabins all with ensuite showers and toilets rents for €2700, €3300 and €3750 in low, shoulder and high seasons, about half the rate per person than for the smaller boat.

One of the great attractions of the rental boats is that they require no boating experience or knowledge, no boating skills or training, no license or qualifications to operate. A brief introduction to the operation of the boat is given at the beginning of the rental period, but effectively, with very little boating awareness, most renters are set free to learn boat handling for themselves.

Another popular way to cruise the canals is aboard a hotel barge. Though a few were purpose-built, most are converted freight or general cargo barges, gutted and refitted with high-quality interiors. There are currently seventy-six hotel barges in France with a total of more than a thousand guest beds. They range greatly in size, accommodating from four to twenty-four guests and they also vary in the quality of the accommodations, amenities and dining provided. Most are fully catered and have organized tours and activities ashore as the barges slowly cruise their itineraries along the canals.

Many of the largest ones are converted péniches or spits and among the smaller hotel barges are converted tjalken, aaken and luxemotors. A common feature is a high staff-to-guest ratio, with the smaller barges often providing higher comfort and individual attention. Weekly rates generally run in the €3000 to €4000 per person range. Some barges with more basic accommodation and self-catering cost under €2000 per person, but for a grande luxe hotel barge, like the Alouette pictured here, the weekly rates are around €5000 per person.

According to the VNF study, in 2011 the hotel barges handled a total of 18,650 guests, 75% of whom were foreigners, mainly Anglophone with a large portion from North America. Assuming an average charge of €4,000 per person per week, this would have generated an annual sales revenue of nearly €75 million.

Most of the hotel barges follow a set itinerary throughout the season, doing a cruise in one direction along the canal one week and retracing the route in the opposite direction the next. A few are more pelagic, their itinerary being along a canal or series of canals with guests joining in one location and disembarking at the end of the week in another as the barge works its way through one or more regions. Some of the smaller barges are known to write their itineraries based where their early-booking clients want to explore and then connect the dots and fill-in the gaps with later bookings. The larger hotel barges fill the majority of their cabins through specialty travel agents.

River cruises form another category of inland pleasure cruising. In recent years the popularity of cruises on the Rhône and Saône have rapidly increased. In 2011 sixteen operators were running thirty-four river cruise ships with a total 4736 passenger beds and they carried a total of 184,700 passengers for 882,200 nights. Many of river cruise itineraries are week long; however, there  are also three, four and five day itineraries. Most of the prices are in the range of €90 to €150 per person per night, though some are much higher, so it is conservative to say that the operators took in revenue in excess of €100 million in 2011.

The final category of commercial pleasure cruising is in the Bateaux Promenade, the short trip boat commonly called Bateaux Mouches and most associated with the Seine in Paris. A simple tour through central Paris lasts seventy minutes and costs €12.50 per adult, with reduced fares for children and groups. Lunch cruises are offered on the weekends at €55 and dinner cruises every evening offer menus at €99 and €140. The VNF report on the 2011 season showed 10 979,810 Bateaux Promenade passengers in France, 78.6% of them in Paris. Annual revenues are in excess of €150 million, and since Paris is the most visited city in the world, it is safe to say that the vast majority of this is from outside France.

I have gone into some boring facts and figures in looking at these various commercial operators. This is because I think it important to point-out the significance of their contribution to the French economy. In 2011 about €400 million was spent by guests aboard the broad variety of commercially operated pleasure boats on the inland waters of France. In each of the categories, the number of passengers or passenger nights was up and continues to rise strongly. In addition, there are the jobs generated in the supply, maintenance, operation and administration of the fleet of 2099 vessels and their bases. The French authorities are not likely to allow this revenue to be endangered.

Not mentioned in the 2011 report were the privately owned and operated pleasure boats. According to recent VNF figures, there are currently over 20,000 active private boats on the inland waterways, fifty percent of which are foreign owned. This private fleet is nearly ten times the size of the entire commercial pleasure fleet, but its impact on the economy is considerably less. In annual canal usage fees it generates less than €1 million. An average of €5000 per boat for annual moorage, maintenance, food, drink, supplies and services would provide another €100 million to the economy, just one quarter of the commercial pleasure fleet revenue. Because of this comparatively low revenue generated per boat, €5000 compared to €190,000, the private boats receive very little support with infrastructure and facilities.

However; owning one's own vessel on the waterways offers the most freedom and flexibility. In 2000 I bought my first canal boat in France. Lady Jane was a 14-metre Dutch motorkruiser built of steel in Groningen in 1970. After a refurbishing refit, we cruised throughout northeastern France on the Saône, the Canal du Rhône a Rhin, the Canal du Centre, the Canal de Bourgogne. We wandered up through the Franche Compté, crossed into the Champagne, spent time in Paris, explored the upper Seine, the Yonne, Loing, the Briare and the Loire.

After six years on the French canals, I grew restless and wanted some wild and remote sailing. While I was still young enough, I wanted to sail through Patagonia and around Cape Horn. I sold Lady Jane and had a new 15-metre cutter-rigged sloop built and christened Sequitur. In 2009 Edi and I sailed south from Vancouver and after three years exploring South America, we rounded Cape Horn and headed up the Atlantic. Along the way, in dealing with stultifying Third World bureaucracies, sparse resources and a hurricane and three Force 11 storms at sea, we realized that we were approaching our best-before-dates for wild cruising. We decided to look at a more sedate and gentle style of boating.

Chapter Six

Buying a Canal Boat

Because I had previously owned a Dutch motorkruiser, our initial thoughts were on buying another one. From what I had seen during my previous years of canal boating, most of the motor cruisers on the French canals had been built in the Netherlands. The Netherlands, with only one quarter of the population of France, has several times as many used boats available than does France; the wisdom almost universally expressed among canal cruisers is that the Netherlands is the place to buy.

As we worked our way up the Atlantic from the Falklands to Uruguay and then around the coast of Brazil, whenever we had an Internet connection we combed the online listings on Apollo Duck, the major international listing site used by both brokers and private sellers. Searching for used powerboats in the Netherlands yielded over three-hundred listings; narrowing these to boats between 14 and 20 metres took the list to fifty-one.

Refining the list further to boats less than twenty years old pared it down to twenty-nine.

As we looked at the listings, we were linked to many brokers' sites, and on these we found other listings. Because most of the online listings have multiple photos, we were easily able to form opinions on boats that weren't suitable and narrow the list further. We looked at many possibilities and dreamed.

Somewhere along the way our thinking evolved to buying a new boat and we began investigating that side of the market. Most intriguing to us was the line of boats that are being built by Linssen in Maasbracht. The company was established in 1949 and has been building a range of very high quality motor yachts that are well-suited to the European waterways. I recalled having admired those I saw on the French canals a decade previously.

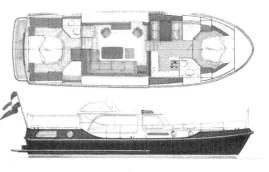

As we sailed across the Caribbean, pausing to relax in Barbados, Martinique, Guadeloupe, Saint Croix and Puerto Rico, our Internet research went into full speed. Since we were thinking of a new boat, we investigated the possibilities of having a new barge built to a classic Dutch barge design. We found many companies building modern versions of the luxemotor or styles adapted from it. Among those that interested us in England were Branson, Piper and Will Trickett and in the Netherlands we found Euroship and SRF interesting. Most intriguing to us was Aqualine, a British company that set-up a factory in Gdansk, Poland to use the skills from their long history of shipbuilding and to take advantage of the lower labour costs.

During the exploration process, our thinking slowly morphed toward buying a converted ex-commercial barge. We pored over the online listings of the many brokers in France, the Netherlands and Britain. We looked at the listings for converted aaks, klippers, luxemotors, steilstevens and tjalken.

As we grew more familiar with the various barge types, we were increasingly drawn to the tjalk, the most typical of all the Dutch small ships. The name is from the old Dutch language and was first mentioned by Witsen in Architectura Navalis in 1690. This painting of a tjalk by Ludolf Bakhuizen is dated 1697. Tjalken are flat-bottomed sailing cargo ships with shallow draft ideally suited to use in the shallow inland and coastal waters of Friesland and Holland.

On the Internet we saw a photo of a beautifully restored tjalk named Owlpen, which convinced us that we wanted a similar barge. The shape of the tjalk, with its tumblehome gunwales and pleasing sheer, is reminiscent of the Dutch wooden shoe. Because of their flat bottoms they were fitted with leeboards instead of deep keels, and they could easily dry-out on the beaches with the tides. Most tjalken had easily lowering masts so they could pass under the low bridges and then re-erect the rigs to continue sailing.

As we sat in St Augustine Florida preparing Sequitur for sale, I began compiling a spreadsheet of suitable tjalken to consider. I began contacting brokers in the Netherlands and refining the list and by the time we had arrived in Friesland in July 2012, I had a complex spreadsheet of data from seventeen tjalken we had chosen to look at. Most of the ones we had selected had been built in the 1890s or during the first decade of the twentieth century, and they ranged in length from sixteen to twenty metres. There are much more rigorous licensing requirements for vessels over twenty metres in Europe, so we wanted to stay under that length.

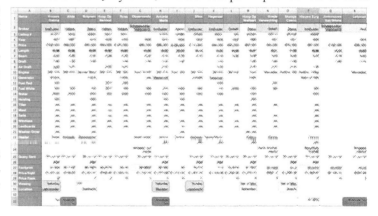

We had arranged for a rental a car at the airport and had booked accommodation in a holiday apartment with a well-equipped kitchen. There was a large supermarket a five minute walk away, so shortly after we had arrived, we went shopping for groceries. We had appointments through their various brokers to view several barges on our list, and we were awaiting responses from four other brokers.

Our first appointment was in Leeuwarden on Saturday morning. After breakfast, our car's GPS took us to the canal alongside our first tjalk. Lady Gazina is 19.98 by 4.60 metres and was built in 1907. She still had her complete sailing rig in working condition.

Her interior was well finished, and fully set-up for comfortable living. However, the systems and galley equipment were very dated and the interior layout was not to our liking. We would have to gut the entire interior and start over. Her high asking price reflected her condition and equipment, much of which we would have to throw away. Also, her generous headroom gave her a very high air draft at 3.5 metres. This meant she would scrape on many of the bridges in France and would be too high for the Bourgogne, the Nivernais and the Midi.

On Saturday afternoon we drove to near Koudam on the shores of the Alde Karre, near the IJsselmeer for an appointment to see the next tjalk on our list, a 19.90 by 4.15 metre vessel built in 1910. From the outside she appeared to have long since lost the love of her owner. This was strongly confirmed by a visit to her interior. The owner explained the wet bilges to be from a leak she had not yet tracked down, and the stains and rotting floorboards forward pointed to other leaks from above and below. She was very quickly scratched off our list.

Making our trip worthwhile, though was the sight of a skûtsje sailing past in a stiff breeze on the Alde Karre. Skûtsje racing is a very active and keenly followed sport in Friesland, where dozens of extremely competitive antique skûtsjes regularly compete in organized races.

Our next appointment was southward in Lelystad to see a 19.80 by 3.80 metre tjalk that had been built in 1903. She had a full working rig in apparently good condition. Her interior; however, was absolutely

basic and this was diminished further by carpentry of a very poor standard and signs of poor maintenance. Her interior would be easier to gut than the first barge we looked at, but she simply did not feel right.

With our day's appointments completed, we drove back by way of a stop in Harlingen. We walked along the canal in the centre of town, in awe of the beautiful old buildings and ad-

miring the obvious pride of the home owners. The canals were filled with boats moored along both sides. Among them were several classic boats: tjalken, Lemsteraken, klippers and skûtsjes.

In the outer harbours were many commercial tjalken, and we watched as one of them arrived and unloaded its day tour passengers and another appeared to be stocking-up for a more extended trip with another group. We counted fifteen restored klippers and tjalken, most over a century old, that appeared to be in the charter trade.

We had an early dinner back at the apartment and quickly went to bed to continue working-off the jet-lag from our eight hour time change. On Sunday we had no appointments, so we went exploring, hoping to find a suitable tjalk with a Te Koop sign, a *For Sale* sign.

We also went looking for one of the listings on our spreadsheet, about which we had not received any response from the broker. This 19.98 by 4.49 metre tjalk was built in 1897. After some questioning, we finally tracked it down alongside a farmhouse outside of Kollum. We barged-in and met the owners on their patio and they gladly showed us their ship. We could find nothing positive to say about it.

We then drove to Warten to look at boats in the marina at Boten en Meer. After sharing coffee with us, Auke van der Meer, the owner of the marina and its associated brokerage showed us around. He had nothing suitable onsite, but we were very taken by a beautiful little 5.4 by 2.2 metre boeier built of oak in 1941 for a Nazi general during the occupation.

Auke was the listing broker for one of the tjalken on our spreadsheet, but its owner had moved the barge to a boatyard in Heeg to have it stripped-out to a bare hull in preparation for a new fit-out. It is a 19.66 by 4.22 metre Pavjonentjalk built in 1898 and still with its full rig, but this

had been removed for the work. The yard is closed on Sundays, so we arranged to meet Auke on Monday morning for a visit.

On Monday we liked what we saw. It was stripped-out, the engine and machinery were removed, the deckhouse had been cut away, the poured concrete ballast had been jackhammered out and work had begun with some bottom re-plating.

We talked in broad terms of various refit possibilities with Auke and the yard manager. The barge was still sufficiently original that it could be easily restored and accepted for listing as an historic vessel. This would allow free moorage at museum harbours throughout the Netherlands. We looked at the leeboards and other bits and pieces of rigging that had been removed, and then we went back to Warten with Auke to talk details.

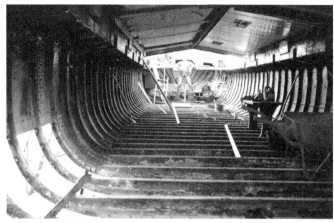

One clog in the works was that, since he had begun work, the owner had rather steeply raised the asking price from what we had seen in the listing. Another detraction was the estimate of nearly a year to complete the fit-out. At least we had found a tjalk that we hadn't rejected.

On Tuesday morning we drove across the Afsluitdijk to North Holland for an appointment with Peter Rood of Scheepsmalelaardij Enkhuizen. Peter had four of the listings on our spreadsheet, two of which we had already viewed through him on Saturday and Sunday. He had made appointments for the other two for us for later in the afternoon and our meeting with him was on our way south to see them. We also had an appointment to see a tjalk from another broker. We sat in Peter's canal front office, sharing coffee and giving him a better understanding of what we were looking for.

One of the better ways to search for a boat is to engage the services of a professional broker. The boat brokers work for, and their commissions are paid by the seller. Their job is to find clients for their listings, since they make their commissions only on completion of a sale. A good broker will eagerly take on serious buyers and search for suitable boats for them. They have their own listings, but they also know what is available in the market from the other brokers and they stand to split commissions if they make a sale of another broker's listing.

First on our list was a 19.80 by 4.20 metre live-aboard in Amsterdam. We found it comfortably finished, but completely wrong for our tastes. We would have to gut it and start over, and because of its level of finish, the asking price was high, making it unreasonable to consider.

The second tjalk on our day's list was in Aalsmeer. It was a 1908 skûtsje of 16.38 by 3.44 metres, the second smallest on our spreadsheet. The pretty little barge had been bought by her current owner in 1975. He had converted and lovingly maintained her for 37 years. Her sailing rig was ashore in a shed, where the owner had been restoring it until he became too ill to continue.

The interior, while rather smaller than we had set out looking for, oozed charm and showed a distinct pride of ownership. The owner talked loving- ly of many years of boating with his children and now his grandchildren.

We now had a second barge on our list to consider; how very different they were from each other.

The final barge of the day was a 19.14 by 4.10 vessel built in 1902. It was in Loosdrecht and was owned by a marine engineer and his wife. He works in the boatyard where they are moored. The tjalk was fully fitted-out, rigged for sailing and was very well maintained, as can be expected from being owned by a professional boat maintenance person.

I was impressed with the engineering fit-out, by the completeness of the systems and equipment and by the orderliness and cleanliness of the barge. Its price re- flected the quality. While the interior is not completely as we would like, its modernization refit would not be such a huge task.

All of a sudden, we found ourselves with three choices, each dramatically different from the others. During the 160 kilometre drive back to Leeuwarden we had much to discuss. Essentially, we had already made up our minds which one we wanted. However, as we drove I played devil's advocate and represented the other two, offering ever decreasing arguments in their support.

We arrived at our apartment at twilight, and before beginning to cook dinner, I sent an email to the broker with an offer on Nieuwe Zorg, telling him we would like to meet in his office on Wednesday to formalize the offer. On Wednesday morning we received an email from the broker informing us that the seller had accepted the amount of our offer, and that he would await our formal written offer.

At 1100 we met with the broker. Among other things, we went over lists of recommended surveyors and insurance agents and looked at possible yards to haul-out for the survey. I was delighted to see on the short lists the names of the surveyors and insurers to whom the previous evening I had emailed requests for quotes. These names I had harvested from the list of links on The Barge Association site. We had rejoined the Association, having let the membership lapse after sale of Lady Jane in 2006.

With paperwork well underway, we headed back up to Leeuwarden, packed our belongings and moved out of the apartment. The week's rental was up, so we moved south to an apartment in Volendam. We had found a rather modern place in a location much more central to our anticipated activities over the following week or so. It has a well-equipped kitchen and a second-floor balcony overlooking a large, active marina.

On Thursday morning we went on a walking exploration of old Volendam, through the labyrinth of narrow back streets and then along the old waterfront. There we admired the traditional Volendamer kwaks, the wooden fishing boats similar to Zuiderzeebotters.

These kwaks fished the Zuiderzee for shrimp, eel, anchovies and herring in the nineteenth and early twentieth centuries, and at its peak in 1910, the Volendam fleet numbered over three-hundred kwaks. With the closing Afsluitdijk in 1932, the former Zuiderzee waters around Volendam became the IJsselmeer, and as the waters slowly lost their salt content, the fishery and the local livliehood changed.

On Friday we drove up to Enkhuizen, where we proofread, amended and eventually initialled and signed the formal offer to purchase Nieuwe Zorg. The HISWA (Netherlands yacht brokers' association) standard contract was clear and concise, as were the nearly four pages of appended special conditions, which had been compiled in face-to-face, email and phone consultations among the owners, the brokers and us.

Peter then gave us an insurance application to complete, and he faxed it to the broker, phoned to see if all was in order, had us redo one page and re-faxed it. Our quote for insurance on Nieuwe Zorg came in at less than eight percent of our just cancelled insurance on Sequitur. It looks like the Dutch canals are a much lower risk than the Chilean ones.

Back in our apartment on Friday afternoon, using Skype and the reception office's fax, I ordered our bank to send a wire transfer of the fifteen percent deposit in Euros to the broker's Stichting Derden Geld (third-party or trust account). Meanwhile Peter had coordinated our chosen surveyor, a haul-out yard and Nieuwe Zorg's owners into a very smooth three-day schedule of events beginning on Monday.

We were up early on Monday to drive to Hoopddorf to the EuropeCar agent to arrange for an extension of four days on the rental car. Then we continued on to Aalsmeer, arriving at Nieu-

we Zorg at 1002, two minutes after the appointed time. We surprised the owners Henk and Madij, who been told that we would be arriving at noon. This was to be the only glitch in the complex schedule involving eleven people, four locations, three days and two languages.

We relaxed onboard having coffee with Henk and Madij and waiting for their daughter, Jacqueline to arrive. Edi and I were feeling comfortably at home onboard as we increasingly realized how suitable Nieuwe Zorg is for us.

We reflected on the meaning of her name: Nieuwe Zorg translates to *New Concern* or *New Worry*, and we thought that she should instead be called Zonder Zorg: *Without Concern, Without Worry, Carefree* as we are.

Jacqueline eventually arrived and provided excellent translation for Henk and Madij. We headed out of the little port and down the canal toward the Westeinderplassen, scooting easily under a low bridge, while other boats lined-up waiting for it to open. Nieuwe Zorg's air draft is only 1.95 metres, which gives her a great exploratory range. Henk gave me the tiller and I quickly gained a feel for how easily she handles.

We arrived at Kempers, and Henk being unfamiliar with the marina layout, headed in through a narrow entrance and weaved his way between lines of moored boats toward a couple of people on the bow of a cruiser to ask directions. The way was back from where we had come, and I was pleased with how easily Hank handled the barge in the confined spaces. She appears very responsive, and I noted she has a left-turning screw, which in astern gear gives the stern a kick to starboard. This has always

been my preferred turn, since it makes very easy mooring with the favoured starboard-side-to. We found the proper entrance and came to bollards on the wharf short of the travel lift.

Marine engineer Rutger Versluijs arrived onboard and began a systematic inspection of the engine and the machinery spaces. He paused from time to time to explain to me what he was doing and what he was finding. First with the engine and generator off, and then with them running, Rutger continued inspecting the machinery spaces for over half an hour, including the engine cooling and exhaust systems, the through-hulls, the electrical systems, the generator, the batteries, the heating system, the propane tank

installations, the engine mounts, the transmission, the thrust bearing, the stern gland and its associated greaser, and so on. During this process, he used an electronic temperature sensor to take readings from a variety of places on the engine and its ancillaries.

He then had Henk motor out onto the lake and we did a half hour sea trial, including ten minutes at full throttle with Rutger down in the engine room with his flashlight and instruments. Back alongside, Rutger performed battery load tests and did inspections of the galley and heads systems. It was early evening by the time we were finished with first part of the survey; the second and third parts, the hull and the rigging were scheduled for Wednesday.

We were delighted with the thoroughness of the surveyor, and with his findings thus far. We drove back to our apartment in Volendam, where we dined well and slept well. On Tuesday morning we arrived back in Leimuiden for the scheduled 0800 haul-out. The weather the past few days had been clear and warm and forecasts had this fine spell continuing for several more days. It was glassy calm as Henk motored Nieuwe Zorg the short distance into jaws of the travel lift.

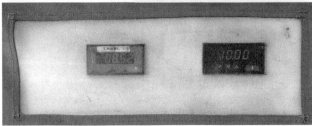

We admired the efficiency of the haul-out process. It consisted of one man with a push-button remote, calmly and methodically doing what we have seen teams of three and more chaotic and scrambling men perform in Vancouver, Callao, Puerto Montt and St Augustine.

Henk told us that Nieuwe Zorg had last been out of the water in 2005, when he had re-plated her bottom. We had expected to see a heavily fouled bottom, encrusted with mussels and other growth. Instead, there was only light vegetation and a few small crops of mussels. As Nieuwe Zorg hung in the slings, the lone operator power-washed her bottom.

The scales on the travel lift showed that she weighs 18.52 tonnes, which, for the benefit of the metrically-challenged, is about 20.4 tons.

With a touch of thumb pressure, the operator single-handedly nestled Nieuwe Zorg onto the stands as he adjusted the wooden blocks and wedges to evenly distribute the old girl's weight. The one-man operation was much calmer and took less time than any of Sequitur's haul-outs.

After taking another series of measurements of her interior, we left Nieuwe Zorg resting on her stands and headed north again. We drove to Alkmaar in central North Holland and explored the range of furniture and kitchen appliances in the crowd of large home decor stores across the canal from the historic centre of town. Shopping craving satiated, we headed across the bridge and strolled through the old town until a canal-side restaurant tempted us to pause for lunch.

Back in our apartment in Volendam on Tuesday evening I prepared a huge pot of mussels. Not the ones from Nieuwe Zorg's bottom; we had found some great-looking fresh mussels in the market in Alkmar. I began with a butter sauté of julienned garlic and shallots and diced red, green and yellow peppers, then added the mussels and a generous splash of beer. The steamed mussels were garnished with chopped parsley and served with melted butter and fresh baguette slices accompanied by a bottle of Champagne Veuve Clicquot. It was a delicious, if maybe a bit premature way to begin celebrating our pending new adventures.

On Wednesday morning we arrived back at the Kempers yard at 0800 to find that Rutger had already begun the bottom survey. He had completed the port side and was halfway back on the starboard with his electronic sounder. Unlike previous versions of this instrument, which I had seen with Lady Jane's surveys in France in 2000 and 2006, this one does not require removal of the bottom protection layers.

Application of a conducting gel to the hull's surface and then applying the sensor to the gel gives an instantaneous reading of the metal thickness. This is a wonderfully non-destructive process, much better than the former necessity of scraping or grinding away the coatings, and dramatically better than the earlier need to drill holes through the bottom, take measurements and then weld closed the holes.

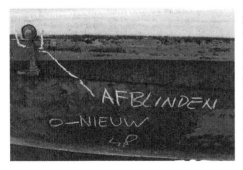

Something that I had quickly noticed when the barge was hauled on Tuesday also caught Rutger's attention. Henk had added a second raw water intake for engine cooling to handle the expected dirtier water before he went to France a few years ago. I saw that the unconventional installation was vulnerable to being compromised or knocked off by large flotsam as well as by canal banks and lock sides. I was pleased to see Rutger think the same way and condemn it.

Rutger found the rudder bearings to be well within tolerance, but found the propellor shaft with a rather large amount of play. The tolerance is two percent of the shaft diameter, so he applied his dial indicator to the shaft as Henk pried the propeller up and down against the skeg. The readings calculated to exactly two percent, and Rutger explained that in a case like this, the owners and buyers should share the replacement expenses. We agreed.

The aluminum anodes showed erosion, not excessive, but sufficient to indicate that they had been doing their duty protecting the more noble parts of the boat. Rutger declared that these and the remainder of the underwater were gear good.

We next went aboard and inspected the inside of the hull under the floorboards. The flash on my camera made this process much easier than contorting behind a flashlight and trying to get a viewing angle. The photos showed a dry and dusty environment with virtually no rust on the century-old riveted iron bottom.

The only place where there was any appreciable amount of rust was in the well beneath the mast tabernacle. The foot of the mast, with its 1100 kilogram counterweight swings through a slot in the foredeck as the mast is raised or lowered, and the cover over the deck slot is very prone to leaking. Rutger called this the weakest part of a skûtsje. He hammered and sounded and declared it still good. Though not critical, Rutger recommended we scale and treat the area. We both remarked that there were no bilge pumps in Nieuwe Zorg, neither here nor in the engine room; there had apparently been no need for over a century. This had been noted in her sale listing.

As we were finishing the hull inspection, Peter, the broker arrived. We all met: seller, broker, buyer and surveyor, and we received the verbal survey report. There were a few things for Henk to correct, repair or replace before the completion date. There was nothing major:

- un-seize, clean and grease the starboard leeboard winch;
- repair a broken cog on the port leeboard winch;
- relocate the secondary raw water inlet and blank-off the old hole;
- replace the propeller thrust bearing rubbers;
- repair a leak in the cooling water pump; and
- repair the interior heating system.

There were two items that we agreed will be shared 50/50:

- replace bow-thruster battery bank; and
- replace propellor shaft stern bearing.

Henk and Edi and I agreed to have Peter investigate the costs involved in the shared items, and we would then come-up with an amount to deduct from the balance owing on the purchase. We arrived at an easy agreement and then we got into our four separate cars and Henk led us around the Westeinderplassen to Hoofddorp, to a warehouse where he has been storing Nieuwe Zorg's rigging. The leeboards had been newly refinished.

We were aware from the listing that some fittings and pieces of rigging were missing and that there is no jib, only a mainsail. We saw that the sail was in good condition, still crisp and as far as we looked, with intact stitching. The mast has a deep split running about half its length, and this had been exacerbated by an earlier repair attempt. Henk had invited a carpenter to attend the inspection, and after a quick examination, we all agreed that it was uneconomical to repair. The boom is in far better condition, though missing a few fittings. In our contract, the seller

is to install the leeboards and deliver the remainder of the rigging onboard Nieuwe Zorg before the closing date. We told Henk that he could exclude the mast from this, but to include the mast counterweight. It was mid-afternoon by the time we had all shaken hands and had driven off in our separate directions. Everything had gone smoothly; totally zonder zorg.

Edi and I drove northward, past Volendam and out across the Afsluitdijk to Friesland and then further northward to Harlingen. We had been researching yards to do our proposed refit on Nieuwe Zorg. Among other yards, we had looked at the marvellously modern, but not-yet-completed new facilities at Kempers, and had met with Willem Dokkum, the works manager. We were now on our way to meet with Lex Tichelaar, a partner at Scheepsbouw & Reparatie Friesland, known better as SRF.

As we left our car and walked across the yard toward a couple of men talking, one of them stepped out to meet us. We asked where we could find Lex, and he said right here, pointing to his chest. Lex is a robust man, very alive and immediately likable.

He showed us around, beginning with a huge loft full of shelves laden with a vast assortment of old boat parts and fittings. Next he showed us a similar sized hall full of new parts, fittings and hardware. We saw a mast and spar building room, in which they build solid and laminated wooden spars and masts. We followed him through huge hangars with a broad range of ship construction, repair and refit projects in progress in wood, steel and composite. He showed us the cabinetmaking shops, the steel fabrication shops and we completed the loop up in his office sharing coffee. We liked the place; they appear passionate in their restoration and refit of traditional vessels, employing as appropriate both the old and the fully modern shipbuilding techniques and equipment.

Lex confirmed that they had space inside for our skûtsje in October to begin a restoration and modernizing refit over the winter. He asked for the current location of Nieuwe Zorg so he could look at her to gain a better understanding as we discuss work over the coming weeks. We left SRF convinced that it fully met our requirements to do a major refit on Nieuwe Zorg.

We were now committed to the purchase of an antique skûtsje that had been built in 1908 in Gaastmeer, just inland from the Zuiderzee. With a spare day until our flight back to Vancouver, on Thursday we played tourist. Among other things, while we were browsing along the Volendam waterfront, we had our portrait taken dressed in traditional nineteenth century Zuiderzee boating clothing.

On Friday we drove to the airport, dropped the rental car, checked-in and boarded a flights to Vancouver. We had driven just over 4250 kilometres in a very relaxing two weeks, during which time we had found a wonderful old boat. We were delighted with the ease of the entire process, and particularly with the clear, concise and efficient system used by the brokers, surveyors and insurers in the Netherlands.

There were a few items arising from the surveys that the owner must address before the closing date, which we had set in our offer to purchase contract as 01 September to allow six weeks for the comfortable completion of any arisings from the survey. Also, before the closing date we need to transfer the balance of the purchase price to the broker's trust account.

Chapter Seven

Researching History

With the details taken care of and having six weeks before our possession date, I began researching skûtsje history in general and that of Nieuwe Zorg in particular.

sold

Dimensions: 16,36 x 3,44 m
Air draft min.: ca. 1,95 m
Built: 1908 Wildschut in Gaastmeer
Accommodation: 2 cabins / 5 berths

Engine: Perkins 6 cil. 84,6 kW (115 HP)
Draft: ca. 0,70 m
Hull shape: flat bottom
Material: steel

On the brokerage offering she was described as having been built in 1908 by the Wildschut yard in Gaastmeer. From our contract to purchase, I found that the sellers, Henk and Madij had bought her in 1975 and Henk later told us that her name had always been Nieuwe Zorg.

I searched online and found a website: www.skutsjehistorie.nl, where there is a listing of registrations for all the iron and steel skûtsjes that had been built. I sorted the list alphabetically by ship names and scrolled through the Nieuwe Zorgs. There are 40 of them plus one Nieuwe Zorgen listed as having been registered between 1895 to 1923, none of them built by Wildschut, nor even in Gaastmeer.

I next sorted the list by registration date and scrolled to 1908. Of the sixty-eight skûtsjes built in Friesland in 1908, four of them were named Nieuwe Zorg, but none of these are listed as having built in Gaastmeer, nor by Wildschut. The two 1908 registrations that had been built by Wildschut in Gaastmeer, Hoop op Zegen and Zeldenrust, had measurements that were different from those of our Nieuwe Zorg.

I then sorted the list by building yard and scrolled to the Gaastmeer section. There I found a listing for De Nieuwe Zorg built in 1901. Things weren't making sense until I noticed that the date sequence was awry; the 1901 listing was sorted with the 1907s, which is where her Registry Number, S831N placed her.

S 818 N	1907	Aag	Workum, Jan de Jong	Makkum, Willem Everts Zwolsman / Amels	Jan de Boer te Weidum
S 819 N	1907	De Twee Gebroeders	Drachten, Albert Hendriks Schokker	Gaastmeer, Wildschut	Jan Overwijk te Oppenhuizen ('Twee Gebroeders')
S 820 N	1907	De Twee Gebroeders	Terhorne, Engele Engelsma	Sneek, Minne Molles van der Werf (vanaf juni 1906)	
S 825 N	1907	De Jonge Afke	Poppingawier, Andries Bouwhuis	Drachten/De Pijp, Bouke Berends Roorda	
▲ S 826 N	1907	De Jonge Douwe	Oosterbierum, Bouke Lodewijk	Franeker, Klaas Draaisma	J. Talsma en Maritieme Academie ('De Jonge Douwe')
▲ S 827 N	1907	Hoop op Zegen	Oppenhuizen, Gosse Aukes van der Veen	Drachten/ Buitenstvallaat, Jan Oebeles van der Werff ('De Nijverheid')	
S 829 N	1908	Verwisseling	Wierum, J. de Vries	IJlst, Jelle Jelles Croles	
S 831 N	1901	De Nieuwe Zorg	Koudum, Age Vaandriks	Gaastmeer, Wildschut	
S 832 N	1908	De Twee Gebroeders	Oppenhuizen, Anne Hoekstra	Sneek, Minne Molles van der Werf (vanaf juni 1906)	
S 833 N	1908	De Tijd zal 't Leeren	Uitwellingerga, Wybe Lolkes Zijlstra	Sneek, Minne Molles van der Werf (vanaf juni 1906)	
▲ S 835 N	1908	De Vrouw Hinke	Follega, Arjen Mientjes Keuning	Heeg, De Jong	Kees Jonker te Woudsend ('Vrouwe Hinke')

De Nieuwe Zorg

Registratienummer:	**S 831 N**
Bouwjaar:	**1901**
Type:	**Roefschip**
Werf:	**Wildschut in Gaastmeer**
Opdrachtgever:	**Age Vaandriks te Koudum**
Lengte:	**16,33 meter**
Breedte:	**3,43 meter**
Tonnage:	**31,064 ton**
Meting:	**Sneek, 20 mrt. 1909**

Tweede eigenaar: Douwe Albert Visser te Stavoren
Tweede meting: Stavoren, 25 juni 1941: l 16,38 m m / b 3,44 m / t 31,971 ton: G 6496 N

I resorted the list by Registry Number, and De Nieuwe Zorg's S831N fell in among the 1908 listings.

I opened the details of the S831N line and found her second measurement from 1941. These are the exact measurements listed for our Nieuwe Zorg in the brokerage listing: length 16.38 metres and beam 3.44 metres. She was calculated in 1941 at 31.971 tons, and the owner was listed as Douwe Albert Visser of Stavoren.

I emailed the webmaster of the site and pointed out the apparent error to him, and asked for confirmation that it actually is an error. A few days later I received a reply from Frits Jansen, the webmaster confirming that the date had been mistyped when compiling the spreadsheet from the original ledger. He told me that it would soon be corrected on the website. Frits attached a photo of a spread of pages of the Sneek registration ledger showing the listing for De Nieuwe Zorg.

I blew-up the high-resolution photo to show the details clearly: 831 | De Nieuwe Zorg | A. Vaandriks / Koudum | Roefschip / yaer | Gaastmeer / 1908.

On the facing page, the registration continues with her measurements all written-out in words. Her first measurement on 20 March 1909 gave her length as 16.33 metres and her beam as 3.43 metres. A later measurement is referenced with new registration number, G6496N. Under Notations, the final column, is an undated entry indicating the registration was cancelled.

The listings showed that the first owner was Age Vaandriks of Koudum. I searched the registry and found that Age had commissioned a second ship from a different yard in 1925, a 19.15 X 3.9 metre skûtsje named Dankbaarheid. To its details page had been added a photo of Age, and with further digging I found that he was born in 1876, so would have been 32 when he had the Wildschut Brothers build De Nieuwe Zorg.

Between 1857 and 1953, four generations of the family Wildschut had a shipyard in Gaastmeer, a short distance from Sneek in southwestern Friesland. Beginning with ship repair and maintenance, they soon grew to building wooden sailing tjalken, and as the demand for more nimble barges grew, they developed the predecessor of the skûtsje.

At the end of the nineteenth century Wildschut began building in iron, and then from 1904 they appear to have specialized in iron and steel skûtsjes, building eighteen of them in the ten years leading up to The Great War. This photo shows the Wildschut facilities in 1907, around the time that De Nieuwe Zorg was being built. The yard also built tjotters, tjalken, klippers, palingaken and a variety of smaller inland water craft.

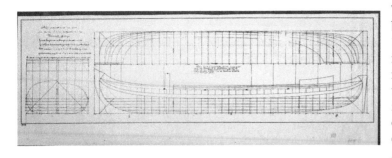

The Friesian skûtsje had been developed between 1855 and 1860 and they were initially built of wood. Then in 1887 riveted iron was introduced, and during the first decade of the twentieth century, the yards gradually converted from iron to steel. A total of 870 iron and steel skûtsjes were built until 1933. There are many line drawings of skûtsjes in the Fries Scheepvaart Museum in Sneek. This one is of built in 1908 by Auke van der Zee in Joure.

They were initially used in the eel fishery and in hauling peat and composted manure from inland Friesland to the coast and along the Zuiderzee. The worldwide depression starting in 1929 decreased the commercial usefulness of the skûtsje and the closing of the Zuiderzee in 1932 sounded its death knell. There were only four skûtsjes built in all of Friesland after 1928, and with the last one in 1933, their production ceased.

During the ensuing years, many skûtsjes were fitted with engines, but even with power, they were too small to compete with new designs, particularly the luxemotor. By the end of World War II, like most tjalk type barges, skûtsjes were commercially obsolete, and were either abandoned, were sold for scrap or were refitted as houseboats.

The houseboat shown in this photo was Nieuwe Zorg in 1975 when Henk and Madij bought her. The snapshot was among the folder of papers that came with the boat. Also in the folder was the bill of sale showing they had paid 15,500 Guilders for her.

Some Skûtskes were converted to sailing yachts, retaining the mast and rigging, removing the small roef aft to make a cockpit and turning the cargo hold into living accommodation with a jachtenroef. Our skûtsje is one of these.

Henk was a professional welder and he spent three years refitting Nieuwe Zorg, starting with scrapping the wooden superstructure and gutting the interior. He added a graceful jachtenroef, which is seen in this 1978 photo. He told us that he had copied the lines from De Groene Draeck, the Lemsteraakjacht that the Dutch people had given to Princess Beatrix on her eighteenth birthday in 1956.

A few skûtsjes were maintained in their original form and used in inter-town races. As the popularity of these races grew, more and more houseboat and yacht conversions were reverted to their original configurations. There are currently about ninety of these historic vessels restored to full sailing trim and competing in regular SKS and IFKS races in Friesland.

Wildschut's twenty skûtsjes are a small portion of the 870 iron and steel skûtsjes that were built by some thirty Friesland yards between 1887 and 1933. Of the twenty Wildschut skûtsjes, we have accounted for fourteen survivors, with ten of these now in full sailing trim. Of these, six have the distinction of having been registered as racing Suûtsjes in one or the other of the two leagues: Sintrale Kommisje Skûtsjesilen (SKS) or Iepen Fryske Kampioenskippen Skûtsjesilen (IFKS). Another is the representative skûtsje in the Zuiderzee Museum in Enkhuizen and another is a registered historical sailing ship. The skûtsjes that Wildschut built are held in very high esteem, and we are proud to own one.

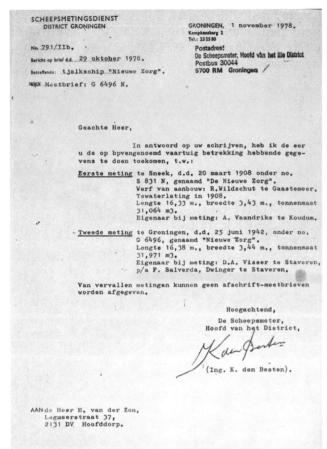

We still had some gaps in our skûtsje's history. The new registration number, G6496 noted on the second page of the Sneek ledger matches a new owner, Douwe Albert Visser of Stavoren.

Among the papers in Henk's file aboard Nieuwe Zorg was a 1978 letter he had received in response to a query on the registration history. It confirmed the measurement data we had already found and confirmed the new owner as D.A. Visser and listed his address as: p/a F. Salverda te Stavoren (in care of F. Salvera at Stavoren).

We tried to trace D.A. Visser or Douwe Albert Visser as he is listed on the De Nieuwe Zorg page at www.skutsjehistorie.nl but we kept coming up with modern versions of the name. Our online searches are seriously affected by there currently being an Albert Visser and two Douwe Vissers as very competitive skûtsje racers, each as skipper of one of the fourteen competing skûtsjes in the annual SKS championship series.

1n August 2013 Douwe Visser, Jzn. skippered his crew in the De Sneker Pan to his third consecutive championship in the fourteen-day, eleven-race series. This was his eighth championship since taking-over as skipper in 1989. Complicating our search further is that a Douwe Visser, Azn. is also an SKS skipper, and he won the series championship twice, 2005 and 2009 in the skûtsje, Doarp Grou. In 2011, 2012 and 2013 he was runner-up to his cousin Douwe. Further confusing search engines is that Albert Visser, Jzn, brother of the Sneker Pan's skipper, had for years been the skipper of Twee Gebroeders, the SKS skûtsje from Drachten, and in 2013 moved to take over as skipper of the Lemster skûtsje. With all the notable skûtsje involvement of these modern Douwe and Albert Vissers, Google couldn't get us back beyond very recent history.

Again I emailed the webmaster of www.skutsjehistorie.nl and again Fritz quickly replied with the family tree: Douwe Albert Visser, 1902-1997 married Tjitske Taekesd Salverda 1906-1998 in 1928. They had five children: Albert, Taeke, Jappie, Immertje and Trijntje. Taeke was a skipper in the SKS on d Halve Maen from 1982-1984. Albert was the father of Douwe Azn Visser who is now skipper on Doarp Grou in the SKS. Jappie is the father of Douwe Jzn Visser, who is now skipper on Sneker Pan in the SKS, and Albert Jzn Visser who is now skipper on Twee Gebroeders in the SKS.

Frits continued with his genealogy: Tjitske the grandmother also comes from a skipper family; her father Taeke Salverda was a fisherman from Stavoren. Her sister Willemke married Klaas Keimpesz van der Meulen, an SKS skipper and four-times champion. Their children Keimpe, Taeke and Ype van der Meulen are or where skippers in the SKS.

So now we know the relationship between Nieuwe Zorg's second owner and the current successful SKS skippers. He was grandfather or great uncle to more than a third of the skippers of the current fleet. The family members have won the SKS championship seventeen times since 1945, when the organization was established.

Now we need to communicate with the Vissers and van der Muelens to fill in the blanks we have in Nieuwe Zorg's history between 1941 and 1975 and to see if we can find out what the skûtsje Nieuwe Zorg was used for.

Chapter Eight

Taking Possession

Toward the end of August, we wired the balance of our skûtsje's purchase price to the yacht broker's trust account in Enkhuizen, and at the same time, we wired the insurance premium to the agent. With all the purchase details taken care of, we began organizing our return to the boat in Aalsmeer, Netherlands.

Although Aalsmeer is at the end of the runways of Amsterdam's Schiphol Airport, Air Canada does not fly there. They do; however, fly to Brussels, about 200 kilometres from Aalsmeer. All the flights to Brussels were overbooked at the end of August; however, on the Tuesday after Labour Day there were flights with many open seats, so short notice booking on our choice of them was easy. Through the broker, we easily arranged to postpone the possession date to 5 September.

There is something about Tuesday and Belgium, so Edi booked flights to Brussels via Montreal for Tuesday the 5th of September and I reserved a car to get us from the airport to Aalsmeer and to use during the first few days for shopping after we arrive.

When I was reserving the car, I clicked the GPS option and was shocked to see that even with my Hertz #1 Club Gold, which still triggers Air Canada Super Elite discounts from a former life, the GPS charge from Brussels for the four days came to just over €70, including taxes. I decided to look at options. When we were in the Netherlands in July, everyone referred to TomTom when talking of driving or walking directions. Online in the Apple App Store I found TomTom with maps for all of Western Europe for my iPad for $89.99, about €72.50.

While I was in the online App Store, I decided to look at Navionics charts for Europe to see if there is coverage of the inland waterways. We had been delighted with the quality of the Navionics charts for iPad and they became a very important adjunct to our chart-plotter aboard Sequitur as we navigated from La Punta Peru southward along the Chilean coast, through the archipelagos of Patagonia and Tierra del Fuego, around Cape Horn and up the eastern coasts of the Americas. Many times the iPad was our primary source of navigational information. I found the Navionics Europe HD application for $64.99, and some quick investigation showed me that the lakes, rivers and canals are all charted. I downloaded a copy to my iPad.

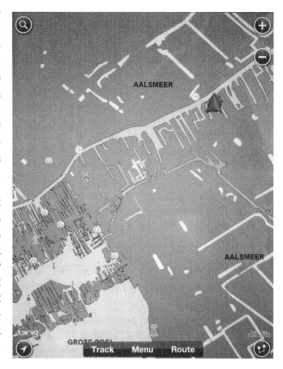

We each packed a piece of checked luggage at 22.5 kilos and balanced our four carryon pieces at exactly 10 kilos each. The total of 85 kilos is much less than the 224 kilos we lugged had back from St Augustine when we had left Sequitur two months previously. However, our current trip was planned for only five weeks, sufficient time to take possession, move aboard and become familiar with the skûtsje as we slowly took her from Aalsmeer, North Holland to Harlingen, Friesland for her facelift.

On Tuesday morning we wheeled our luggage the two blocks to the SkyTrain station and rode to the airport. Because of a late arrival of the inbound plane, our flight was delayed leaving Vancouver, and we had run to make the connection in Montreal. Of course, our Vancouver flight arrived at one end of the terminal and the Brussels flight departed from the other end. Fortunately, Trudeau Airport is rather compact, so the run was not so bad.

Customs and Immigration in Brussels were a snap, our luggage had made the tight connection and our car was waiting for us at the Hertz gold counter. The TomTom worked well on my iPad, and shortly before noon, we arrived at the marina in Aalsmeer. Henk was aboard Nieuwe Zorg ready for our noon appointment.

During the past few weeks he had completed the work arising from the survey, which included mounting the leeboards. They look wonderful. We did a walk-through and a systems familiarization, and then we signed the transfer papers, formally taking possession.

Henk and Madij's attention to detail, their care and their pride were all so obvious from the moment we first saw Nieuwe Zorg. She took possession of us, and now we had reciprocated.

In July, after we had contracted the purchase of Nieuwe Zorg, we had encouraged Henk and Madij to take her out cruising during the five weeks until the completion date. They had spent three weeks cruising with their extended family, during which time Henk must have spent many hours maintaining and fine-tuning the skûtsje; she was in even better condition than when we had left her after the survey.

We then spent a delightful couple of hours with Henk learning the idiosyncrasies of the vessel's systems and listening to stories from their thirty-seven years of restoring, upgrading, maintaining and enjoying this wonderful historic skûtsje.

After Henk left, Edi and I lay down for a nap to try to catch-up from having been up and travelling for over twenty-four hours and to start adjusting to the eight hour timezone change. We were expecting Lex and Klaas from SRF to arrive onboard sometime in the early evening to discuss preliminary ideas for Nieuwe Zorg's refit and for her restoration to sailing.

Lex and Klaas arrived shortly before 1800, waking me from my slumber on the salon couch as they arrived. We showed them through the skûtsje and threw ideas around with them for the better part of two hours. They took measurements, made notes, did calculations and we all scratched our heads and pondered the possibilities. They left with a good idea of what we wanted and a better understanding of how to achieve it than they had gleaned from the emailed list of items we had sent them a couple of weeks previously.

A little before 2000 we rushed off following directions on my iPad's TomTom to the closest Albert Hein for some groceries and cooking utensils. It was a smaller version of the huge Dutch supermarket chain, and they had no cooking utensils. From the store's information counter we were given the address of a much larger Albert Hein store in Amstelveen, which we punched into TomTom and allowed the program's mellow voice to lead us there. Their cooking equipment supply was limited, so I punched in Ikea's address in South Amsterdam and TomTom took us there with 45 minutes of shopping time left before the 2100 closing.

From Vancouver, we had brought sheets, pillow cases, duvet cover and towels, plus cutlery, stemware and our favourite coffee cups and saucers, so we needed everything else. As we hastened around the circuit, we loaded into our cart an assortment of pots and pans, cooking utensils, plates, bowls, pillows, a duvet and whatever else we could think of before the closing announcements began. We were back in the car with our load of goodies shortly before 2115 and following TomTom back to the larger Albert Hein. With a bit more than half an hour until closing, we set a more relaxing pace selecting sufficient groceries and supplies to settle us into living aboard until, after some much-needed rest, we could conduct a more organized laying-in of basic goods.

During the following days we alternately measured and remeasured spaces aboard, rested, went on shopping trips and drew preliminary layout plans for Nieuwe Zorg's interior makeover. As much as we love the craftsmanship and design of Nieuwe Zorg's interior, it is dated. It is a third of a century old, as are her systems and her construction technologies. Our intention was to totally strip-out her interior down to bare riveted iron and start over. The makeover includes making the bedroom the full width of the hull, rather than two-thirds the width. Also, we wanted to move the shower to the centreline to take advantage of the higher headroom there. Because of the low curved roof, using sliding doors instead of hinged ones will make access to the bedroom and heads much easier.

The current galley had extremely limited countertop space, the counter being mostly taken-up by the gas cooktop and the sink. We thought of adding an island to increase the countertop workspace, but there was insufficient room, so we reworked the design to accommodate under-counter convection-microwave oven, dishwasher and fridge-freezer. Because of the easy and frequent availability of fresh produce along the inland waterways of Europe, we won't need two fridges and two freezers like we had in Sequitur; a single under-counter combo unit will be sufficient.

For breakfast on our third morning aboard, Edi prepared some pain perdu au jambon. We had settled-in quickly, and we began organizing for a slow trip northward to Harlingen, Friesland for Nieuwe Zorg's facelift. At 104 years of age, the old girl is past due for her hundred-year makeover.

We figured that along the way, as we became more accustomed to the old lady, our ideas of what we wanted and how we wanted them would slowly evolve.

Chapter Nine

Northward Through Holland

I hauled out the portfolio of ANWB charts that Henk had left aboard and began looking at possible routes northward to Harlingen. The first leg was easy; turn right and follow Ringvaart van de Haarlemmermeerpolder to Rieker plas, through it to Nieuwe Meer and along it to Nieuwemeersluis, through the lock and into Schinkel of Kostverloren vaart, which is followed northward to the Noordzee Kanaal.

I also looked at the route on the Navionics app on my iPad. It confirmed that the lowest bridge along the route was 2.44 metres, so with our air draft of 1.95 metres, we would not have to wait for any bridges to open for us. I looked at jachthavens close to downtown Amsterdam, and seeing that SixHaven, directly across the IJ from Central Station was the most convenient, I phoned the number listed on the iPad app and made a reservation for three days from mid-afternoon on Tuesday, 11 September.

It was drizzling on Tuesday morning when I called Henk; he had asked to be there when we cast off and headed out. Henk arrived and suggested to me that I put on some rain gear, otherwise I'd be drenched by the time we got to Amsterdam; the erected canopy is too high to pass under some of bridges. He dug down into a locker and pulled out a suit that he had left onboard for me.

At 1224 we slipped and headed out as Henk watched his cherished skûtsje motor slowly away. For just over thirty-seven years, more than half his life, he had poured his heart and soul into Nieuwe Zorg, and now she was leaving. We all felt lumps in our throats and had wet cheeks.

At 1337 we arrived at Nieuwemeersluis and sat alongside some pilings awaiting the cycling of the lock. At 1349 we entered and temporarily secured, waiting for the two small craft ahead of us to move further in so that we could squeeze forward and leave room behind us for a large commercial barge.

Pauline Anette moved in behind us and secured, then we all rode up about half a meter as the lock filled. The rise was to bring us up from the level of the canals in the polder south of Amsterdam to the level of the IJ. Of the many hundreds of locks that I have transited in Europe, this first one with Nieuwe Zorg was the lowest level change of all.

After we were through the lock, we allowed the commercial traffic to overtake us as we motored slowly along the canal enjoying the passing scene. The parade of boats ahead of us all needed to have the bridges opened for them, but at only 1.95 metres in height, Nieuwe Zorg could slip under all the closed bridges on this canal.

Once the last boat ahead of us passed through each of the bridge cuts, the bridgekeepers all lowered the bridges ahead of our arrival, knowing it wasn't necessary to hold-up road and pedestrian traffic for us. We ducked under eleven bridges as we slowly motored through Amsterdam, admiring the wonderful variety of architecture.

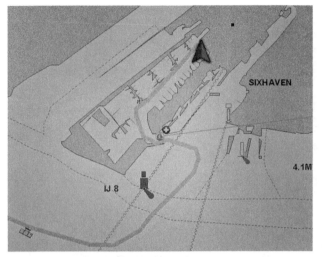

At 1513 we left the canal, entered the IJ and turned eastward through the heavy commercial traffic across the north waterfront of Amsterdam. We located the entrance to SixHaven and threaded our way in through a gap not quite a metre wider than Nieuwe Zorg and then all the way along the narrow alley past jutting bows and sterns to the back of the marina to lie alongside the end wall, directly under the havenkantoor.

When we arrived there had been boats secured alongside all four of the T-docks, narrowing the passage to under four metres. Fortunately, Nieuwe Zorg handled it superbly, squeezing by with less than thirty centimetres to spare. I was delighted with her manoeuvrability and responsiveness.

We checked-in and paid €87 for three nights, including electricity, water and wifi. We asked the Havenmeester for directions to the local supermarket and then walked the kilometre or so to it. Disappointingly, it is in a low income neighbourhood, and the selection is not what we were looking for. We were able to find sufficient to make do.

On Wednesday we walked the few hundred metres from the marina to the free ferry, which crosses the IJ to Central Station. From there we took the Metro southward to Ikea to finish our laying-in of basic equipment and supplies. Unlike in Canada, Ikea here is easily accessible by public transit.

On Thursday we celebrated my sixty-eighth birthday with a visit to the Van Gogh Museum. We took the ferry across the IJ and walked a crooked route about five kilometres through central Amsterdam, enjoying the varying scene. At the museum, instead of the €14 per person entry fee, we opted to each buy €49.90 passes good for one year for entry to over four hundred museums throughout the Netherlands.

On our way back, we took a different route to see more of the city and along the way we paused near the flower market for koffie en appeltaart in a street café. We also did some shopping to strike-off the last few items from our list, and arrived back onboard at the end of the afternoon, refreshed from our ten kilometre walk.

The weather forecast for Friday called for rain with winds above 30 kph. We decided to see if we could stay another day. The Havenmeester readily extended our stay and we settled in aboard, nicely warm and dry as the rains began. By early afternoon on Friday, the hour-by-hour online forecast was predicting sunny periods with a slight chance of rain, so at 1300 we walked to the ferry and rode across to downtown.

As we came out the front of the station, we passed seemingly endless racks of bicycles. There were thousands of them. Most commuting is done by bicycle and public transit, either train or bus. Car parking is scarce and expensive, while bicycle parking is everywhere and free. There are more bicycles in the Netherlands than there are people, about 1.12 bicycles per person. Nearly 30% of all trips in the Netherlands are by bike, and traffic patterns reflect this. The order of priority seems to be: pedestrians, buses, cyclists, boats and then cars.

Through Google, we had located an Albert Hein supermarket just across the Martelaarsgracht from Central Station. We found it a rather narrow, but block-deep supermarket fitted into a patchwork of several old buildings. Because of the confined space, the selection is a bit limited, but what is there is nicely skewed to the upscale end and toward the quality we were looking for. We were still trying to accustom ourselves to buying for only a day or two at a time, rather than for weeks or months as we had been doing the previous three years sailing around South America. We held our purchases to only a few days supply and were ready to continue northward on Saturday morning.

We waited until nearly 1030 on Saturday, 15 September for the boats on the slip across from us to leave. We then had room to swing Nieuwe Zorg's bow across to port the eight or so metres to the corner of the pier, from where it could be squeezed by hand past the corner. My calculations had been correct; she was about ten centimetres shorter than the space available, and with her bows past the corner, we were be able to motor forward out of the marina rather than having to back out. Once back out in the IJ, we almost immediately left it and entered the Noordhollandsch Kanaal and the Willemssluizen. In the lock we were joined by a cruiser named Stormvogel. The skipper pointed to his 't Eiland burgee from Aalsmeer, and pointing to Nieuwe Zorg, said: "that's Henks old boat".

We locked through and slowly made our way past an amazing assortment of liveaboard vessels in a decreasing level of quality and care the further from the city centre we went. The vessels gradually decreased in frequency, and then ended with a few derelicts. We were out in the open country, with the cattle and sheep, the farmhouses and the windmills.

Shortly before noon we entered the Monnickendam-Edam Kanaal and a short while later we were motoring along a very narrow waterway past a near-solid line of dike houses in Broek in Waterland. Each of the houses has a foot ferry to cross from the road on the one side to the otherwise isolated house on the other.

At 1220 we arrived at the first bridge than needed to be lifed for us, and we moored to a bollard and a pounded stake on the left bank while we waited for the bridgekeeper to arrive. After about ten minutes the keeper arrived and let us through the bridge, and then through a second one a bit further along.

In Monnickendam, we stopped in the approaches to the lock to await the lock keeper's return from lunch, and then shortly after 1400 we began locking through. Two other boats came through with us, both of them turning right and heading through Monnickendam toward the Markermeer, while we turned left up the Stinkevuil of Purmer Ee for a kilometre or so until turning right up the Purmer ringvaart and bypassing the two low bridges on the Trekvaart Het Schouw. A bit less than an hour later we turned off the ringvaart and into the Oorgat through Edam.

At 1520 we secured starboard side to on the right bank in a residential area of Edam, just short of the start of a series of six low bridges that we needed to have lifted in order to continue. It is a very peaceful spot, and on the bank are coin-operated water and electricity outlets.

Among the bridges we needed to have lifted for us is the Kwakelbrug, for which Edi's great-grandfather and grandfather were once the toll keeper. We walked the short distance along the canal through Edam to the bridge. Next to the bridge is the house in which Edi had always been told that her grandfather once lived. Beside and in the rear of the house is a small shipyard.

On the shipyard gate is a sign signifying that Scheepswerf Groot has been in business since 1768. We later learned that it traces its roots back further to the golden era of shipbuilding in Edam in the seventeenth century. Edi knew that her great-grandmother's maiden name was Groot, but in her tracing of the family genealogy, Edi had not run into this connection with shipbuilding. On the surface it made sense that her great-grandfather had married a daughter of the shipyard owner. More investigation is required.

We continued along to the Edam Museum, which is housed in a house built in 1550. Our museum pass gave us entry and the loan of small audio guide players triggered by proximity switches to explain the various displays. Edam's harbour was readily accessible to the main cities in Holland and also to international trading routes.

Shipbuilding became an important industry; by the sixteenth century there were thirty-three shipbuilding establishments in Edam. The city grew in prominence, and with Enkhuizen, Hoorn and Amsterdam, it was one of the most important cities of North Holland. The harbour opening on the Zuiderzee allowed flooding inland, so in 1569 the harbour mouth was closed with lock gates. Unfortunately, the harbour very gradually silted in, and by the end of the seventeenth century, the ship building industry was in rapid decline. However, because of its right granted by Emperor Charles V in 1526 to have a weekly cheese market, the city continued to prosper. In 1594 the right to hold the Edam cheese market was extended for eternity.

We wound our way back through the old city to Nieuwe Zorg and in the evening we relaxed over dinner aboard. On Sunday morning we explored more of the back lanes and small streets of Edam and in the afternoon we walked along the dikes to Volendam. We wandered through its old streets, browsed the shops along the historic harbour and enjoyed a fried sole sandwich from a waterfront fish shop.

We had spoken with the bridgekeeper on Saturday and learned the routine for passing through Edam. The descending schedule is 0930, 1130, 1400, 1600 and 1800, so on Monday morning at 1130 we set off. The first lift is a pair of wide, heavy traffic bridges, which leads to a short pound of about 25 metres length, where we needed to stop and wait.

The keeper had to close the two bridges behind us and restore traffic flow, then he pedalled down through a tunnel under the main roadway and began working on the third bridge while Edi held our bows to a pylon and I held the stern to another.

Once we were clear of the third bridge, we motored and drifted very slowly toward the Kwakelbrug, while the keeper pedalled along the canal bank to prepare the bridge for us. The scene was idyllic as we glided through the still waters along the narrow canal lined with impeccably maintained homes.

Looking back after passing through the Kwakelbrug, we saw a kwak on the ways in the shipyard having its bottom re-planked. We saw also how much a unit are the bridge, Edi's grandfather's house and Scheepswerf Groot.

As we slowly drifted down canal, the keeper closed the manual bridge astern of us and lifted the gates to restore traffic. He then pedalled past and began preparing the fifth bridge for us, manually closing gates to stop traffic, unlocking the mechanisms and activating the electric winch.

The canal is narrow, and passes through marvellous scenery, including the patio of the Hotel Fortuna, where we had sat on Sunday afternoon enjoying koffie en appeltaart and watching the boats passing by on the canal.

The sixth bridge is opened by hand, and as we passed under it, the bridge-keeper told us we could duck under the next bridge, the last one before the lock which would lead us out into the Markermeer. As we approached the lock, the lights turned red and green, indicating that it was being prepared for us. We easily locked-through, and at 1221 we entered the Markermeer and turned northward.

On the lake with us was a great variety boats, mostly sailing craft. Among the sailing craft were many old vessels, and as we motored north at 6 knots, we were slowly overtaken by a tjalk under sail. The wind was blowing offshore about 12 to 15 knots and the tjalk had its jib furled on the bowsprit, but was flying a full main and staysail. It was a wonderful beam reach for all of the boats sailing north and south along the coast.

Without rig; however, Nieuwe Zorg had to contend with motoring with a steep chop slapping at her port beam. I lowered the starboard leeboard to offer us some stability in the quick waves of the shallow meer.

At 1400 we were off the entrance to the harbour of the city of Hoorn and deciding which place to try first for moorage. As we neared, Grashaven appeared the natural choice, so we entered and quickly found a guest dock with a small cabin and an intercom to the office. We were given a berth across the end of a finger and we moved to it and secured.

We were in Hoorn, the place after which Cape Horn had been named, so in a way we were closing the loop on our rounding of the Cape in February.

Chapter Ten

The Zuiderzee

After we had organized onboard, we walked up the floats past ten fingers of mostly occupied slips. The marina is a fully modern and very well maintained facility of 710 slips, and in the havenkantoor we checked-in and paid €49 for two nights including electricity, water and wifi. We asked for directions to a museum that would give us some background on the discovery of Cape Horn.

We continued ashore and followed the directions into the centre of town, where we found the Westfries Museum. Actually, it appeared to be leaning out to greet us as we approached; one certainly gets a different slant on architecture around here. We used our passes to gain admission to the museum and searched in vain for any mention of the connection to Cape Horn. The displays are mostly inward looking depictions of life in the town, with very little on the far-reaching exploits of its former citizens, whose activities included the discovery of Cape Horn and the running of the VOC. We had to look further.

The VOC, Vereenigde Oost-Indische Compagnie, is the Dutch name for "United East India Company", more commonly known in English as the Dutch East India Company. It was a chartered company established in 1602 and granted an initial twenty-one year monopoly to carry out colonial activities in Asia. It is considered as the first multinational corporation, it was the first company to issue stock, the world's first publicly traded company on the world's first stock exchange. It began with the spice trade in the Far East and expanded, quickly eclipsing all of its rivals in the Asia trade.

Between 1602 and 1796 the VOC sent almost a million Europeans to work in the Asia trade on 4,785 ships, and handled more than 2.5 million tonnes of trade goods. By comparison, between 1500 to 1795 the remainder of Europe combined sent only 882,412 people. The fleet of the British East India Company, the VOC's nearest competitor, was a distant second with 2,690 ships and only one-fifth the tonnage of goods carried by the VOC.

The power of the company was in its ships; the Dutch had become the finest shipbuilders in the world. By 1669, the VOC was the richest private company the world has ever seen, with over 150 merchant ships, 40 warships, 50,000 employees, a private army of 10,000 soldiers, and a dividend payment of forty percent on the original investment. In 1637 its value was 78 million Dutch Guilders, which adjusted to 2012 Euros is €5.5 trillion, far surpassing any of its contemporary companies and all those since, including today's Exxon, IBM, Microsoft and Apple.

The VOC traded throughout Asia. Silver and copper from Japan were used to trade with India and China for silk, cotton, porcelain, and textiles. These products were either traded within Asia for the coveted spices or brought back to Europe. They built an artificial island off the coast of Nagasaki, Japan and for two centuries this was the only place where Europeans were permitted to trade with Japan.

The VOC had a monopoly on all Dutch trade with the Orient via the Cape of Good Hope and the Straits of Magellan, then the only known sea routes. Seeking an alternate route, Isaac Le Maire a prosperous Amsterdam merchant and Willem Schouten, a ship's master of the town of Hoorn formed a joint venture and received additional financial support from merchants of Hoorn. Two ships, the 360-ton Eendracht and the 110-ton Hoorn left Holland in June 1615. Hoorn was destroyed by fire while burning-off barnacles on the Argentine coast, and the expedition continued in Eendracht.

In late January 1616 Endracht sailed around the south tip of South America and in honour of the Dutch city, they named the most southerly point Kaap Hoorn. The name was later corrupted by English cartographers to Cape Horn because of its shape. In Chile, where it is located, it is charted as Cabo de Hornos, which translates as: Cape of Ovens.

To investigate the VOC further, on Tuesday morning we walked to the train station and bought return tickets for €4.40 each for the twenty-one minute trip to Enkhuizen. With Edam, Hoorn and Amsterdam, it was one of the four most important cities of North Holland in the sixteenth and seventeenth centuries. From the Enkhuizen station we walked past the fortified tower, the Drommedaris, which was built in 1540 and then we continued through the old town to the canal and along it to the Zuiderzeemuseum, which is housed in a string of seventeenth century buildings that were once East India Company warehouses.

Our museum passes gave us entry and soon we were learning the geography and history of the Zuiderzee. It was an arm of the North Sea that had gradually evolved with the rising sea levels caused by the slow global warming and melting ice sheets from the last ice age twelve thousand years ago. Global

warming in not a new thing invented by pseudo-scientists and popularized by Al Gore; it is one of the natural cycles of the earth's climate.

At the end of the ice age, the area now known as the North Sea was dry land. About five thousand years ago, the rising sea levels from the melting and recession of the last of the ice sheets that had covered northern Europe, created the North Sea and the melting polar icecaps soon increased it to its current shape. The topography of the areas inland from the coast in what is now the northeastern portion of the Netherlands was a shallow depression. Drainage here was slow and the area filled with peat.

The continued warming trend caused the North Sea levels to rise further. Gradually there were inundations over the low lands inland, and flooding during major storms accelerated the erosion of the coastal dunes. The two maps on the previous page show the approximate land form of what is today the Netherlands. The one on the left shows the coastline during the first century AD, the one on the right depicts its shape in the tenth century.

Storms in 1282 and 1287 broke through the coastal barriers and the sea flooded inland. The name Zuiderzee entered general usage around that time. The size of the inland sea remained relatively stable from the fifteenth century onwards because of improvements in dikes. There were continuing disastrous floods, one in 1421 broke a seawall and incoming waters flooded seventy-two villages and killed about ten thousand people.

Dikes and seawalls continued to be built and upgraded and around the Zuiderzee many fishing villages grew. Some of these developed into fortified towns and established important trade connections with ports in the Baltic Sea, England and in the Hanseatic League.

Kampen in Overijssel grew in prominence, as did several villages and towns in Noord Holland, such as Naarden, Amsterdam, Edam, Hoorn, and Enkhuizen. The formation of the Zuiderzee had created many large protected ports that were connected to the sea and started the ascendancy of the Dutch to the status of world super power in the sixteenth and seventeenth centuries.

Th map on the facing page was drawn in 1818 and it shows the extent of the Zuiderzee at that time. The Dutch continued to extend and reinforce its system seawalls and dykes and look at ways to reclaim land from the sea. In the seventeenth century there was a proposal to harness the waters, but its concept was too ambitious and impractical for the available technology of the time. In nineteenth century serious attention was given to controlling the waters and reclaiming land. Plans were proposed in 1848, 1849, 1866, 1873 and then Cornelius Lely began serious planning in 1886.

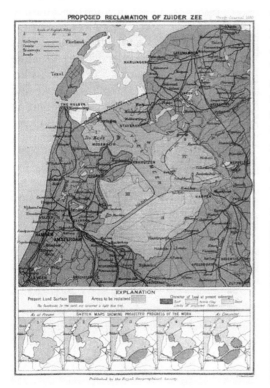

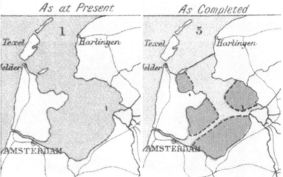

This map was used to illustrate an article in the March 1893 edition of the Geographical Journal of the British Royal Geographical Society. The article had been written by Pieter Hendrik Schoute of Groningen, Friesland. He wrote of plans developed by a technical research team under the guidance of Cornelius Lely, who in 1891 had become the Minister of Transport and Water Management for the Netherlands.

The plan called for the closing of the Zuiderzee with a dyke running from the tip of Noord Hol-

land to western Friesland, making the contained waters into a freshwater lake. Once this was stabilized, internal dykes would be built encircling some of the shallowest areas and then draining these to reclaim the land. It was a very ambitious project.

The project sat on the shelf through the recession of the 1890s and continued to gather dust into the twentieth century. In 1913 Cornelius Lely regained his seat as Minister of Transport and Water Management. After severe flooding along the Zuiderzee coasts in 1916, the plans were resurrected and in 1918 the Zuiderzee Act was passed. Works began in 1920 and they progressed in stages. By 1924 the first dike, just 2.5 kilometres in length was completed. Between 1927 and 1932 the 23 kilometre Afsluitdijk was built between Noord Holland and Friesland, cutting off the newly formed IJsselmeer from the Noordzee. The polders were drained between 1930 and 1968.

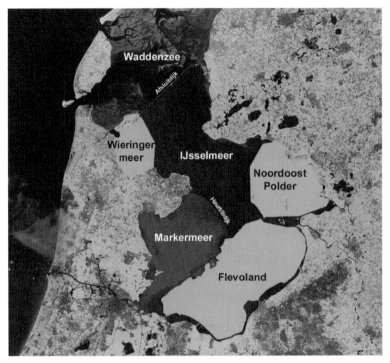

The newly created lands of Wieringermeer were absorbed into the province of Noord Holland. Those of the Noordoostpolder and the Flevolands were united in 1986 to form the new province of Flevoland. A total of 1650 square kilometres of new land was created. About fifteen percent of this is now used as housing, nearly seventy percent is for agriculture use and the remainder is parks, nature preserves and infrastructure. The plans to dyke and drain the southwest portion of the old Zuiderzee to form a polder named Markerwaard was indefinitely postponed in the 1980s.

With a better understanding of the background of the Zuiderzee, we went into the schepenhal to examine the collection of wooden boats packed like sardines into the fifteen metre high room. Although in the photos they look like models, they are beautifully preserved, full-sized vessels.

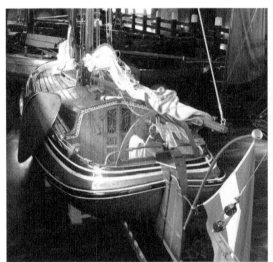

Viewing is from floor-level, beneath the boats, from a deck-level balcony and from a balcony at mid-mast height. The collection consists of both work boats and yachts. There is a Fresian bol, two tjotters, fishing boats, including a Marken smack and one similar to the kwaks we saw in Volendam. There is a small tjalk, which appears to be a predecessor of the skûtsje.

After a couple of hours, we left the indoor exhibits and headed across the street and along the dike to the entrance of the outdoor museum. This begins with a recreation of a fishing harbour, modelled on the one in Marken. In the harbour is a wonderful collection of boats dating back nearly a century and a half.

I had promised Edi that among the things that would be included in our skûtsje's renovated galley is a dishwasher. I showed her one hanging on the quarter gunwale of a tjalk in the harbour, but she said that she wanted one a tad more modern.

One of the things we were looking for among the exhibits was Hoop op Zegen, the skûtsje built in 1904 by Wildschut in Gaastmeer. Along with our Nieuwe Zorg, it is one of the fourteen known survivors of the twenty skûtsjes built by Wildschut. It was not in the schepenhall and the ladies at the desk knew nothing about it. It wasn't in the fishing harbour, nor did anyone there know where it might be.

A man at the net-mending hut told us of a small tjalk on one of the canals in the recreated town. The town is divided into several districts, each a reconstruction using original spacial planning and layout from various towns and villages around the Zuiderzee. Hindeloopen is the model for the church district, the polder slope is modelled after Urk, a former island in the Zuiderzee. The town canal in the museum village is on one side modelled on Noord Holland styles, while the other side depicts the Friesland style. The Noord Holland side is an urban depiction with a row of merchants' shops; apotheek, slager, bakker, kaaswinkel and so on.

The Fries side is a more rural setting with houses set back from canalside gardens. In front of one of the houses sits a small skûtsje.

We immediately saw similarities to our Nieuwe Zorg that told us the vessel had been built by Wildschut. The more we looked, the more convinced we were. However, unlike everything else we had seen in the museum, there was no placard describing the skûtsje, nor was there any identification on her.

On the Noord Holland side of the canal, directly across from the skûtsje sits a prosperous merchant's house. We went in for a look at the opulent rooms and elegant furnishings. While we were coming down the porch steps on our way out, we spotted a small placard on a stake. It described the skûtsje across the canal as: Hoop op Zegen, Wildschut, Gaastmeer 1904. While only 35 centimetres narrower than Nieuwe Zorg, it is nearly seven metres shorter, and is the smallest of the twenty skûtsjes built by Wildschut.

HOOP OP ZeGen

Wildschut, Gaastmeer, 1904

9.46 x 3.09 m

Besides the skûtsje, we also spotted other sailing clogs. These were on a bench where we paused to buy a couple of smoked kippers. The fish were very oily and they continued to repeat for a long time after we had finished eating them. We decided that they were otherwise not a repeat. Among the fascinating things about the Zuiderzeemuseum is that craftsman, artisans and other interesting and display-related people participate in the museum. Smoked eel and herring are available at the smoking demonstration.

Cheese is available for purchase in the cheese shop, handmade brushes and brooms are for sale by the maker in his old-fashioned shop, the sailmaker can be commissioned to handmake a new sail or mend an old one and his working becomes part of the museum exhibit.

It was late afternoon by the time we had finished our tour around the museum park. We walked back into the centre of town and paused at Vishandel van der Veen and sat on their canalside patio enjoying delicious broodje scholfilet en koffie. The sole was so good that on the way out we bought two fresh filets to cook for dinner. and caught a train back to Hoorn.

Chapter Eleven

Onward to Friesland

At noon on Wednesday the 19th of September we slipped from alongside a guest pier in Grashaven, Hoorn. It was time to move on; we had a long way to go to get our skûtsje to Harlingen for her second century facelift.

The weather was a bit unsettled as we left; though it was raining lightly, there were blue patches among the large billowy clouds that were following the nimbus system moving off to the east. The winds were about 15 kph from the southwest with occasional gusts to about 25.

We had decided that rather than crossing the IJsselmeer, we would to head south, back down the Markermeer and then make our way around the chain of lakes and canals that follow the former Zuiderzee coastline. If conditions deteriorated, we could poke back into the canals through Edam or Monnickendam and take the longer but calmer inland route.

We watched as a thunderstorm engulfed Hoorn astern of us. Ahead, it didn't look so nice either. We continued southward, favouring the western side of the Markermeer to make our exit inland shorter and easier if we needed to take it.

About midway to the entrance to Edam, we were hit by a heavy thunderstorm and Edi wisely retreated to the dryness below. I lowered the port leeboard to offer better stability in the building chop. The waters of the Zuiderzee were notorious for their rapidly building into short, steep waves. The old sea was very shallow, and the IJsselmeer and the Markermeer inherited those waters.

The maximum depth of the IJsselmeer is 7 metres, though most of it is only 3 to 4 metres. In the Markermeer, the depths are similar, but its maximum is only 5 metres. This shallowness causes very steep, short-pitched waves to quickly build.

The thunderstorm had passed and the rain was slowly abating as we passed Volendam. The sea was a bit lumpy with leftover chop from the system's 50 or 60 kilometre winds, but the sun was breaking through.

Ahead beyond the Marken light, the sky showed more blue than cloud. We decided to press on down the Markermeer. As we passed the Marken light, we committed ourselves to a thirteen kilometre crossing to the next protected waters in Flevoland. The wind was southwest 25 to 30 and would be on our starboard bow for most of the crossing.

We could, of course, turn and run back to the protection of Marken if conditions deteriorated too much during the first part of our crossing. Fortunately, the thunderheads moved past us to the north and the south, and spared us the heavier winds and downpours. It did; however, continue to alternately rain and drizzle with few dry respites.

About half-way across we had to cross the main commercial traffic lanes, up and down which seemed a nonstop flow of huge barges. The regulations call for crossing traffic lanes at a large angle, so that as little time as possible is spent in the lanes. We were crossing at an angle of about 30°, which is rather shallow, but with the sea conditions as they were, we would have the seas too much on the beam with a broader crossing angle. I picked a gap between the fast traffic and with very little course alteration we popped through.

As we approached the Flevoland coast, the sun broke out through the western clouds and gave some colours to the eastern ones. It continued raining as we entered more protected waters, passed under the Hollandse Brug and into the Gooimeer. I was very thankful that Henk had left his foul-weather suit aboard for me.

At 1645 we arrived at Jacht Haven Naarden and secured to the reporting pier. We pushed the call button on the speaker and were answered by a female voice. Edi asked in Dutch for moorage for two days, received confirmation of space availability and was told to go to the Westzijde. The posted map is oriented at 45°, so there are two Westzijdes, northwest and southwest. The slip and moorage arrangements in both looked plausible.

Edi asked for directions. An impatient voice told her to go left and then left. Edi asked left facing which direction and got no reply. We noted that the office was open until 1700, so we still had a good ten minutes to walk to the office and get better directions. After a brisk walk, we arrived at the office a few minutes before closing time to find the door locked, but still occupied by a woman. We gave-up, writing her off as an extremely rare example of an unfriendly and non-cooperative Dutch person. As we descended the stairs, we were met by a sympathetic man, who told us to wait a minute, and he went off to a storage shed and came back with an area brochure and a layout of the jachthaven, showing where Westzijde is located. We walked back to Nieuwe Zorg and moved her to a wharf on the northwest side of the marina.

Naarden, in the province of North Holland is a wonderful example of a star fort, complete with fortified walls and a moat. It was granted city rights in 1300 and later developed into a fortified garrison town with an important textile industry. Because of its distinctive shape, the town was a visual rally point for Allied bombers returning to England after raids on Germany during WWII.

On Thursday morning we walked to the office to register and pay for two days moorage. We met the woman with whom Edi had spoken when we arrived at the reporting pier. She was just as forthcoming and helpful as she had been previously. Edi asked her directions to Naarden and was told where to find the bus stop, so we walked about half a kilometre to it and waited for the hourly bus. Fortunately, we had arrived a few minutes before its scheduled passing and when we boarded the driver refused to take any fare, telling us the trip was too short. He drove us back past the marina and another kilometre to one of the gates leading into Narden.

We walked along the defence walls above the moats and wandered through the arsenals, which have been converted into upscale interior decorating boutiques. In the centre of town we admired the city hall, which on its intricate facade proclaims that it was built in 1601. We visited the baker for bread and rolls and the small centre-of-town supermarket for vegetables and meat and so on for a couple of days. We had finally become accustomed to shopping for a day or two at a time, rather than stocking-up for weeks or months at a time. We wandered a circuitous route exploring the old city looking at a charming mix of old and new. Then we walked along the foot and bicycle path the kilometre or so back to the marina.

On Friday morning at 1050 we slipped and headed out into the Gooimeer and turned eastward. At 1320 we secured alongside the wharf in front of the Havenmeester kantoor in Spakenburg, squeezed in between a fishing boat and two dinghies. The Havenmeester was not in, so we walked the two hundred metres into the centre of town for a look around.

We passed a seeming unending line of century-old wooden boats, dating from the nineteenth and very early twentieth centuries. Most were botters, but there were also Lemsteraaks, Staverse jols and bons.

We watched old wooden ships moving in and out of the harbour and counted forty-nine alongside in port. There were several slips open and there were three boats hauled-out for repairs on the antique marine railway. We thought of the Vancouver Wooden Boat Festival and laughed.

As we were looking at the old boats, a woman in traditional Spaken dress rode past on a bicycle. We learned that there are still several dozen regularly wearing the costume. We saw another in the super-market as we were picking-up some items for din-ner and breakfast.

After our circuit through town, we went back to the boat to stow our purchases and to top-up the water tanks. While the tanks were filling, flotillas of ducks gathered around our boat looking for handouts. We settled-in for the evening in an idyllic setting among a wonderful selection of antique boats in an historic fishing town on the ancient shores of the Zuiderzee.

Saturday is market day in Spakenburg, so early in the morning we walked into town to expe-rience it. Stalls were set-up all along the broad avenue that runs each side of the canal through the centre of town. We wanted some sole for dinner, so we looked at the collected viswin-kels and chose the one with the largest crowd.

Their sole appeared to be the freshest, so we had the young chap behind the counter select a couple of large fish. He weighed them, jotted down some figures and then proceeded to filet them for us, very shortly presenting us with four nice filets in a small plastic tray for less than €3.

We stowed our market purchases aboard and then walked back to the museum. Our passes gave us free admission, and we spent a couple of hours thoroughly engaged with the story of the transition of a coastal fishing town on the Zuiderzee into an inland port cut-off from its historic fishing grounds.

Shortly after 1100 on Sunday the 23rd we slipped and headed out of Spakenburg, totally enthralled with the wonderful little town. We turned eastward and fifty minutes later came to the Nijkerk lock, which took us up about 30 centimetres to the level of the Veluwemeer. We had been in the province of Utrecht, now we entered the province of Gelderland, while along our port side passed the new province of Flevoland.

There was a steady parade of boats, mostly pleasure cruisers and sailboats. Most of the commercial barges were taking a weekend break. Along the tops of the dykes on both sides of us were steady streams of cyclists following the paved bicycle paths.

The lake turned to the northeast and we followed the marked channel around its northern shore. As we neared Harderwijk the lake became increasingly crowded with small boats out for a Sunday afternoon sail, paddle or cruise. We arrived in Harderwijk mid-afternoon and were met at the passenten melden pier by the Havenmeester, who directed us to a spot in the inner harbour to moor.

We secured and walked into town past the historic ships and windmill. We continued to be amazed with the number of beautifully restored and maintained boats that there are in the Netherlands. Where in much of the rest of the world, a boat a hundred and more years old is a remarkable sight, here they are commonplace.

Through the sixteenth century gate we went and continued into the wonderfully preserved old town. Among the old buildings, some have been modernized, and we were charmed by a century-old art deco storefront among three, four or five hundred-year-old buildings.

Back onboard, our furnace had failed to run. I had spent a couple of hours troubleshooting without success. I had installation instructions in Dutch only, plus a multi-lingual operating sheet. The English on the multi-lingual sheet was clear enough; the problem was that the heater was British.

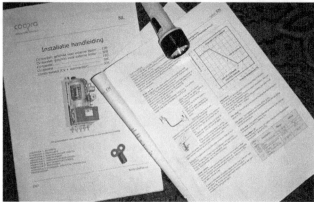

I dug back in my mind to my days of sorting-out Lucas wiring and other British engineering labyrinths from my days of trying to keep running various models of Austin Healey, Triumph, Jaguar and Lotus. I finally resolved to bring a water hose into the engine room and through a likely-looking spigot try to add some pressure to the system's water tank. It worked. We had heat again.

We slipped our lines shortly before noon on Monday and continued northeastward. Two and

a half hours later we had secured to the guest wharf in Elberg. We locked-up and walked into town to find the Havenmeester and to look around. Elberg is a delightful town, filled with charm and with houses that reflect their owners' pride.

Everywhere we looked we saw an eclectic mix of decor; old, new, organic, inert. Among the things we were shopping for was an inexpensive handcart to haul our empty propane tank to the service station for a refill. We found a passably robust model for €14 and we also bought some lamp oil.

We needed a new wick for the lamp, but the shop had none suitable. The clerk pointed-out a couple of shops along the street that had wicks. The mentioned shops had nothing near what we wanted. Edi thought of the marine hardware shop we had seen next to the city gate, and we went back out to it. There was a large selection of wicks in many styles, including one ten centimetres wide, which to me appeared what we wanted.

We bought a half metre piece and chatted with the owner for nearly an hour before we hauled ourselves away. The wick fit perfectly, and in the evening we dined by lamp light.

After breakfast on Tuesday I put the empty propane cylinder our new shopping cart and wheeled it about 400 metres along the paved walking path on the dike to the Esso station and pulled-up at the AutoGas pump. I added 28 litres of propane to the tank, paid the clerk the €22 and wheeled away back to the boat. How wonderfully convenient this process is compared to our experiences in finding propane in North and South America.

We slipped mid-morning on Wednesday and headed back out to follow the Drontermeer as it gradually bent northward. Just over an hour later we arrived at the Roggebotsluis where we were lowered about half a metre to the level of the Ketelmeer. There was a heavily laden commercial in the approaches as we exited the lock. It was filled to the combing tops with sand and its gunwales were awash in the ripples.

The marked channel led us to the north-west, and as we passed the mouth of the IJssel, we bent our way westward toward the Ketelbrug and under it. As we passed under the bridge and into the IJsselmeer, there was a parade of antique klippers and tjalken lowering sail to await the opening of the bridge.

The IJsselmeer was very choppy. The short, steep wind waves combined and interacted with waves reflected off the shores to offer a very confused sea. The wind was about 50 kph from the southwest, nearly on our beam for the remaining 6 kilometres of our passage to Urk.

At times Nieuwe Zorg got into a rolling rhythm when the pitch of the waves matched her beam. I lowered a leeboard and steered a tacking course, putting the slop alternately on our bow and our quarter. The pressure on the tiller was very strong and I needed to brace myself to steer. The winds had increased and Edi was below clearing away things that had shifted, when we heard and felt a very loud bang. We quickly searched for its source, but found nothing. There were no signs of problems, so we continued.

After nearly an hour of fighting the confused seas, at 1440 we entered the protection of Urk and secured in the lee of a wharf near the centre of town. While Edi was forward handling the bow lines, she noticed that the mast counterweight, which had been placed athwart the centreline, had slid across to the port gunwale. That explained the loud bang. The 1100 kilogram weight had broken loose from its temporary blocks and had crashed into the gunwale.

It had struck the mooring cleat there with sufficient force to shear its two robust mounting bolts. We were listing to port, so with the aid of some mooring lines, I slowly moved the weight back closer toward the centre of the foredeck and blocked it there. Our onward route would be all inland, so there was no need for further securing arrangements.

We secured and went into town to explore Urk and visit its museum. The town is first mentioned in historical records over a thousand years ago in 996. At that time it was an island in the Almere, a lake that would become part of the Zuiderzee in the thirteenth century after a series of inundations by the North Sea. The island was about 80 hectares in size and composed of a high clay hump and a pasture. The hump was about 12 hectares and on it was built the town. The low-lying meadow flooded regularly and the island slowly eroded until it was little more than the small town.

With the closing of the Afsluitdijk in 1932, the waters around Urk slowly reverted to fresh for the first time since the flooding in the thirteenth century. In 1939 a dike connecting Urk to the mainland was completed, ending the town's island status. In 1942 the surrounding land was drained to become the Noordoostpolder. Today, Urk has the largest fishing fleet in the Netherlands and boasts many large, modern fish processing and packing plants.

At 1110 on Wednesday we slipped and headed around into the lock, where we were lowered 5.5 metres to the level of the canals in the Noordoostpolder. In the lock chamber are conveniently spaced pipes set in vertical slots in the walls. Edi looped a line around one forward and I around one aft, and we enjoyed a smooth, well controlled descent.

As we motored slowly along the canal through Urk's new suburbs on the polder, we passed many large fish-packing plants, all with their owners' houses, wharves and jachts on the canal side. There is obvious prosperity.

At 1435 we arrived at the entrance to the Friesesluis, the lock that would take us back up the 5.5 metres out of the Noordoostpolder to the level of the IJsselmeer and into Friesland. There was another pleasure boat in the lock ahead of us, and I needed to snuggle very closely up to its stern so that our tiller and flagstaff would miss the bridge as we rose. In this lock, instead of the vertical pipes to handle our lines, there are 3cm ropes fastened top and bottom and spaced every 3 or 4 metres.

As we came up, I thought I would need to remove the flagstaff, but in the end, it cleared the bridge by about 20 centimetres.

We exited the chamber and slowly motored into Lemmer and up to its entrance lock just as the keeper was opening the gates for us. We entered and secured to the chamber wall as she came over to collect the €5.50 fee for the lock and a series the bridges through the city.

After we were lowered about half a metre to the level of the canals in Friesland, we exited the lock and motored to a mooring on a wall in the heart of the historic section, where we secured at 1520.

Our skûtsje, Nieuwe Zorg was back in Friesland and we decided to pause for a few days to look around and relax.

Chapter Twelve

Northward Through Friesland

Lemmer is the home of the Lemster-aak, and down the wall from our mooring were two beautiful examples. We walked along the wharf to admire them. These boats have a more rounded bottom than do the skûtsjes, and the leeboards are narrower. They evolved from Frisian visaak and the more ancient boeier. The first of the design were built around 1875.

The first pleasure version was built in 1907 with a gracefully curved jachtenroef with glass windows and decorative carvings. As the leisure class grew, the jacht style gradually replaced the fishing version.

There are many elements of the jacht version of the Lemsteraak that make it easy to see where jachtenroef conversion of skûtsjes drew their design inspiration. It was this design that the people of the Netherlands chose in 1956 to give to Princess Beatrix, the future Queen, as a gift for her eighteenth birthday.

At 1030 on Thursday morning we slipped and headed through town. We had been moored about a hundred metres short of a bridge, which needed lifting for us. We had spoken

a couple of times with the bridge-keeper the previous day, and he was watching us as we prepared to get underway. As soon as we let go our lines, he initiated the process to stop traffic and raise the bridge. We passed through and wound our way along the canal to the next bridge, which was open for us.

As we rounded a bend we saw the third and final bridge opened with three boats passing through it. However; we were too far back for the bridgekeeper to delay traffic and he closed it. We waited for a few minutes while road traffic cleared and the bridge could be reopened. A large tjalk came up astern of us as we cleared through the bridge. We moved along at 6kph, the speed limit on this section of the canal, but it was obvious that the tjalk's skipper found this much too slow and we were soon overtaken.

We shortly joined the Prinses Margriet Kanaal and followed it northward. Close to the junction we spotted a sign indicating a wharf for the landing of barge automobiles. Next to it on a tall pylon was a modern version of the Dutch windmill. Barging certainly has changed since the days our skûtsje was built.

We followed the tjalk up the Groote Brekken, keeping up with it with the increased speed limit of the broader waterways. Further ahead was another tjalk under sail, and there was a rather steady down-bound traffic, both pleasure and commercial.

The sailing tjalk turned off into the Rijnsloot and appeared to be sailing through the fields as it headed toward Sloten.

Across the dikes from the canal we saw rich agricultural lands stretching beyond the horizons.

Dotted among the fields were typical Friesian farm buildings with their low walls and high, steep roofs. We continue to admire the sense of order, the apparent care and the obvious pride of ownership of the land and the buildings.

We turned off the Prinses Margriet and into the Witte Brekken and the Woudvaart toward Sneek. Just short of the toll bridge we spotted a marina with a sign announcing free wifi. We stopped, backed and went alongside its melden wharf. There was nobody around; it was 1315 and we assumed everyone was at lunch. We shut down and were in the middle of our own lunch when the Havenmeester arrived and knocked on the hull.

He showed us to a spot across the way and pedalled around the marina to take our lines when we moved across. He gave us the wifi code, pointed-out the marina's laundry facilities and gave us directions to the supermarkets.

We finished our late lunch and then walked the short distance into the centre of the old city, passing along the way the Waterpoort, which was built in 1492 as a part of the city ramparts. We went browsing and shopping among the wonderfully maintained historic buildings in the heart of town and couldn't resist making some purchases from among the broad selection of upscale shops.

Toward the end of the afternoon we located the Fries Scheepvaart Museum, but there was too little time to give it the attention it deserves. We bookmarked it for a long visit the next day and then walked back to our skûtsje to relax. We were the only barge in the marina. It is next to the plant where Aquanaut builds modern cruising yachts and the marina is mainly their new and used boat display and sales area. Guests welcome.

On Friday morning our passes gave us free access to the museum. We asked the receptionist some questions specific to our skûtsje's builder and early owners. She called the Librarian to set-up a meeting with us and then sent us off to the library. We had a delightfully informative meeting with Jeannette Tigchelaar, the Librarian, and among other things, she gave me some links to research sites to pursue later. We then spent a couple of hours exploring the museum before we headed into the skûtsje rooms.

There are many superbly detailed models on display, which show the skûtsje's design features. I spent a long time closely examining these and took dozens of photos for later study.

In one display case is a skûtsje alongside a tjalk, and this close juxtaposition makes it very easy to compare and contrast the designs. The skûtsje is obviously more sleek; it is narrower and has a shallower hold. The leeboards are broader and shorter to allow very shallow water navigation. To make-up for the narrowness, the roef is slightly longer and a bit higher.

Among the exhibited models is a very finely rendered skûtsje half-section, which clearly shows the internal structure of the ship. At the after end of the cargo hold is a watertight bulkhead. This forms the forward part of the roef, the ship's accommodations. Often it was the home of the barge owners and their family.

It is flat-sided with a curved top, two shuttered windows on each side, a pair of portlights aft and a companionway topped with a sliding hatch. Growing out of the forepart of the roef is a crutch to cradle the boom.

In the museum is a restored skûtsje roef, which shows the typical layout and style. The interior design makes maximum use of the small space and it is very well appointed and finished. In the centre of the forward bulkhead is a fireplace, which serves for both cooking and heating. On each side of the fireplace is a storage cabinet, each with twin doors. The wood panelling and trim appear to be ash or beech, which is lightly varnished.

A table sits in the centre of the room and around it are chairs for the family. There are cabinets along the sides, which make full use the spaces under the side decks. Overhead, in the centre of the roef is a pigeon box skylight, which affords lighting as well as cooling and ventilation when required. An oil lamp hangs from the ceiling and there are decorative lace curtains on the windows and portlights. Leading aft from the room, tucked under the aft deck is a bed platform, extending back into the round of the stern. In the stern are two circular portlights adding some light, and sometimes there was a pigeon box skylight.

A framed drawing on a nearby wall in the museum shows the scale of the interior of the accommodation space. It also shows how important and multifunctional the central table was to the room. In this space lived the family that owned and operated the barge. The skûtsje was both their home and their business.

Their business consisted of finding loads to carry. Often times this was cut peat to be carried from inland across the shallow lakes and through the narrow sluices to seaside ports. Sand, gravel and compost were also regularly carried, as were eels, both fresh and smoked.

The skûtsje was designed as a sailing vessel, and it was fitted with very broad, but relatively short leeboards to better navigate the shallow waters. Other tjalk-types had narrower, longer leeboards that extended deeper into the water. The mast on a skûtsje is fitted with a counterweight to make easy the process of lowering the rig to pass under low bridges and of re-erecting it once clear.

When there was no wind, or when the wind was adverse, the family donned harnesses and pulled the barge along the canal. As small engines became economical, some skûtsjes were fitted with auxiliaries. With the coming of purpose-built powered barges, such as the luxemotor, the usefulness of the skûtsje declined.

A few kept on working, some were scrapped, some were converted to houseboats, some were converted to pleasure yachts with extended roefs over the hold and some were preserved and maintained for racing. Skûtsje racing is huge sport in Friesland, with two leagues: the prestigious SKS and the newer IFKS.

Near the entrance to the skûtsje rooms in the museum is a trophy case, and among the trophies is a retired SKS Championship trophy. It shows the names of the series champions from 1988 to 2007. On the trophy's plaque, Douwe Visser of Sneek is shown as the SKS champion for 1995, 1996, 2002, 2003 and 2007. Douwe won the championship again in 2011, 2012 and 2013.

In the 1930s and 40s his grandfather, Douwe Albert Visser had raised his family aboard our skûtsje, Nieuwe Zorg. Another of his grandchildren, Douwe Visser of Grou won the SKS championship in 2005 and 2009.

We had thoroughly enjoyed the Fries Scheepvaart Museum and our eyes, minds and souls were filled to the brim with wonderful images. It was time to move on. We slowly wandered through the downtown core of Sneek, browsing in the many upscale shops, shopping and gathering ideas for the interior decoration of our restored skûtsje as we made our way back to Nieuwe Zorg to relax for the remainder of the day.

At 1125 on Saturday morning we slipped from our berth and headed back down the Woudvaart and Witte Brekken to the Prinses Margriet Kanaal, which we then followed northeastward to the Sneekermeer. Along the way we saw windmills and sailboats. Set back in the fields along the banks were typical Friesland farmhouses and in the water and in the air were ducks and swans.

Some of the farms had their buildings sited directly on the side of the canal. Many of them had wharves, which at one time may have been the easiest access for sending produce to market.

It was Saturday and there were many pleasure craft out on the water. As we approached Sneekermeer, the number of sailboats we saw quickly increased. We could see at least two class-boat races in progress, with many dozens of participants sailing courses around the markers.

Also out sailing were several skûtsjes, most with crews eight or more. It was rather windy with sudden gusts, and we saw reefs in the mains on some of the skûtsjes and watched as one dowsed its jib.

91

Most of the skûtsjes we saw appeared to be fully restored to their original configurations, with small roefs aft and canvas-topped shutters over the cargo holds. They all looked very well maintained, and we assumed they were part of the SKS or IFKS racing fleets. We headed into the long, narrow harbour of Grou and found an empty mooring place along a town wharf. Once we had secured and hooked-up to the shore power, we went off to explore the small town. Very prominent near its centre is a Romanesque church dating to the thirteenth century. We stopped in for a look. On our way toward the church we saw several more racing skûtsjes.

From the church we headed in search of a supermarket, and along the way we spotted a viswinkel. The displays looked inviting and they tempted us to purchase two large pieces of halibut. We found the supermarket and bought a few items, reminding ourselves again that we needn't buy more than a day or two's supply of food at a time; the markets are everywhere and all so far have been excellent.

For dinner I coated the halibut in crumbled beschuit seasoned with salt, pepper and dried dragon and lightly fried it in butter. The fish was accompanied by butter-roasted baby potatoes and steamed fine green beans and garnished with sliced tomato with shredded basil.

We continue to search for inexpensive wines to add to our list of favourites. Among the whites we have found a wonderful Sancerre-styled New Zealand Sauvignon Blanc by Seagull Mountain and a refreshing Spanish Chardonnay Macabeo blend from Freixenet. Both are in the €4 range.

At 1100 on Sunday morning we slipped and headed out into the continuation of the Prinses Margriet Kanaal. The canals are well marked, with signposts at junctions indicating the branch to follow. Some of the signs are rather complex, and we have learned to take photos of them as we go by, so that we can continue to gather information from them after they have disappeared in our stern.

One of the things we have been noting as we moved along the canals in the Netherlands is that we have seen no raptors. As we were again commenting on this, we spotted a bird perched on a fence post ahead. We thought that we had finally seen a hawk, but as we approached, we saw that it was a duck. I cannot recall ever having previously seen a duck standing on a post, but I supposed that if the raptors don't use the posts, the ducks may as well.

As we entered Leeuwarden, we turned up De Tynje Wide Greons and squeezed through a low, narrow bridge cut. Both on the chart and on the Navionics app on my iPad, the clearance was given as 2.4 metres, so with our air draft of 1.95 metres, we continued toward it. When we were close enough we could see the clearance sign posted over the opening.

Beyond the bridge a few hundred metres we turned and took a mooring along the bank in the entrance to Jachthaven De Nieuwe Leeuwarden. Directly across the entrance canal from us was the tjalk, Vrouwe Geziena. She is the first boat we had looked at in July as we began our search for a barge. We had visited her in a mooring along the Emmakade in the centre of town. Seeing her here was like closing the loop on our adventure.

We spoke with the couple aboard, who were the previous owners, and from them we learned that their tjalk had been recently sold to a young French couple. As a part of the sales contract, they were to assist in the moving of the barge to Paris and they were ready to leave the following morning.

Early on Monday morning we watched as Vrouwe Geziena maneuvered from her slip to begin her estimated ten-day passage to Paris. Looking at her, we were pleased that we had passed on her and had waited until we had found Nieuwe Zorg. The tjalk is 3.5 metres high, compared to Nieuwe Zorg's 1.95 metres, and this would mean not only having to wait for many more bridg-

es to be opened for us in the Netherlands, but also scraping through most of the canal bridges in France and having to forego navigating on many of Europe's smaller canals, including three of the most scenic and historic canals: the Bourgogne, the Midi and the Nivernais.

Shortly after noon we took our umbrellas and set off to walk into the centre of Leeuwarden, arriving in the heart of the shopping district just as the shops began opening; most don't open until 1300 on Mondays. We browsed a few shoe stores, looking for more seasonal footwear; I was still in sandals and Edi was in light runners. We both found fashionable boots that are much more suited to the climate and the barging environment.

On Tuesday morning we slipped from our berth and headed back down the canal. There were boats waiting for the bridge to be lifted and blocking the 2.4 metre side, so we went under the even lower span. We had a couple of decimetres clearance to spare.

We were soon out in the countryside and passing typical Friesian farmsteads. The weather continued heavily overcast with occasional showers as we motored along on our final leg to Harlingen.

The canalside scenery looked as if it had been lifted from textbooks on Friesland. There were Friesian horses, Friesian barns, Friesian autumn skies. We passed many windmills.

Most were the huge modern structures with automatic feathering three-bladed propellers sitting atop tall steel pylons. Here and there we also passed old wooden mills, some intended for grain grinding but mostly they were to drive water pumps to keep the fields dry.

As we approached the town of Dronrijp we saw a three-masted ship on the horizon. It slowly grew and as we drew closer we saw it was secured alongside. As we passed we saw a very long-in-the-tooth ship that was obviously far beyond her best before date. To us she appeared ready for the cutters' torches, though there were some young people aboard who appeared to have dreams of a better future. We have over the years seen many projects like this energised mostly by visions and dreams. These dreamers will need many buckets of sweat from their brows and many more buckets of Euros and still more of good luck to realize their dreams.

We passed under the bridge at the west side of Dronrijp and had gone about half a kilometre when the engine hesitated and stopped. I tried to restart it without luck. As we drifted, I slowly steered toward the right bank, which was slightly to leeward in the 15 to 20 kilometre breeze. At 1346 we came to an emergency mooring on three pins pounded into the soft clay of the canal bank.

The sight glass on the fuel tank in the engine room showed the tank was low, and I suspected that the fuel pump had picked-up some sludge from the tank bottom. Access to the fuel filter involves major disassembly and panel removal in the engine room, so I began toward the other end of the system. I cracked open the line from the fuel pump and turned the engine. Fuel sprayed out. I repeated the process at the first and sixth injectors, which also resulted in spraying fuel. As I turned the engine there were random firings, but none sufficient to kick it into action. I suspected the injectors were clogged. Nieuwe Zorg was telling us she was tired and needed a makeover.

We were at kilometre post 15 on the canal, just 12 kilometres short of SRF in Harlingen. With my cell phone, I called the SRF office and explained the situation to the person who answered and asked if a tow could be arranged. A few minutes later Lex returned my call and told us a boat has been arranged and it would arrive at our location in about an hour and a half.

Shortly before 1600 a small work boat from SRF arrived skippered by a young SRF employee, accompanied by his eight and a half month pregnant wife and an old boat dog.

We discussed towing arrangements and were shortly taken in tow. I steered Nieuwe Zorg in the tug's stern as we began the final two hours of our passage to Harlingen.

Along the way we passed through the town of Franeker, where we again saw canalside homes with private bays for their boats, much as we have driveways and garages at home. Throughout our travels in the Netherlands we have seen many similar arrangements, as well as private wharves with mooring arrangements directly on the canal in the front or rear of the homes. It seems nearly everyone in the Netherlands boats.

As we approached Harlingen we came into an industrial area, including a huge yard filled with many heaps of scrap metal. Among the piles of scrap we could see cutup ship parts. We are delighted that Nieuwe Zorg is a long way from needing to be put to rest here.

A little past 1730 we arrived at SRF on the outskirts of Harlingen. We were towed to a berth outboard an old converted workboat, which was awaiting work on the wharves at the rear of the complex. The yard closes at 1630, so after we secured, we went for a walk and then relaxed onboard for the remainder of the day.

It was Tuesday, 02 October, four weeks since we had arrived in the Netherlands and took possession of Nieuwe Zorg. We had just spent three wonderful weeks bringing her 298 kilometres from Aalsmeer, Noord Holland. During the following few days we needed to refine our plans for the proposed refit, which will restore her exterior to 1908 appearances and her interior to twenty-first century systems and conveniences.

Chapter Thirteen

Planning a Metamorphosis

After lunch on Wednesday, Wychard Raadsveld, one of the four partners in Scheepsreparatie Friesland came aboard to begin gathering information from us to gain a better understanding of what we wanted done and how. We were shortly joined by Lex Tichelaar, another of the partners we had earlier met, and the four of us continued the long process of planning Nieuwe Zorg's second century facelift.

We discussed ways to gain interior space. My head brushes the ceiling in the heads and the bedroom. Among the ideas were to use thinner insulation in the ceiling and to try to lower the floor, but the possibility and effectiveness of these needed to await the gutting of the interior to see what the old girl's underpinnings were. If we could gain some headroom, we could move the shower all the way over to the port side and reduce the length

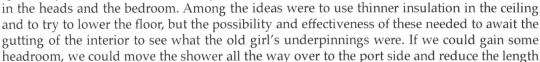

of the room by 15 centimetres. By also rearranging the forward bulkhead in the master cabin and putting the bed athwartships, we could fit a bed with a 200cm X 140cm mattress, possibly even a 160cm one.

With all of the shuffling to fit-in what we wanted, we still needed to find an additional metre or so of interior length. The easiest way to gain this was to shorten the engineering spaces. Wychard remeasured our engine room and machinery spaces to see

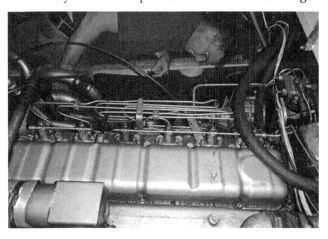

how much room we could liberate by installing a smaller engine. Nieuwe Zorg had a six-cylinder Perkins, which is rated at 86 kW. Besides being nearly half a century old, the engine is much more powerful than the 50 or 60 kW that the skûtsje requires. A smaller engine will allow us to reduce the length of the machinery spaces and to lengthen the living spaces.

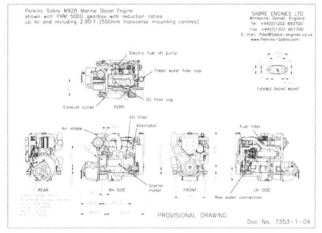

Wychard proposed the Perkins-Sabre M92B with a PRM 5000 gearbox. At the propeller shaft, it develops 50 kW at 1500 rpm and 64 kW at 2400 rpm. The engine is a normally aspirated, low revolution unit with its maximum torque of 320 Nm produced at 1400 rpm. At that speed, the fuel consumption is 4.5 litres per hour and at canal cruising speed, 3 litres per hour. With these specifications, it appears to be the ideal power unit for our skûtsje.

The first step in determining the amount of living space we will have available is to plan the space required by the mechanical installations. Wychard took more measurements in the after spaces as he gathered information to begin designing the layout of the equipment. The engine and transmission, the fuel tanks, the generator, the battery banks, the isolation transformer, the inverter-charger, the water heating and the central-heating systems all need to be laid-out in the most compact arrangement that is consistent with easy inspection and maintenance access.

Edi and I walked the 2.5 kilometres into the centre of Harlingen each day to absorb the wonderful town with its many sixteenth and seventeenth century buildings and its historic harbours, canals and bridges. Harlingen received its city rights in 1234 and rapidly grew in importance as a trading port. It was first mentioned in port registers of England in 1311.

Among the fascinating structures is the Raadhuistoren, the old city hall tower built in 1587. Running through the central part of the old city are pedestrian-only shopping streets, which add immensely to the charm of the area.

We did our daily food shopping in the markets along the way and in the Jumbo and Albert Hein supermarkets. We continue to be amazed at the wonderful selection, the great quality and the low prices of everything from bakery items, meats, fish, dairy and fresh farm produce and of course, wine.

After a week of planning, measuring, head scratching, re-drafting, proposing ideas, listening, discussing, thinking and dreaming, we received an itemized quote from the office. It covered the removal of equipment and gutting the skûtsje down to an empty hull, moving the engine room bulkhead aft, lifting the roef and moving it aft, re-engineering and rebuilding the interior, installing plumbing, lighting and appliances, re-rigging for sail, finishing and painting. We were ready to leave things in the hands of SRF and head home.

On one of our walks through the centre of Harlingen, we saw in the window of a toy hospital a teddy bear of the same vintage as Nieuwe Zorg. It was in for a facelift and make-over, just as was our skûtsje. We wished both of them success.

On Monday and Tuesday we had packed into three large and one huge storage bin everything in Nieuwe Zorg that we wanted to keep. Because all our cooking and dining goods were packed, we went out to dinner for the first time in more than a year. Food aboard Sequitur and Nieuwe Zorg had been so good that we were never tempted to dine out.

We got up at 0400 on Wednesday, packed the bedding, towels and the last bits of stuff into our luggage and drove a rental car the 325 kilometres to the airport in Brussels for our 1040 flight. We had a long wait in Montreal for the connection onward to Vancouver, where we arrived near midnight. Fortunately, our 69 kilograms of checked luggage hadn't make the flight, and after an easy registration with the baggage agent, we walked our carry-on bags to the SkyTrain and to our loft without the huge encumbrance of heavy luggage. The wayward luggage was delivered to our door the following day.

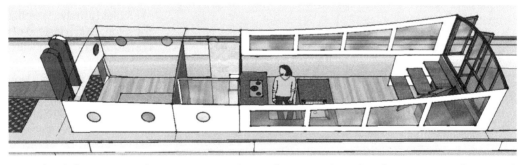

During the following weeks we continued to refine our ideas for the interior. I downloaded a free version of Google SketchUp and taught myself how to use the software to create some three-dimensional drawings and then to look at the implications of various layouts.

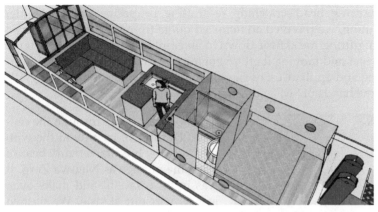

I played with ideas to see how much additional room we will gain by incorporating the hallway with the master cabin and by getting rid of the clothes closet. With this layout, there is room for a full-size European bed with room to walk around forward of it and beside it; whereas, in her current configuration there was room in the bedroom for a 130cm x 200cm bed and for only one person at a time to stand on the tiny patch of floor.

Instead of a closet taking valuable floorspace, we will use the space under the starboard side deck for our clothes storage. The side-by-side washer and dryer will sit beside the mast step and extend forward under the foredeck.

Though the space planned for the heads is smaller in area than in the existing configuration, by getting rid of awkward jogs and using a narrow-profile sink, will be able have a larger shower stall, better ergonomics and more useable floorspace. In the galley we wanted to install granite countertops and I played with ideas to expand the work space by adding two wings. The wing along the port side, partially under the side deck would house the dishwasher, while the new transverse wing would have the fridge-freezer and the sink. The fridge-freezer door would be in the end of the wing, with its hinges to the left for easy access and to reduce space conflict.

We looked at a shorter settee in the salon, 200cm instead of the current 260cm, which will easily convert to a full-size guest bed. This reduced length, combined with the space liberated from the engine room and the heads, allows the larger galley and master cabin. The graceful compound curved jachtenroef provides the main accommodation space. It extends a total of 8 metres of the 16.38 metre length of the skûtsje.

Forward of the master cabin, under the foredeck, there is a space nearly 4 metres in length. The headroom here varies from 100cm to 120cm, and we will utilize the space mainly as storage and occasionally as overflow guest accommodation. Access is

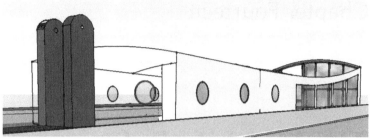

through a door in the forward part of the master cabin and through a hatch at the forepart of the foredeck. Our bicycles can be easily lowered into the space by removing the cover over the mast slot.

The windows, of course will be double-glazed. The ones that I had drawn here may have been optimistically large; however, we wanted them to be as large as possible consistent with proper engineering, offering a very bright and airy feeling to the new interior.

At the end of November we were sent photos of Nieuwe Zorg being hauled out of the water by Scheepsreparatie Friesland. They began stripping out her interior in preparation for her second century facelift. At the middle of December she was moved inside a hangar to begin her metamorphosis.

We would have loved to have been aboard our skûtsje to decorate her for Christmas, but with her in Harlingen under the plastic surgeon's knife, and with us 7700 kilometres away in Vancouver, I instead resorted to PhotoShop to do the decorations.

Chapter Fourteen

The Mid-Life Refit

In Vancouver we kept busy doing presentations on various aspects of our three-year voyage down the west coasts of the Americas, around Cape Horn and up the east coasts. Among the diverse venues were some of the Canadian Power and Sail Squadrons, yacht clubs and the Bluewater Cruising Association. We were experiencing our first Winter in several years; our cruising had us in the Southern Hemisphere for their Springs, Summers and Autumns and we commuted north to Vancouver for three months of Summers as each Winter had happened south.

In mid-December, Edi and I were presented the Cape Horn Award by the Bluewater Cruising Association, only the third time that this award had been presented since the Association was founded in 1978.

We were sent some progress photos from Friesland. Our skûtsje had been gutted. The interior that had been so lovingly installed, maintained and decorated for the past thirty-seven years by Henk and Madij was completely removed. She was taken down to bare 1908 riveted iron so that we could install completely new electrical, mechanical and plumbing systems. With the many changes to systems, equipment and technology over the decades, it makes much more sense to begin with a clean slate, than it does to modify the existing installations.

Corner braces were installed on the inside of the roef to stabilise it and tangs were welded in place along its lower sides. The forward portion of the cockpit deck was cut out About a metre aft, a new watertight bulkhead was fabricated to separate the expanded accommodation area and the reduced machinery space. The top portion of this bulkhead forms the new position of the roef, just forward of the hatch over the engine room.

The roef was cut between the first two portlights and the cut was extended to the rear along a line just above the side decks. With the roef detached, it was slung aft about a metre and stabilised in its new position with the tangs.

The new positioning of the roef gives us not only a longer living space, but also raises the interior clearance by a few centimetres, allowing me full standing headroom throughout the salon, heads and bedroom.

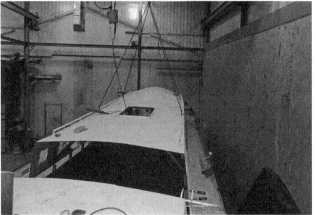

The cockpit is a bit shorter now, but in its former incarnation at over 3.5 metres, it had been rather longer than we saw necessary. A new smaller four-cylinder engine will replace the former larger six-cylinder one and the machinery spaces will be completely reorganised to make efficient use of the still very generous area beneath the cockpit.

To see the progress to date and to give us a better idea of the newly expanded interior space, at the beginning of February Edi and I flew back to Europe, rented a car and drove northward to Harlingen. Work appeared to be progressing well on raising and lengthening her roef; most of the steelwork and welding had been completed.

We were very pleased with what we saw. With the additional 11 centimetres in height and the extra 1.15 metres of length, the interior space seemed so much larger. Of course, with the interior stripped-out, the space appeared even larger.

We were delighted with the condition of the 105-year-old riveted iron. It looks as good as new, and if an observer didn't know it was over a century old, it could be easily mistaken for rather recent construction. After spending Monday evening getting over our jet-lag, we spent much of Tuesday and Wednesday measuring, sketching and planning interior layout details, and in meetings with Klaas and Wychard discussing mechanical, electrical and plumbing systems, cabinetry, appliances and interior materials and finishes.

With exact measurements of the interior, we could now do more detailed planning of the interior layout. Among the many things we decided was to forego the third wing of the galley counter and reshuffle the appliances. We determined the countertop style and colour, chose the wood for the interior flooring, selected the exterior paint scheme, redesigned the salon windows, picked the portlight styles, numbers and placements. We discussed plans for an anchor winch, a spud leg, the engineering spaces layout and many other details.

On Thursday morning, leaving Klaas and Wichard to work-out the engineering details of the engine room, galley and heads, we brushed the snow off the car, scraped the ice off the windshield and headed south in search of a warmer climate. We paused for the night in Meaux and Cognac, France, Pamplona and Morella, Spain before stopping for a few days in Calpe on the Costa Blanca, where temperatures were in the upper teens and low twenties. The view from our balcony on Valentine's Day had the sun rising directly out of the Mediterranean over Peñón de Ifach.

Suitably warmed, after four wonderful days we drove the back roads to Andora, where Edi crossed-off her 85th country and I did my 76th. We then continued on into France to Carcassonne and Narbonne to look for winter moorings for our skûtsje for the end of the coming cruising season.

We headed slowly back to Friesland with overnight stops in Gigondas, Beaune and Reims for tour and tasting appointments with Louis Bernard, Jaffelin and Roederer. Suitably refreshed, we continued northward through Belgium and back to Harlingen to see what work had been accomplished in the two weeks since we had headed south.

The first thing we saw was that the salon windows had been removed and the holes had been enlarged and reshaped. Also, the three various sized and styled portlights on each side of the forward part of the roef had been removed, their holes filled and two larger new portlights let in on each side of the house. The steelwork on the house had been completed and ground. We were very pleased.

In the bottom of the engine room, a part of the hull had been cut away and a well constructed to accommodate the new engine and transmission. Even though the new engine is smaller than the old, because of the lengthening of the house by 1.15 metres, we are moving the engine mounts aft by that amount. This necessitated the construction of a bubble beneath the existing hull so that a proper shaft angle could be maintained.

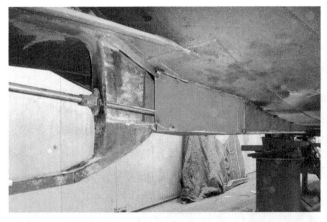

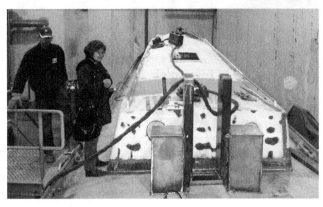

On the exterior, there will be a slight widening of the keel leading to the stern bearing and the rudder skeg. To compensate for the small disruption in water flow around the fatter keel, a larger 22 x 20 propeller has been ordered. I specified a left-hand screw, preferring its characteristics for coming to and leaving moorings starboard-side-to.

The scheepstimmerman had begun work on the interior by laying the subfloor and he told us he would shortly begin stringing battens for the interior sheathing. On the foredeck, the two vented lockers for the gaz bottles had been constructed, one on either side of the mast tabernacle.

Also on the foredeck, pads had been welded in place to take the new anchor winch. The winch, which is a new-built replica of an antique design, meant to take a wire rope around its spool. It is hand operated and has a free-fall feature, which allows quick deployment in an emergency.

We next went to the carpentry shop to look at the new frames for the enlarged salon side windows. The timmerman was just glueing the last pieces on the sixth and final mahogany frame when we arrived. The other frames were standing on the floor on either side of his workbench, waiting for their double-glazed inserts. We were very pleased with the progress, and with the quality of the work that had been done.

We met with Klaas and decided on a few more details. With most of the design decisions made, we felt easy leaving Nieuwe Zorg in the hands of SRF and heading back to Vancouver.

On Saturday we drove southward to look for a place to stay within an easy drive of the airport in Brussels. It was threatening to snow, and we wanted an easy drive on Sunday morning for our 1030 flight back to Canada. Just past Antwerp we left the highway to head into Mechelen to find some accommodation. We drove for many kilometres through the very bland city and its urban sprawl and saw no hotels, inns or any other form of lodging. As we continued through mundane linear communities, we became increasingly convinced that people mustn't stop in Belgium; we could find no public accommodation. Finally, after more than an hour of urban and suburban traffic, we found an Ibis Hotel in the centre of Leuven, about 20 kilometres from the airport.

Sunday morning as we swept the snow off the car, we were pleased that we had stayed so close to the airport. As it was, it took us nearly an hour to drive the short distance. The flight was nearly an hour late departing because of weather, so we missed our connection in Montreal and had to wait over four hours for the next flight to Vancouver, which was also weather-delayed. Finally, at just past 2300 we arrived home after more than 24 hours in transit. We were travel weary, but very upbeat from our wonderful three weeks of adventures in Europe.

Chapter Fifteen

Monitoring the Refit from Afar

We were sent frequent photographic updates on the progress of the work. The first week of March the subfloor had been completed, the interior electrical wiring had been run, the ceiling had been installed, the insulation and vapour-barrier was in place and the interior sheathing battens were fitted.

Work was also obviously progressing in the engineering spaces, with the fabrication of plumbing parts for the hot water system, which will incorporate waste heat from the engine and generator as well as input from the diesel-fired central heating furnace.

The following week photos showed that the new mahogany window frames had been dropped into the roof and installation of the interior sheathing had begun. We had chosen off white panelling with minimal wooden trim to add to the lightness of the interior and to the sense of spaciousness. I have always equated dark wood panelling to the interior of a coffin.

The new Fischer-Panda generator had arrived and was unpacked and readied for installation. It is one of the new Hybrid Power-er models and it is rated at 6000 Watts DC. It is designed to be interlinked with battery bank, inverter and shore power through intelligent controls so that the most efficient power source, or combination of sources, is used to meet changing power needs.

Most of the time the smaller amounts of 240V power will come from the batteries through the inverter. The battery levels are automatically monitored and recharged from shore power, or when not connected, then automatically by the generator. By intelligently monitoring the battery bank, the generator's operating time is significantly reduced, reportedly by more than 70%. In reading through the manual, I see there is an available easy override of the automatic system, which I will likely use most of the time.

Among the email exchange back and forth with SRF was a discussion on the cook top layout. I wanted a large wok burner and at least two, preferably three other burners. Wychard searched the catalogues and came up with this one from Candy. It fit our requirements perfectly, but not being familiar with the brand, I researched it on the Internet. It is a privately-owned Italian company that owns Hoover, Kelvinator and so on. I decided to dig further.

Rather than installing over-priced and under-performing 12 or 24 volt yacht or camper appliances, we had decided to install domestic 240 volt ones. We needed to find an under-counter fridge-freezer, a dishwasher, a microwave-convection oven and a washing machine and clothes dryer, so I looked at online reviews. Candy placed extremely high in customer satisfaction, with many of their appliances receiving 100% ratings and most of the remainder above 95%. We decided to install Candy.

The photos we received the last week of March showed the progress of work. The first one gave a general view of the interior looking aft through the framing for the bulkhead between the galley and the heads. We could see that the sliding doors had been fabricated and installed on the cupboards under the side deck. Also, the new window frames had been removed to be fitted with double glazing.

In a view looking forward we could see that the bulkhead between the heads and the master's cabin has also been framed, and beside the worker's head, we caught a glimpse of the toilet. Again for ease of maintenance, convenience of use, and attractiveness, we had chosen to install a domestic version, rather than a cantankerous, ugly and over-priced boat one.

We chose a bulkhead-mounted model and a Saniflow, which we see beside it in this photo. Because of the difficulty of taking plumbing through the ancient floors of many European buildings, the wall-mount and the Saniflow pump are commonplace. The pump automatically moves the waste to the blackwater tank. This is dramatically better than the marine toilets with clunky fixtures, hand pumps and the attendant complexity of levers, valves and clogs.

Moving aft into the salon, we saw that the hot water radiators for the heating system have been installed. Beside the radiator in the port aft corner of the salon we could see a spaghetti plate of wiring. This is lead through from the engine room and will eventually be connected to the circuit breaker panel, to the generator control panel and to the switch panel.

The framing of the salon settee had begun. Under the seat cushions and behind the seat backs will be large areas for storage. The interior work appeared to be progressing well and we began pressing for a completion date at the end of April. SRF talked of early June; there was still much engineering to do and all the painting.

The batch of photos that arrived in the second week of April showed more details of the work in progress. One showed a detail of the port forward corner of the galley and the bulkhead separating it with the heads. The line in the upper centre of the picture is the drain from the blackwater tank going through a very robust gate valve and thru-hull. Also shown are some of the electrical runs and copper plumbing from the hot water tank.

The above shot showed us that more of the freshwater plumbing had been installed, with runs for the dishwasher and the galley sink and continuing through the bulkhead for the shower, washbasin and toilet. Drains, traps, vents and valves were also in place.

This view shows two SaniVac systems, the one on the left under the galley sink will handle the graywater from the sinks, dishwasher and shower, and the other on the right will serve the toilet. Also in the photo we saw the propane lines had been led for the cooktop.

Here we see that the installation of the galley cabinetry had started. Because there are few if any square corners in a boat and also because of generally smaller spaces than found in a house, the modern pre-fabricated cabinets that are found in kitchen shops will not fit. Nearly all boat cabinetry has to be custom built in place.

In the view looking aft from the galley, we could see that the construction of the salon settee was nearly complete. The photo also shows the huge storage spaces that will be easily accessible beneath the seat cushions and behind the backs.

The old rear window had been removed to be replaced with a new double-glazed version. Through the window is a crane hook and sling, lowering the engine into place for a fitting session and to more accurately map-out the remainder of the engine room. Klaas told me that the engine was then removed so that they could begin the installation of the other engineering components: generator, inverter, battery banks, furnace and hot water heater.

She was scheduled to be moved to the painting hall on 30 April so completion of work, both inside and outside was moving ahead at a pace to have her ready for then. On 9 April the timmerman began installing the appliances in the galley and we were sent another batch of photos, which showed the oven and dishwasher had been placed.

On 10 April more photos arrived to show that the cabinet doors had been hung. It looked like the timmerman had been busy and the galley cabinetry is awaiting only drawers and countertops. We liked the clean appearance of the cabinet fronts.

Other photos showed us that mean while workers were scraping the paint on the roef back to bare steel, getting the old girl ready for her appointment with the painters. The existing paint layers there were not compatible with the two part finish we had chosen.

Another photo showed the completed bed platform in the master's cabin. On its top we saw mattress vent holes and some inspection hatches for access to the domestic water tank.

While we were in Friesland in February, we had visited the recommended upholstery shop to select fabrics for the salon settee. With the interior now ready, we emailed to tell them they could now visit and measure the bed and the salon settee for mattress and cushions.

On 23 April we received some more photos. We could see that the scraping of old paint had been completed and that the roef has been primed. Through the salon windows we could see that work was continuing on the interior.

The iroco planks had arrived and were stacked on the top, ready for installation as our new floor. When we were at SRF in February, Klaas had shown us a large selection of flooring samples. We were attracted to the look and feel of the iroco and Klaas told us that with a good treatment of oil, it was very simple to maintain. We like simplicity.

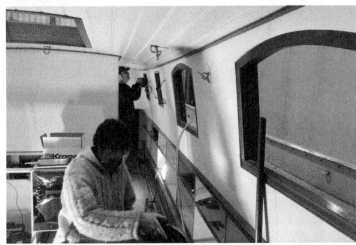

Looking inside we saw signs of much activity. Trim had been tastefully added, leaving a very bright and clean-looking interior, without the ponderousness of too much wood. While we like wood, too much gives a boat interior a sombre coffin-like feeling. We're still much too young for coffins.

Some nice detailing had been added to the area around the settee. Here we see the vent on top of the central heating radiator along the aft bulkhead of the salon.

Work was progressing at a very pleasing pace. In the middle of the final week of April we were sent the following schedule:

- This week we are finished with the woodwork.
- Next week we start the interior painting.
- Following week we start the outside painting.
- Techniek we try to finish by the end of May.
- So I think you can come over the first week of June.

This is one month later than we had originally anticipated, but we must remember that it is a boat; things always seem to take longer with them. Without today's easy communications it would be rather difficult to monitor a boat's refit from 7700 kilometres away. Fortunately we have been able to keep an eye on her while we remained in Vancouver.

With this schedule we received another batch of photos. Among them we saw that the new iroco floor had been laid. We could also see that the wood trim had been finished and that the double glazed windows had been installed in the frames. We were delighted with how attractively her interior had evolved.

On 3 May we received another group of photos. We saw that the new aft window had been installed and that some of the wiring had been pulled from the engine room to the place where the new monitoring and control panel will be fitted.

From the cockpit, we could see how well the newly built window frame matches the elegant curves of the roef. Its inward opening feature will allow a nice cross breeze with the opening skylight above the galley and the six opening portlights forward. We could see that it was still awaiting the completion of the lattice work of double-glazed panes.

Another interior shot shows the sliding pocket door leading to the heads. We designed it as a sliding door because a hinged door would take way too much room. The previous interior had used hinged doors and they conflicted with the curved ceiling and would not open fully. It is the only door in the interior of the barge, we having decided on an open plan to give us better use of the space. All along the starboard side are storage cupboards set in beneath the side decks. The photo shows them with their sliding doors removed for the installation of the trim.

On the technical end of things, we see that the stern tube has been fitted and is awaiting the propeller shaft, which is awaiting the installation of the new Perkins M92B engine and PRM transmission. In the engine room machinery and equipment was being placed around the periphery of the space, leaving room in the centre for the engine.

We received photos showing the new generator being lowered into the after end of the engine room. It was then moved aft and onto the bed that had been prepared for it. Other views showed that the Marine Booster diesel furnace had been installed as well as the Victron inverter charger and an 876 amp-hour, 26.4 volt battery bank made up of 2.1 volt cells.

On 7 May some new photos arrived showing her still in the work shed with the masking and priming of her roef looking complete and the hull draped in plastic sheeting. She appeared to be ready to have the first of the top coats applied to her roef.

There was a photo looking aft over the mast tabernacle, showing us the graceful curves of the newly-extended roef. Another view showed us details at the mast tabernacle. Between its uprights, a caisson for a spud leg is unobtrusively fitted in place. When deployed, the retractable spud leg will extend a little bit more than two metres below the bottom of our skûtsje.

With her bottom three-quarters of a metre below waterline, this will give a quick and convenient mooring to the canal bottom in water depths of two-and-a-half metres or slightly more. Since most small canals are less than two metres in depth, many of them much less, the spud leg be useful for remaining in position while waiting for a lock or a bridge and will also be ideal for securing alongside the usually rough and irregular canal banks that are found in most places except the organised moorings.

The spud leg is just a little more than five metres aft of the bow, so mooring lines ashore from the bow and stern cleats will have more than ample leverage to hold her aligned to the bank. Our three-metre aluminium gangplank, which attaches to the gunwale at one end and has large casters on the other, will easily bridge the gap to the canal bank.

The placement of the spud leg between the pillars of the tabernacle precludes our fitting a mast. While our initial intention had been to re-rig the skûtsje for sail, we decided that we were getting to an age where sailing her would be too much of a chore. With traditional rig, a crew of four is considered minimal, so we would need to take on crew when we wanted to sail. Additionally, our thinking was that for the few times we would have sailed her, the clutter of folded mast, boom and gaff and all the associated shrouds, stays, sails and other rigging would be in the way on the canals. Our voyage through Patagonia and around Cape Horn had satisfied our thirst for sailing. We decided to forego the mast and go for a more relaxed boating adventure.

During the second and third week of May a few more batches of photos arrived. These showed the continuing work in the engine room. The installation of the generator appeared to have been complete. It is at the after end of the engine room, centred above the propeller shaft, and thus will be easily accessible through the aft engine room hatch.

Clockwise from the generator we see the start battery for the generator.. Next along from this is the Maritime Booster diesel-fired central heating and hot water system. This system is linked to thermostats that control both the domestic hot water and the central heating. The unit also has a burner to provide hot water on demand.

Running along the port side up to the forward bulkhead is one of the two interconnected diesel oil tanks. To monitor the fuel level there is a sight tube. Around on the forward bulkhead is the raw water strainer for the main engine and next to it we see that a switchable pair of Racor diesel fuel filters had been installed. These and the strainer are readily accessible through the hatch.

Continuing clockwise across the bulkhead is the raw water strainer for the generator. Around the corner in front of the starboard diesel oil tank we see the Victron MultiPlus 24/5000/120. This 5 kilowatt pure sine wave inverter-charger provides many automatic functions, including up to 120 amps of charging to the 24 volt bank of house batteries as well as for the bow-thruster battery and the start batteries for the engine and generator. Beneath the unit is the engine start battery.

Aft of the Victron is a very beefy switch and breaker panel linking the inverter-charger to the 876 amp-hour, 24 volt house battery. We chose to go with gel cell because of its greater availability of power, greater forgiveness and lower maintenance.

In front of the battery bank is the propeller shaft's stern gland greaser. Its location appears to make it very convenient to give the crank a turn or so after each day's run. Immediately aft of it is the heat exchanger to heat domestic hot water with waste heat from the engine and generator. It appeared that the only things missing were the engine and its transmission.

The Perkins-Sabre M92B is a 4.4 litre, 4 cylinder in-line, vertical 4 stroke water cooled and naturally aspirated diesel engine with a fresh water heat exchanger. Among the things I like about the engine is that its maximum power and torque are developed at low revolutions. The torque curve is rather flat, with its maximum developed at only 1400 rpm, where the fuel consumption is about 4.5 litres per hour. With a properly matched propeller, this will allow us to cruise at the 8kph speed limits of most small canals at around 1200 rpm or so, while burning about three litre per hour.

On 21 May Klaas sent us some photos showing the engine being lowered into the space that had been left for it. It was then fitted onto the mounts that had been prepared for it, and in short order, the raw water cooling, exhaust, fuel and electrical systems were connected. our skûtsje again had mechanical power.

The next day we again received photos from Harlingen. These showed us that the custom-made Marlan® countertop had been installed. Marlan® is a Dutch product that is non-porous, dirt repellent, stain resistant, hygienic and food safe. Unlike the Corian®, which we had in our sailboat, Sequitur, Marlan® is also flame resistant and has a high resistance to scratching.

We had initially wanted granite countertops in the galley; however, once Klaas showed us samples of and specifications for Marlan®, and explained the seamless

fabrication and shaping, our decision to go with Marlan®, even though it is more expensive than granite, was easy. To coordinate with our iroco flooring, mahogany trim and the pale cream cabinetry and bulkheads, we chose the Himalaya Bronze colour. The cooktop was ready to nestle into its position above the convection-microwave oven. In his email, Klaas told us that the interior would be completed at the end of the week and the iroco flooring would be oiled the following week.

On Friday 24 May we were sent some photos showing the progress with the painting. We had chosen an ivory colour for the roef, for us a more pleasing and slightly warmer colour than the previous white. We were told the first finish coat had been applied a few days before. The rubbing strake, gunwale tops, winches, bollards and other deck gear are in black. Our thinking here was that with these being the most commonly chipped, chafed and worn areas as the barge is operated, black would be the easiest colour to match and the simplest to apply touch-up without looking too patchy.

The photos we received 25 May showed how well our other colour choices work. For her hull beneath the rubbing strake, we chose a navy blue, and for the topsides we decided on a rich burgundy. We opted for these darker colours on the hull because the previous white too easily showed rust weepings. We thought that we could find better things to do than frequent cosmetic touch-ups.

The photos showed that the first finish coats were all on as were some of the top coats. The decks were waiting for the surrounding paint to dry, so that they could be masked in preparation for painting with a non-skid layer. A few days later, on Thursday 30 May we received another batch of photos showing the completed paint job. We thought that our skûtsje had a rather fine complexion for a 105-year-old lady.

Proudly wearing her new colours, she was transferred onto a low crawler and rolled out of the hangar and into the yard to be prepared for re-launching. She was moved to the edge of the water and was slung in the travel lift.

For the first time in six months her bottom was wet again. We had decided that at this moment we would rename her **Zonder Zorg**. Zonder Zorg is Dutch for *Without Worry, Without Care, Carefree.* We feel that this name more aptly describes us and our style of boating than did Nieuwe Zorg, which means *New Worry* or *New Concern.*

Before she was even out of the slings, work resumed aboard. There were still many details to be attended to make her liveable. It was already Thursday afternoon and were scheduled to arrive on Monday to move aboard. We were assured that we would be able to move in upon arrival. Even then, we knew there would be small things needing completion, tweaking, adjusting and refining. We were looking forward to settling-in and making Zonder Zorg our home.

Chapter Sixteen

Moving Aboard and Settling In

On Sunday morning, 02 June we rolled our ten-piece luggage train the block and a half from our Vancouver loft to the SkyTrain for the ride to the airport. Our flights took us without hitch via Montreal to Brussels and we breezed through Immigration, with Edi's new Dutch passport allowing us to do the very short *EU Passports* line; the *Other Passports* line looked thirty or forty minutes long. Our luggage arrived promptly and our car was waiting for us at the Hertz Gold Counter.

Within three hours we were looking across the canal at Zonder Zorg, looking wonderful in her new colours. Her leeboards had not yet been installed, and we could see work underway with hatches open fore and aft, an entry door standing on the side deck and the carved artwork leaning against a shoreside hangar wall.

After a quick visit aboard, we went up to the office to announce our arrival to Klaas and to get an update from him on the progress of the work and to find out where our stored bins were. We were shown to a third-floor loft in one of the hangars, where from our pile of belongings we selected two bins in which we could see tableware, stemware, cutlery and cooking utensils and vessels. We lugged them down to the boat. We then hauled our ten pieces of luggage onboard from the car and drove into town shopping for ingredients for dinner and breakfast.

Back onboard we unpacked and began organising. The rough sorting was easy with all the sliding doors removed from the fronts of the compartments. There are twenty-two compartments running all the way along the starboard side. With six each in the salon, galley and bed-

room and four across from the heads, sorting by place of use was simple. The five drawers and two cupboards beneath the galley countertops easily swallowed everything we threw at them and still seemed almost empty. The bins beneath and behind the settee are huge and they remained nearly empty.

While Edi continued to sort, I prepared dinner. There were no cooking pots in the bins we had brought down from storage, and the hangar was locked for the night. I decided against driving into town to look for a small pot, so with just a wok and a sauté pan to work with, we skipped the green beans amandine and had a simple meat and potatoes dinner. At 2200 we dragged ourselves to bed, thirty-one hours and 7700 kilometres after we had sprung out of bed in Vancouver. The new mattress was very comfortable and we were very soon asleep.

The next morning we saw Sfinx sitting in the slip around the corner from us. She was one of the three tjalks we had winnowed onto our short list from the seventeen we looked at. Looking at her and at Zonder Zorg now, we are delighted with our decision. Looking at the tangle of rigging on Sfinx, we are thankful that we decided not to restore Zonder Zorg to sail; the rig would have been in the way most of the time for the style of boating we want to do now.

Through the following four days, as the yard workers tended to some of the remaining small details aboard, we hauled more things down from the storage loft, We also shopped around in Harlingen for an espresso machine, a bean grinder, a toaster and other comforts of home. On Wednesday and Thursday we made trips to Ikea in Groningen and each time came back with

a stuffed car. Thursday afternoon we bought two lightly used bicycles in a shop in downtown Harlingen, and in the evening we tried them out with a grocery shopping trip into town. On Friday we returned the rental car to the Hertz office in Leeuwarden and took the train back to Harlingen.

On Saturday morning we headed out in Zonder Zorg for a shakedown cruise to try out her various systems. We found a very simple and practical way to secure the bicycles aboard, with a fender on the mast tabernacle and a bungee cord. The sluit cover makes a perfect wheel chock. The bicycles came fitted with wheel locks, which also incorporate a robust cable lock.

We headed along the Van Harinxma-kanaal toward Leeuwarden under scattered clouds in gusty crosswinds. Among the many boats we saw were a few sailboats on beam or broad reaches along the canal. Zonder Zorg's new larger diameter propeller gives her helm a much more stable feel. Where Nieuwe Zorg's tiller needed to be tended full time, and with considerable effort, now the tiller can be let go for short periods and is much easier to handle.

We motored through Faneker and shortly beyond it we turned off the main canal into a narrow one heading southward. The sign at the canal entrance confirmed the notations on the chart that gave the maximum bridge clearance of 2.4 metres, but with Zonder Zorg's low air draft, we easily passed under.

We wound our way through pastures and tiny villages for a few kilometres, and then turned off the small canal into a tiny one and secured alongside in a tiny wilderness park. Earlier in the week we had paid €12 for an annual membership in De Marrekrite, a recreation group that provides 3500 free mooring spots at 285 locations throughout Friesland. For the fee we received a map to all the locations and burgee which allows us a year of free moorage. We settled-in and relaxed. It may take us a while to become accustomed to this pace, but we are confident that with practice, we eventually will.

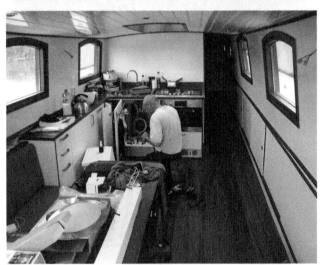

We arrived back in Harlingen midday on Monday after our weekend shake-down cruise. With us we had a short list of arisings that needed attention. While Zonder Zorg is a hundred-and-five years old, that is on the outside only; inside, she is completely new. As with many new installations, there are tweaks and adjustments necessary that are discoverable only with use. We found several. One of these was the hand sink in the heads; in the standard Dutch fashion, it was plumbed for cold water only. The easy fix was to add a mixer to its feed line under the galley sink.

Another item that needed attention was that a right-hand propeller had been installed instead of the left-hand one that I had specified. I much prefer a left-hand screw because of the ease of handling when going alongside starboard-side-to. When the engine is put astern, the stern kicks to starboard, nicely pulling it alongside. When leaving, the forward turning screw pulls the stern to port, moving it nicely away from the wall and allowing a clean departure.

We motored Zonder Zorg around to the travel lift to be hauled and have the propeller exchanged. The lift was quick and very efficient. With Zonder Zorg out of the water, it gave us an opportunity to again familiarize ourselves with her underwater architecture. The bottom of the rudder extends a metre and a half aft of the pintles, but is protected by being ten centimetres above the skeg. The propeller is also protected from shallow bottoms by the skeg.

The retaining nut was heated and undone. The propeller was then heated and thumped off the tapered shaft end. While the shaft was cooling down, the crew went for their koffie break. With the shaft cool, the new 22 X 20 LH screw was introduced to the tapered shaft, heated and snugged up with the retaining nut, which was then locked in place with a setscrew into a shaft dimple.

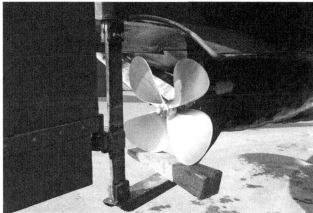

While the barge was out of the water, we had a good look at the original registration number stamped into her side in 1908. The S831N signifies that she was the 831st ship registered in Sneek in the Netherlands. Above the number is a line of original rivets joining iron plates in her century-old hull.

Also while on the hard, we had a new through-hull installed just below deck level on the port bow. This is to reroute the water tank breather line, which had been badly routed and had allowed water to overflow into the bilges when we had filled-up the fresh water tanks.

After the very quick and efficient work, we went back into the water and motored around to work wharves on the south side of the site. Shortly after we secured, a Lemsteraak rafted outboard. We counted seventeen boats being worked on in the water and on the hard. Plus inside the hangars there were another eleven vessels being built or refitted. Every space was full. SRF is an extremely busy yard with over fifty workers and seemingly more work than they can handle in what was widely reported as a continent-wide slowdown. Many of the other yards were struggling to find work; some were completely idle.

On Zonder Zorg work immediately resumed, with such things as adding re-enforcement webs to the main engine room hatch and installing sound-deadening insulation to the undersides of both hatches. We had a locking latch installed, so that we can secure the engineering spaces when we leave the boat.

While work progressed, we kept ourselves busy fine tuning and adding interior details. Being now the full width of the interior, the bedroom is spacious and comfortable, with lots of convenient hanging points. The washing machine and the clothes dryer are nicely tucked-in under the foredeck; convenient to get at, but out of the way. We gave them several loads to work with.

On our first trip to Ikea we had bought a MemoryFoam pad to put on top of our mattress, and this made the very comfortable bed even more luxurious.

We love the clean simplicity of the interior, and the wonderfully convenient cabinets behind sliding doors all along the starboard side. There is more than enough storage.

The arrangements of fixtures in the heads has allowed for a very spacious shower, with more than ample elbow room. The water heating system provides hot water for as long as the two large water tanks and the supply of diesel fuel hold out. The toilet is well placed and being wall-mounted, it takes very little space. The electric flush through the Saniflow is quiet and efficient.

The galley is very well laid-out, with everything ergonomically arranged and conveniently placed. We have thoroughly tested the dishwasher. At 45 centimetres width, it is just large enough to swallow in a single load everything that we use to prepare and enjoy breakfast, lunch, snacks and dinner.

The fridge sits conveniently under the port side-deck and is sufficiently large to store several days of food. Although with shops and supermarkets being very plentiful often within a short walk or cycle from the canals, we don't need to stock-up like we did during our years of wild and remote sailing.

The seven-month refit had been completed and the last few adjustments and details were being addressed as we settled-in and made Zonder Zorg a home. Of course we tried-out the new galley repeatedly and it has consistently produced wonderful meals. It is such a joy to work in and the appliances far exceed our expectations.

By late afternoon on 18 June the most of the items on the list had been tended to and completed. There were just a couple of things still unfinished, and the workers were confident that they would be completed the following morning. The last of the testing would be done and everything would be ready for us to head out to begin our cruising.

In the evening we again tested the galley to ensure everything was working properly. It produced another splendid meal. We were looking forward to many years of zonder zorg cruising in Zonder Zorg.

Chapter Seventeen

Which Way to Go?

On our way back from Spain toward Friesland in February, we had stopped in the Midi region of France to see if we could arrange winter moorage. To hedge our bets, we applied to the capitaineries in both Carcassonne and Narbonne. In mid-May, after three months of communicating and negotiation, a place was confirmed for Zonder Zorg in the Port de Carcassonne.

The Port is located at the edge of Ville Basse, which is referred to as the New Town. New because it dates only to 1247, when Louis IX founded it across the River Aude from La Cité, the fortified citadel on the hill that was built by the Romans dating the first century BC.

Carcassonne is home to about 50,000 people. It is about mid-way along the Canal du Midi from the Mediterranean to Toulouse, and is within a few kilometre from being the most southerly part of the French canal system. A major portion of its businesses is tourism, centred around La Cité and the Canal du Midi, both of which are UNESCO World Heritage Sites. Wine growing is also a major focus here, it being in the heart of the Languedoc-Roussillon wine region, with many famous areas, such as Minervois, Corbières and Limoux nearby. We look forward to a pause there.

However, Carcassonne is about 2000 kilometres south of Harlingen, across the Netherlands, Belgium and France. We had a long way to go and we had a very large variety of routes from which to chose to get us there.

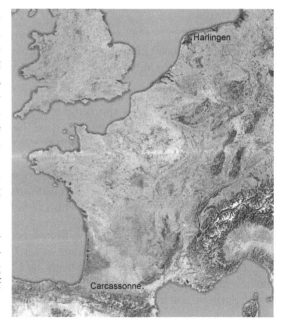

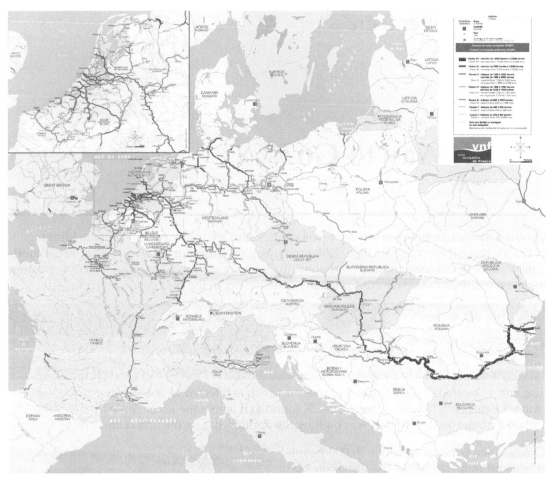

There are over 45,000 kilometres of navigable rivers and canals in Europe. That is more than a global circumnavigation's worth of inland waterways to explore. In France alone, there are 8,800 kilometres.

Our intention was to do a thorough shake-down of Zonder Zorg by wandering around the canals of Friesland. Once we were satisfied that all systems were working properly, we thought to follow a meandering route through the remainder of the Netherlands to Maastricht on the Maas at the border with Belgium. The river changes names at the border of Walloonia, the French portion of Belgium; it becomes la Meuse. This is the shortest route through Belgium and it is reputed to be very pleasant in its southern portions. There isn't time on this trip to explore in Flanders, the Dutch-speaking portion of Belgium, where the pleasure boating excellent.

Once we enter France at Givet, we will be faced with many choices of routes to take us through northeastern France, but it was a rather safe bet that whatever way we chose, our first destination would be the Champagne. Onward from the Champagne, we can opt to continue via Paris, with the decision of whether to go by way of the Marne or the Aisne, Oise and Seine. From the Seine above Paris we can choose to continue on the Loing, Briare, Loire and Centre to the Saône, which

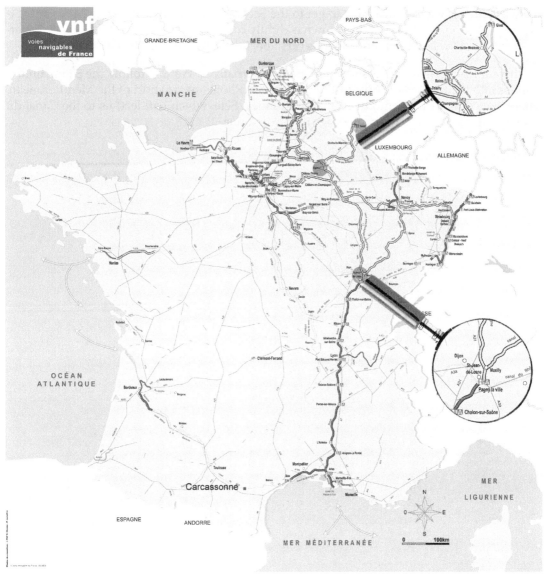

entails 554 kilometres and 157 locks; or possibly take the more scenic Yonne, Nivernais, Loire and Centre, which is a bit longer and has a few more locks; or we can take the Yonne and Bourgogne to the Saône, which is shorter at 401 kilometres, but involves more work with 214 locks.

Alternatively, if we decide to give Paris a miss on this trip, we can follow the Aisne a la Marne, the Lateral a la Marne and the Canal entre Champagne et Bourgogne to the Saône, or we can do the Marne a la Rhin and Canal des Vosges to the Saône. An additional eastern alternative is to continue along the Marne a la Rhin into the Alsace, then southward and take the Rhône au Rhin to the Saône. The route we take will depend on many factors: how much time we have, how many locks we feel like doing, what history and culture we want to see, and what we want to eat and drink.

Whichever route we take, we have to get to the Saône. Six different routes meet at or near St-Jean-de-Losne on the Saône, and the town is rightly considered the centre of the French waterways system. We had based our previous canal boat there between 2000 and 2006.

Southward from St-Jean-de-Losne, there are no alternatives. We will follow the Saône until it empties into the Rhône at Lyon and then follow the Rhône to just short of the Mediterranean, where we will branch off into the Canal du Rhône a Sète, which will lead us to the Canal du Midi and along it is our winter moorage in Carcassonne.

Chapter Eighteen

Southward Through Friesland

On Wednesday morning, 19 June we went up to the office of Scheepsbouw & Reparatie Friesland to bid our farewells. We had the rare good luck of finding the three partners, Lex Tichelaar, Wychard Raadsveld and Klaas Koolhof in the office at the same time. After we had thanked them for the wonderful work they had orchestrated, I posed for a photo with them. I am not a short person, but with the Dutch having the tallest average height in the world, these three men at 195 to 200 centimetres tall towered over me. Their work seems to tower over that of other yards in our experience.

We flashed-up Zonder Zorg's new engine, and at 1015 slipped our lines and headed out. As we motored past the yard, André shouted a "bon voyage" from his perch on the foremast of Avatar, his new 23-metre topsail schooner. After nearly two years it was nearing completion in the SRF yards. We had watched the previous week as the masts were stepped, and now we saw the yards being rigged. There is still considerable interior work to be completed, but she is looking very shippy.

Within ten minutes we were at the In-dustriebrug waiting for the bridge to be opened for us. We had decided to take the narrow Harlinger Trekvaart, which winds through farmland and small villages to Bolsward. Along the way are several low fixed bridges, the lowest being 2.16 metres and the nar-rowest 4.5 metres, but before we can get to them, we have five movable bridges that need to be lifted for us. We phoned the number on the bridge sign and were informed it would be about ten minutes; they were just fin-ishing at the other end of the series.

The second bridge was 6.9 metres wide, but it required a 90° turn to port from the narrow canal, so it was a good test of my barge-handling skills. I surprised myself with the ease of the manoeuvre, and I am delighted that we had taken the time to insist that the left-hand propeller we had originally specified was fitted.

The third bridge, which is shown as number 7 on the inset from the chart, is a 5.5 metre wide swing bridge with an immediate 80° port turn into the 6.6 metre wide road bridge and the adjacent 6.4 metre wide rail bridge. It was all wonderful barge handling practice and Zonder Zorg handled it all very well.

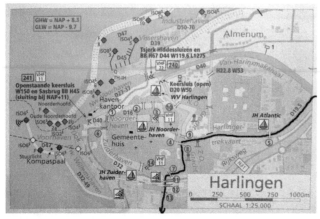

At 1059 we were through the rail bridge and then very quickly into ru-ral Friesland, with no more movable bridges until the city of Bolsward. There were; however, many fixed bridges, mostly with 2.5 metres of clearance above water. We had not ac-curately measured our air draft since the refit; rough measurements show us to be about 2.05 metres. We had room to spare.

Along the canal banks were herds of grazing cattle, needing no fences to keep them in. The canals and drainage ditches also provide them drink. The canal wound through several tiny villages where we admired the wonderfully kept homes alongside the canal. Many of these had life-sized livestock sculptures as lawn ornaments, likely representing their owners' livelihood. And everywhere, there were boats moored.

The water was glassy calm as we neared the village of Kimswerd shortly before noon. The day was very hot, with temperatures in the 30s and all morning the sky had been cloudless. We were relieved to have a layer of cirrostratus begin to move in and offer some protection; our bodies were still very pale from a rather cloudy spring.

We wound our way around some tight turns in the village and through some narrow and low bridge holes. Just beyond the village, we saw a very pleasantly sited wooden wharf, and decided to secure alongside to pause for lunch. The structure is about 60 metres long and it has solid mooring bollards spaced about 4 metres apart.

Alongside the canal runs the old towpath, now a paved bicycle route. We surmised that because the canal is so narrow and winding through Kimswerd, making moorage there impracticable, the wharf has likely been built to offer passing boats a place to stop to visit the village.

After a leisurely lunch and a relaxing hour, we slipped and continued along the canal.

Shortly past 1500 we arrived in Bolsward and paused briefly as the Jansbrug was lifted for us to pass through. The bridge keeper then pedalled along and prepared the next two bridges for us, and each was ready for us as we arrived. Within twenty minutes we were through Bolsward and back out into the farmland. Four more lifting bridges and about eleven kilometres brought us to Workum just past 1800.

We secured to bollards on a low wharf along the canal bank at the northern edge of the city. We had come 32.7 kilometres in about seven hours of motoring. Unlike in our sailboat Sequitur, there is no autopilot in Zonder Zorg. Steering is a constant hands-on affair with a huge oak tiller, and we were a tad weary.

When the municipal toll keeper came by in the early evening, we paid her for two days, and said we would likely stay for a third. We needed a rest after the rather hectic schedule of the past three weeks, with leaving Vancouver, setting-up house in Zonder Zorg, wrapping-up the last bits of the refit and preparing to head south. We needed some time to unwind and to catch our breath.

To mark the beginning of our new cruising life, I prepared chicken tarragon and served it with fine green beans almandine and sautéd small potatoes garnished by sliced Roma tomatoes with shredded fresh basil. With dinner we enjoyed a celebratory bottle of Cava Codorniu Classico.

We are increasingly convinced that we will quickly learn to enjoy this style of cruising.

The thin cirrostratus that we had welcomed as a sun blocker on Wednesday afternoon had changed to a solid altostratus by evening. Thursday morning we were under low nimbostratus and rain appeared inevitable by mid-afternoon. Nonetheless, after a luxurious sleep-in and a late breakfast, we unloaded our bicycles from the foredeck and pedalled through Workum and out the other side, and using TomTom on my iPad, we chose to follow the bike path on Oude Dijk that runs southwest toward the coast. After nine kilometres we arrived in Hindeloopen.

Hindeloopen was built on a group of three mounds in the saltwater marshes along the western coast of Friesland beside the broad delta of the IJssel. In the twelfth century its mariners began voyaging out of the IJssel and along the North Sea and Baltic Sea coasts fishing and trading. It was granted city rights in 1225 and became a member of the Hanseatic League in 1368. The trade grew and reached its greatest extent from 1650 through 1790. At its height, a fleet of eighty trading ships called Hindeloopen home.

Their strong overseas connections with foreign countries and infrequent contact with those of the hinterland across the marshes, caused the development of the Hindeloopen language; a mixture of West Frisian, English, Danish, and Norwegian.

We pedalled into the tiny city, pausing frequently to admire the views. Everything that we saw was tidy and well-maintained. There is an evident pride everywhere here. We circled the church to get the best angle to see its leaning steeple.

Though not as impressive as Pisa's leaning tower, it is certainly out of plumb. We locked our bikes in the convenient racks beside the church and went in for a visit.

We then took our bicycle panniers up onto the sea dike and down the seaward side to sit on the large blocks of riprap and have lunch. Edi had prepared ham and cheese croissants and we enjoyed them as the sheep and lambs around us grazed on the lush grass.

After lunch we left our bicycles on the racks and went wandering the city and browsing the shops. We bought a few things for Zonder Zorg. I bought a spare Friesian flag for the jackstaff and Edi bought some of the famous Hindeloopen fabrics and some Douwe-Egberts Hindeloopen cup and saucer sets from the artist who had designed them. Then it started to rain.

We walked back to our bike rack, which was nestled between the church and the museum. The continuing heavy rain convinced us that this was the prefect time to visit the museum, which is in the building that was the City Hall from 1683 to 1919. The receptionist told us that with all the shipping trade in the seventeenth and eighteenth centuries, the citizens had become quite wealthy and spent a great amount of money in Amsterdam on precious fabrics, furnishings and decorations.

Many of the goods they bought had been imported from Asia through the Dutch East India Company. The rich town developed its own distinctive costume with its fabrics and designs showing a distinct Asian influence.

As the prosperous times waned and oak could no longer be afforded, furniture and panelling were made with simpler, less expensive woods. These were decoratively painted by the locals to replicate the intricate carving of the oaken pieces. Thus the now famous Hindeloopen decorative style evolved. The museum is full of wonderful early examples.

After nearly two hours we were filled to the brim with this wonderful art. We left the museum and scurried fifty metres through the downpour to Restaurant Sudersee, where we had a koffie en chocoladecake to help the rain diminish. As the rain persisted, the owner, Piet Bakker offered his wifi code and a link to a weather radar site so we could watch the progress of the storm on my iPad.

After an hour in the restaurant, the radar showed the heavy downpour easing to a downpour, so we took that weather window and pedalled back the shorter six kilometre route to Workum. It was less scenic, but with heavy, wind-driven rain, we weren't really into looking around. Back onboard Zonder Zorg we enjoyed very long, hot showers and relaxed.

Zonder Zorg had been built in Gaastmeer in 1908 and we wanted to visit her birthplace. Gaastmeer is only six kilometres east of Workum and the easiest way to get there is by water. However, with the continuing heavy rain and howling winds, we decided to stay a third night in Workum, hoping for better weather.

On Saturday morning we pedalled into the centre of the old town to do some browsing and shopping. We con-

tinue to be struck by the cleanliness, the tidiness and the order of the buildings and the settings, both public and private. Windows are clean, walls sparkle, gardens are groomed. House windows usually have no curtains, inviting our eyes inside. Everywhere we have been in the Netherlands has shown this obvious care and pride.

Back onboard I monitored the evolving weather with the buienradar.nl site, which showed the passing of the main nimbus system we had been under for days. After 1400 there were just a few smaller patches of rain heading our way, so at 1500 we flashed-up the engine and headed out.

We wore around in the narrow canal and headed southeastward along the Lange Fliet toward the Friesian Lakes. Light rain alternated with heavy drizzle as we motored along the canal and there was a strong crosswind from the south. Taking advantage of the winds were many sailboats, in a wonderful mix of new and old, large and small. This century-old classically maintained wooden botter was among them.

As we reached the lakes the winds were building through Force 6, so we decided to seek shelter. At 1552 we secured to a wilderness wharf on the lee side of an island on the western edge of Grote Gaastmeer. This mooring place is part of the De Marrekrite system, for which we have a burgee.

Overnight, the rain eased, but the winds remained strong. In the early afternoon on Sunday as we were planning our onward trip across the lake to Gaastmeer, we were told by a man from the boat astern of us that the winds were predicted at Force 7

late in the day. Looking at the charts and seeing no good protection in Gaastmeer from the forecast winds, we decided to seek better shelter in Heeg. At 1429 we slipped from the wharf and crossed the Gaastmeer in building winds. We lowered the leeboard to stabilize Zonder Zorg in the short, steep breaking chop. Across Gaastmeer, we entered the short Yntemasleat, which lead us to De Fleussen and shortly into Heegermeer. There were many sailboats out on the meeren scurrying for home from a Sunday sail with deeply reefed sails.

As we approached the entrance to Heegerwâl, we had to crab a full 30° to maintain our track in the cross-wind. At 1530 we found lee in the basin and shortly we secured to a solid wharf with a thick stand of old trees breaking most of the wind. The winds increased overnight, but we were snugly comfortable with a good wifi signal from the office just across the way.

The rains had stopped by the time we arose on Monday. After a large breakfast of local sausage, scrambled eggs on toast with tomato slices and fresh basil washed down with steaming cups of espresso, we headed out.

We pedalled into strong headwinds the five kilometres to the village of Gaastmeer. Thankfully, our bicycles are seven and eight speed, so the pedalling was eased, though rather slow.

Near the centre of the village Edi spotted a sign indicating that the Wildschut Werf was down a small side street. It had moved a few dozen metres around the bend of the canal from where it had been when the Wildschut Brothers had built our skûtsje in 1908.

We pedalled into the yard and introduced ourselves to a worker. He told us that the owner was out, but should be returning shortly. As he spoke, the owner drove in. He was a bit rushed, but we interrupted him for a short while, telling him that we owned the skûtsje that his company had built in 1908 as De Nieuwe Zorg. He confirmed that he was a descendant of the Wildschut family, but in the rush we didn't even get his name, though we did remember to give him our boat's calling card along with a few questions, which he promised to answer by email.

In the single slipway of the yard was a skûtske casco from the same era as ours, although it had been built by a different yard. It had been completely stripped-out and primed and was waiting for someone to buy it and have it fitted-out to their own specifications.

We told him we were looking to fill-in some missing pieces in the Wildschut family history and that of the company, which is now called Jachtwerf Wildschut. We asked him to look at Zonder Zorg's website and to email us any additional Wildschut details he might have. We left optimistic that he would be in touch with us; however, as I write this six months later, we are still waiting to hear from him. It will likely take another visit.

Our pedal back to Heeg was down-wind and very much easier. When we arrived back in the basin, two skûtsjes were moored just ahead of us on the wharf. Each was overflowing with teenagers on deck, excitedly preparing for a sailing adventure on the meeren. With the wind still a bit high, we opted to stay another night in Heeg, relaxing and enjoying the good wifi signal.

At 1050 on Tuesday 25 June we slipped from the wharf in Heeg and headed out into Heegermeer, across it and into Wâldsinster Rakken to Woudsend. As we arrived in Woudsend, we passed a dozen racing skûtsjes moored on piers alongside the canal. It is wonderful to see so many century-old vessels in such fine condition, and to know that each is raced hard in the many Friesland sailing competitions.

As we continued through the town, we passed the line-up of boats waiting for the bridge to open, and easily ducked under the 2.45 metre span. With our leeboard down for stability, we crossed Slottermeer in a strong crosswind and entered Slotergat. A short distance along, in the centre of the town of Sloten, we came to the Nieuwe Langenbrug, which at 1.11 metres was too low for us.

The keeper had opened the bridge for us as we approached, and as we passed through, he swung a wooden shoe out on a pole and line for Edi to drop in the €2 bruggeld, the bridge money. While most bridges are free in the Netherlands, on some of the smaller canals that run through the historic centres of towns and villages, tolls are often collected.

145

The scene behind us as we left Sloten was definitely the Netherlands. There was a windmill, many red tiled roofs, a stone bridge, two canals and a variety of boats old and new. South of town we turned eastward into Wâldsleat, crossed Brandermar and then followed Hjerringsleat and Reinsleat to Grutte Brekken, which we followed southward.

From its southern end we turned into Stroomkanaal and then followed Zijlroede into downtown Lemmer. Here there are three bridges that require lifting. At the first one Edi put the posted €5 bruggeld into the clog-on-a-line and we confirmed that this fee was for all three bridges plus for the lock at the far end of town that will take us up to the level of the IJsselmeer.

As we entered the centre of town, we saw the canal banks lined with visiting boats. It was still early in the afternoon and the havenmeester obviously hadn't yet been around to condense them; they were loosely spaced with many 10 and 12 metre gaps. However; since we need 18 or more metres for Zonder Zorg to squeeze-in, we continued through the third bridge. We were hoping to find a place on the wall in the basin before the lock, where we had stayed on our arrival in Friesland in September.

We were fortunate in finding a space of more than 20 metres just down stream of the bridge. At 1358 we secured against a 3-metre high stone wall with a stout wooden rubbing strake along its bottom and solid bollards along its top. We were in the heart of the city; the bridge is main cross street of old city and downtown Lemmer. We had come to the southern edge of Friesland and we decided to pause for a couple of days.

Chapter Nineteen

Around the Old Zuiderzee Coast

We spent some delightful time in Lemmer, browsing the shops for small things for Zonder Zorg's galley gadgets drawer and some decorative items to make her more a home. On Thursday we had a light lunch of broodje gebakke schol from a booth in the weekly street market that sets up just in from the canal. Then at 1415 we slipped, backed and slowly turned while the Lemstersluis was being prepared to take us up to the level of the IJsselmeer. We didn't have long to wait and there was only a small sailboat in the lock with us. The lift was less than two metres and the entire process of waiting, entering, lifting and exiting took less than a quarter hour.

About a hundred metres onward from the lock we turned east and entered the Friesesluis that would take us down about seven metres to the level of the Noordoostpolder. Through the lock is the province of Flevoland, and we watched behind us as the doors closed on Friesland. We have very fond memories of our time in the land of the skûtsje, and we were taking Zonder Zorg away from her homeland again.

We motored out of the lock and followed the Lemstervaart through fields of crops on rich farmland that just three-quarters of a century before had been reclaimed from the seabed. At Emmeloord we came to a T-junction; leading to the westward was the canal to Urk and the IJsselmeer, from which direction we had come in October.

Instead of retracing our route, we turned eastward onto the Zwolsevaart. We motored past fields of potatoes and grains and along the way we passed a great assortment of waterfowl. Among these were ducks of various sorts, plus coots and swans.

A little over twenty kilometres along from Lemmer we came to the Marknessersluis in the centre of the town of Marknesse. As we approached, the lock was prepared for us, and we entered without pause. We were lifted about three metres to a higher level of the polder, and continued through rich farmland for a couple of more kilometres, where we turned southwestward into the narrow Enservaart. We stopped for the night in a peaceful setting, secured to a solid wilderness wharf.

After a leisurely breakfast on Friday morning we continued along the Enservaart. It is a narrow, shallow canal, which by the spread of lily pads across the channel, is apparently little used. We followed it to its end at the edge of the village of Ens. There we turned in the small basin and secured to the well maintained wharf. We had come to the end of this cul-de-sac because it is the closest approach to Schokland, which is only four kilometres away by bicycle.

Schokland is a former island in the Zuiderzee, which has a very long and complex history. The landform of the island, a low hilly ridge, that as one of the banks of the ancient River Vecht, had originated as a glacial esker at the end of the last ice age. It was home to wooly rhinoceros, aurochs, mammoths, Irish elk and European bison. As the ice receded the ridge became the occasional home to roaming hunters and fishermen, with evidence of encampments ten thousand years ago. More permanent settlement of the area dates from about 6500 years ago. Archeological finds show that the Roman armies also camped here.

With the gradual inundation of the low lands and the formation of the Zuiderzee, the area around Schokland became marsh, and by the end of the fourteenth century with the rising sea, the ridge had become an island.

The island was low and farm land was disappearing. Diking and draining were attempted, but the sea continued to erode the island. The inhabitants had been harvesting peat from the land, which had caused its further subsidence. The written history of the Schokkers dates to the early 1500s and most of the record concerns the erosion of their island as hillocks and dikes were washed away during storms. The few hundred inhabitants retreated to small hillocks on the eastern side of the island. Soon there was little more than three tiny settlements: Emmeloord, Molenbuurt, and Middelbuurt and some protective dikes.

The population had become severely inbred and impoverished; seventy-five percent of the islanders were on welfare. By Royal decree in 1859, King William III ordered the island evacuated and the residents distributed among many communities along the Zuiderzee coast.

With the diking and draining of the area and the creation of the Noordoostpolder in 1942, Schokland was reclaimed from the sea. In 1995 Schokland became the first UNESCO World Heritage Site in the Netherlands. Today the former waterfront of Middelbuurt appears as an island in a sea of potato fields. The splendid small museum that is housed in some of island's the old buildings tells the story much better than I can here.

With our minds filled with images, we retreated to the security and comfort of Zonder Zorg in Ens to relax and to ponder what we had seen.

At 1000 on Saturday the 29th of June we slipped from the wharf in Ens and headed back out the blind Enservaart to the Lemstervaart and turned southward. Shortly after noon we arrived at Voorstersluis, which brought us back up out of the level of the Noordoostpolder. From De Voorst we followed the Kadoeler Meer southeastward to Zwarte Meer, which we crossed using the buoyed channels to the Scheepvaartgat, which led us in a strong cross wind to the Goot and along it to the Ganzen Diep.

Along the way we wound a sinuous route through idyllic rural scenery. Although Kampen is only 10 kilometres from Ens, the water route we had to follow linked together several canals and lakes and took us 36.3 kilometres.

We arrived in Kampen at 1825 and secured to the melden pier in Jachthaven Seveningen to fill with water, and were told we could remain in place on the pier overnight.

Kampen was a very important seaport during Medieval times. Remains of wooden buildings date to 1150 and it received its city rights in 1236. With its location on the busy trade route between the Zuiderzee and the Rhine, the it quickly developed to become one of the most powerful Hanseatic cities in northwestern Europe. Its old city centre is remarkably well preserved.

The distance from Kampen to Elburg is thirteen kilometres overland; however, the shortest water route is 32.1 kilometres. The route follows the IJssel downstream to the Ketlemeer, where it goes around the end of a long dike and heads in the opposite direction up the beginning of the Randmeeren, the chain of lakes between the old Zuiderzee coast and the newly formed province of Flevoland. There were many huge commercial barges on the IJssel, but also a few smaller vessels.

As we headed around into Drontermeer there was a rather steady stream of pleasure craft coming and going, many of them under sail in the stiff breeze. The weather continued cold and bleak, with heavy mist alternating with rain showers throughout the day.

At 1305 we secured to the wharf in Elberg after a three-hour trip, the first part of which was aided by the current running in the IJssel. Although we had visited here on our way up to Friesland the previous September, we were fascinated by this medieval moated and walled city and we went exploring.

We admired the beautifully kept homes that abut the insides of the city's fortified walls that date to the 1290s. The lanes are a profusion of flowers interspersed with patio furniture; the residents obviously enjoy their tiny front yards. The lanes invited us to explore further into the old town and we spent two days relaxing and enjoying this wonderful place.

Mid-morning on 2 July we slipped and headed out to continue our way around the Randmeeren, the former Zuiderzee coast. We followed the buoyed channel along Veluwemeer, passed through the open sluis at Hardewijk into Wolderwijd and followed its buoyed channel to Nuldernauw and then through Nijkerkersluis to Nijkerkernauw, which took us after a 42.6 kilometre day to Spakenburg. Not long after we secured to the wharf, a line of wooden botters paraded past.

There are about four dozen of these marvellously restored and maintained old fishing boats here in Spakenburg, many of them dating from the late nineteenth century. Most of these seemed to be heading out for an evening sail on the Eemmeer. On some, crews were busily raising their sails as they went by us.

We watched the parade go past and then walked along the dike to its end at the edge of the meer. We stood watching for a long while as two and a half dozen antique wooden sailing vessels, ex-fishing boats, played with each other, tacking and gybing in the light evening breezes. As we retraced our steps along the dike to Zonder Zorg, we thought of watching evening sails on Vancouver's English Bay, then immediately dropped the thought.

In a light drizzle at 1400 on Wednesday we continued around the Randmeeren, first northward along Eemmeeer and then northwestward along Gooimeer and finally north under the Hollandsebrug and into the southern end of Markermeer. It was raining rather persistently and the wind was gusting into Force 4 from the northwest, the direction we needed to go.

We decided to seek shelter on the south side of a tiny uninhabited island, named Hooft. At 1620 we tied to small trees on a dilapidated wharf, secured out of the wind for the night. It continued to rain heavily.

After a leisurely breakfast on Thursday morning, we slipped our lines and headed across Markermeer toward Buiten IJ and the entrance to Noordzee Kanaal. Marine traffic is nicely separated, with the central lanes for large commercial vessels and side lanes for smaller and recreational ones. The locks are also segregated, and we were the first to arrive and wait for the next cycling of the non-commercial side of Oranjesluizen.

We waited for about fifteen minutes as the lock keepers shepherded nine boats of various ages, shapes and sizes into the chamber. After all the juggling, we were lowered only about 20 centimetres.

We were then in the Noordzee Kanaal, which leads across Amsterdam and out into the North Sea. We motored with heavy traffic past central Amsterdam under clearing skies. Westward, we were in the zone of the deep sea ships and passing the heads of many busy side harbours. Traffic became increasingly heavy and fast.

The wind built and we were butting into building chop. After about 30 kilometres we turned off the Noordzee Kanaal into Zijkanaal, which led us southwestward to Noorder Buiten Spaarne and onward into Haarlem.

With our travels in September to Edam, Hoorn and Enkhuizen, we had now visited nearly the entire coastline of the old Zuiderzee. We had found the area so rich in history, with stories everywhere of the struggle of the Dutch people to work with the forces of nature and to build for themselves a nation that during the Dutch Golden Age had become the wealthiest and one of the most influential in the world.

At 1650 we secured to the canal wall in the centre of the old city of Haarlem. We had left the old Zuiderzee coast and were in the heart of the art, the culture, the innovation and the wealth of the Dutch Golden Age.

Chapter Twenty

A Pause in Haarlem

We were at the foot of the street up which 150 metres is the magnificent Sint Bavokerk, which has dominated the city skyline for at least six centuries. Beside us was Teylers Museum, the oldest museum in the Netherlands. With Zonder Zorg in such a wonderful place, and with the weather finally looking a bit more summer-like, we decided to pause for a week and explore the area.

In the four weeks since our arrival in the Netherlands, we had been going rather steadily, moving into Zonder Zorg and making her our home. While we still had some fine tuning to do, we were finally ready to slow down and enjoy.

We enjoyed a leisurely breakfast on Friday morning, watching the passing parade of boats in the canal. We were just upstream of Gravestenenbrug, which is a small pedestrian and bicycle bridge that opens with a double bascule. It is 3.45 metres above the water in the centre, but toward the sides of the 10.7 metre span, the clearance is not much more than 2 metres. All the local tour and rental boats pass easily under it, as do many of the pleasure cruisers and barges.

Sailboats, of course need the bridge lifted, as do the large commercial barges. We watched as an unladen 40-metre barge came around the corner upstream and slid past us. The brugmeister from Melkbrug, the swing bridge just upstream of us, cycled past us and opened Gravestenenbrug. We watched as the barge from Dortmund glided through.

We were midway through our breakfast when a converted luxemotor flying a French flag passed us heading downstream toward the closed Gravestenenbrug. I immediately spotted its navigation sidelights fixed atop the wheelhouse somewhat like Mickey Mouse ears. They looked to high to make it under the sloped bridge decks. As the barge approached the bridge, the crew went forward to lower the burgee mast, but the skipper ignored the navigation lights until the last moment. With a belching of diesel smoke, he managed to stop before any damage was done, except to his ego.

A standard pleasure boat height for France is 3.40 metres to fit under the usual 3.50 bridges, so I assume that the skipper, reading the 3.45 metre clearance on the chart, considered he would clear. After an embarrassing pause, the bridge was lifted for him and he continued down canal. The shape of a bridge span is often more important than its listed clearance.

We finished breakfast without any further excitement and in the late morning we went walking in the old city. We walked past Sint Bavokerk and into Grote Markt looking for a good angle for pictures of the church. Narrow streets and tall buildings make this the only reasonable place from which to shoot. The sun angle on Sint Bavokerk was not at its best, but we did get a fine shot of de vleeshal, the old meat market that opened in 1604.

Along at the western side of the square stands the Stadhuis, the old city hall which dates to the 1350s. In the fourteenth century Haarlem was the second largest city in historical Holland after Dordrecht but ahead of Delft, Leiden, Amsterdam, Gouda and Rotterdam.

Haarlem is situated on a thin strip of land above sea level that is called the strandwal, *beach ridge*, which connects Leiden to the south to Alkmaar to the north. The early settlers here struggled against the waters of the North Sea on the west and those of the IJ and the Haarlemmermeer to the east. The protected inland waterway became a very important trading route and Haarlem was in position to control it.

We wandered the many walking streets, which are lined with a grand selection of shops of mid and upscale merchandise. Not being in a shopping mode, we concentrated on the small lanes that weave a maze between the larger, though still very narrow streets.

Late morning on Saturday the 6th of July, we hopped on our bicycles and pedalled northward out of Haarlem. We followed strandwal on wonderful bicycle lanes and paths to and through Santpoort, Driehuis and Ijmuiden and came to the Noordzee Kanaal. With many dozens of other cyclists, we boarded the ferry for the free ride across the waterway.

On the other side, we followed the cycle route signs to Beverwijk and then to Wijk aan Zee and pedalled past the house in which Edi was born. We continued up onto the dunes, and overlooking the North Sea, we paused on a restaurant patio for croquette broodje en bier to refresh ourselves from the eighteen kilometre ride.

In the dunes around Wijk aan Zee many bunkers still remain of the defensive line that had been built by the German occupying forces between 1940 and 1944. These were part of Festung IJmuiden, *Fortress IJmuiden*, which was to protect the nearby steel works against attacks from the Allies. After a wander among the dunes, we retraced our route back to Haarlem.

On Sunday morning we dawdled over break-fast and were again too late in Grote Markt to get the sun on the east side of Sint Bavokerk. We did, however take a respite from the mid-day sun and went into Grote Sint Bavokerk to cool off. This was once the Catholic Cathedral of Haarlem, but in 1579 it was taken-over by the Protestants. The interior is finely decorat-ed and the entire floor is made up of grave markers. Most noteworthy in the interior is the immense pipe organ, which was once the largest in the world. Herman Melville, in his novel Moby Dick compared the inside of the whale's mouth to the pipes of the Haarlem organ.

Many famous mu-sicians have played this organ, among them Händel, Men-delssohn and Mo-zart. On the rear wall, beneath the pipes, is a plaque  indicating that the ten-year-old Mozart played it in 1766.

Toward the altar, among the many hundreds of grave markers, is the tomb of Frans Hals, the most famous painter of Haarlem. It was easy to find, with an advertising banner from the Frans Hals Museum standing over it. The banner announced a special exhibition comparing the painting style of Hals with those of Rembrandt, Rubens and Titian. We had already planned to visit the museum in the early afternoon, and this spurred us on.

We followed Grote Houtstraat for three blocks past the fashionable shops, then turned along Gedempte Oude Gracht a couple of blocks across to Groot Heiligland, which we followed past lines of row houses. These were once the city's old folks homes. In one of them Frans Hals lived late in his life, and a series of them have now become the Frans Hals Museum.

Frans Hals was broadly admired early in his painting career for his bold approach, with large single brush strokes and for his rare ability to capture facial expressions, particularly smiles. A prime example of this is his *Jester with a Lute*, painted between 1625 and 1630. He was also acclaimed for his ability to paint directly, without the need for preliminary outlines and sketches. His paintings are alive and fresh, particularly when compared to those of most of his contemporaries and predecessors.

On display for comparison were portraits by other artists. Later in his painting career, Rembrandt adopted some of this bold and more casual brush stroke style. This is seen in his *Bust of a Laughing Man in Gorget*, which he painted in 1629 or 1630.

Among the many paintings by Frans Hals in the museum, I was intrigued by this one of the *Regents of the St. Elisabeth Gasthuis of Haarlem*. Hals had been commissioned to paint an official portrait of them in 1641 and the more relaxed poses in the work suggests that he had studied some of Rembrandt's historic themes and probably his 1632 *Anatomy Lesson of Dr. Nicolaes Tulp*. It was interesting to see the influ-

ence that these great masters had on each other's works.

Later, as we were passing the former old folks home on our way back to Zonder Zorg, we wondered whether any of these men were still serving as regents when years later Frans Halls appeared before the board for admission to the home.

Though not by Frans Hals, one painting caught our attention. It is a scene of the canal bank in central Haarlem painted by Gerrit Adriaensz Berckheyde in 1670. Its central theme is the De Waag, *the Weigh House*. There, goods were offloaded from barges, craned in through the front door, weighed for taxation, then moved out the side door and onto wagons or barges. Our skûtsje, Zonder Zorg was moored in front of De Waag, almost exactly where the wooden predecessor to our skûtsje with sails is moored.

The scene has certainly changed today, with more modern boats along the canal side and some new buildings, such as Teylers Museum with the huge verdigris copper sculpture above its imposing facade. De Waag is still there, though now it serves as a popular tavern.

There were several guilds formed to protect the professional status of the artists, the most prominent among these was the Saint Lucas Guild, with Frans Hals as one of its members. The Saint Lucas Guild went through many changes as the demand for paintings decreased and it was dissolved in 1795. It was revived in the early nineteenth century and then finally dissolved in 1860.

An artist group was established in 1821 and later honoured by royal decree as the Federated Holland Societies of Artists, Sculptors and Engravers. Since 1821 the group has rented the top floor of De Waag. To become a member of the society, an artist had to submit a work to be juried by a panel of nine art professors. Five votes of the nine were needed for acceptance.

Edi's father had joined the group before the Nazi occupation in 1939 and he resumed his participation at the end of the war, after he returned from forced labour in Germany. He was trained and mentored. His first work was not accepted; however, he was encouraged by other artists to try again. As a second presentation, he submitted his self-portrait. This time he was honoured with all nine votes, a first in the group's history. His self portrait became his masterpiece.

160

If his ghost were to have looked out the studio windows where he trained and painted in the 1930s and 40s, and surveyed the scene on the Sparne below, it would have seen our skûtsje, Zonder Zorg moored on the wall.

Monday again dawned clear, and the day quickly warmed into the mid-20s. Our entertainment from the cockpit was supplied by the antics of the many rental boaters. We are always a tad nervous when rental boats approach; fortunately, most of these are small and plastic and cannot inflict much damage. Every day eight or ten large commercial barges passed by, but even though they could cause huge damage, they gave us no concern; their skippers are very competent.

In the afternoon we pedalled up into the industrial area to the northeast of the city centre. We were looking for the last few bits and pieces for Zonder Zorg. We followed signs to Gamma, the Dutch answer for HomeDepot, where we picked out a few small items and a three-metre diameter patio umbrella for the cockpit table. With the umbrella strapped to my bike, we took a shorter, more scenic route back, which led us through the old Amsterdamse Poort, one of the few remaining pieces from the fourteenth century walls, which had been removed in the seventeenth century as the city expanded.

Just before noon on Tuesday, 9 July we slipped from our wonderful mooring spot, turned in the narrow canal and headed back downstream. We passed under Gravenenbrug and Catharijne-brug, then turned about again to secure on the fuel barge. We took on 100 litres of diesel for €155, delighted with how much easier it is to refuel here,

compared to the endless hassles we had endured in South America during our three years cruising there.

We then moved back under Catharijnebrug and around the bend, where we secured to the wall next to the water point. We filled the tanks for only the second time since we had left Harlingen on 19 June, an average of ten days per fill.

Within an hour we were secured back in our great spot on the wall. We had chosen to do our replenishing trip at midday because since our arrival, we had been observing that boaters usually leave mid-to-late morning and seldom settle-in until mid-to-late afternoon. We wanted our spot back, and Zonder Zorg was again centred between De Waag and Teylers Museum.

For six days we had looked up from our cockpit at the imposing facade of the museum, and we could no longer postpone a visit. The guard accepted our now ten-month-old museum passes and gave us free admission to the oldest public museum in the Netherlands.

It was founded in 1778 to honour the last will of Pieter Teyler van der Hulst (1702-1778), a wealthy linen manufacturer and banker of Haarlem. He had been intensely interested in the sciences and the arts and he had a vast and diverse private collection. His collection formed the initial content of the museum.

Immediately we entered the first display room, we were transported back in time. The displays have been organised and maintained in the same style for more than two centuries. We were effectively in a museum of a museum.

To house the collection, the executors of the estate commissioned "a cabinet of books and art" to be built in the rear of Teyler's former residence in Damstraat. The Oval Room was opened to the public in 1784. It is an impressive space, with cabinets around the walls to display physics instruments. The original pyramidal cabinets are still used to house globes, and the central display cabinets are filled with fossils and minerals. The cupboards beneath the central cabinets originally housed the portfolios of the art on paper collection. A part of the library was kept in the bookcases on the upper level. The room is today kept much as it was when it opened in 1784.

In 1821 the museum purchased its first painting by a contemporary artist and the directors began planning a room for the display the work of "living Dutch masters". The Paintings Gallery was built and it remains today dedicated to paintings from the last quarter of the eighteenth century through the first half of the nineteenth.

The impressive facade along the canal was built as a centenary project in 1878, along with rooms behind it, linking to the original Oval Room and Paintings Gallery. With the rapid expansion of the art collection through the nineteenth century, Paintings Gallery II was built and opened in 1893. This room now displays paintings from 1780 to 1930. The museum has continued to expand, and it now is composed of twelve display rooms, two coffee shops and a gift shop.

Among the many fascinating paintings in the galleries, this one of De Waag stood-out. Along Damstraat, the street leading away from the canal, next to the small tree at the centre, is the house in which Pieter Teyler had lived. In its back gardens was built the original museum, the Oval Room. The bow of our skûtsje was about where the large

tree on the right stands. The dual treadmill crane stood on the quayside for four centuries.

In the evening we walked the three blocks past Sint Bavokerk and into Grote Markt to catch the late day sun on the north and west façades of the church. The bells in the steeple were alive with an evening carillon recital as a prelude to a free organ concert, which was scheduled to begin at 2015.

We arrived inside the church about twenty minutes before the concert and had our choice of seats.

We sat as close as we could determine was the acoustical centre of the huge space. The chairs had all been turned around, and we were facing the organ, with our backs to the altar. Very shortly the church began filling, and with most arrivals settling-in very near us, we confirmed we were near the sound epicentre.

Without announcement, the guest organist, Thomas Trotter began playing, and continued for over an hour, interrupted only by the few seconds needed to change music scores. The huge instrument shook the bats out of their slumbers and they fluttered about above us as we were transported into wondrous realms by the music. As the concert progressed, increasing flocks of birds swirled outside past the upper windows. The only sound other than the organ was the long standing ovation at concert end.

Back onboard we counted our blessings as we dawdled over an assortment of cheeses, salamis, olives and breads with glasses of wine. We love this lifestyle.

Chapter Twenty-One

To Gouda

We had spent a wonderfully relaxing eight days in Haarlem, absorbing the culture and history of the city. As enjoyable as the city is, we decided it was time to move on lest we be painted into the scene. At 1025 on Friday, 12 July we slipped, turned in the narrow canal and went back under Gravenenbrug to the watering point. Although our tanks were still well over three-quarters full, we decided to top them off before continuing our voyage. A habit we try to maintain is topping-up the tanks at every reasonable opportunity, to give us as much independence as possible.

While we were filling, two large commercials came through heading downstream. Also in the canal nearby was the regular flotsam cleaning barge. We had seen it making regular runs a few times each day, cleaning flotsam and detritus from the canals of the city.

With our water tanks full, we turned again and headed upstream back under Gravenenbrug and along to Melkbrug, where we waited for the bridge to be swung open for us. Its clearance is listed at 2.0 metres above the water, and with Zonder Zorg's air

draft not yet accurately measured, but thought to be two or three centimetres either side of two metres, we decided to join the line of other waiting boats, rather than trying the yellow light lane. One of our priorities was to measure the barge's height, but until we did, I assumed it as 2.10 for safety. As we passed through the opening, I tried to compare the height of our highest point, the mast tabernacle with the bottom of the bridge. Angles and distance made it inconclusive.

Once clear of Melkbrug, we looked back at the skyline of old city, dominated by Sint Bavokerk and listened to the carillon striking noon. What a splendid time we had here. The eight days were so full, and we will long cherish fond memories of our time in Haarlem.

We followed the Zuider Butten Spaarn to its junction with Ringvaart van de Haarlemmermeerpolder, which we followed southwestward. Along the way we passed first through mainly pasture land, then increasingly past flower farms. There were grazing cattle and sheep, windmills, stately homes and small villages. We were able to pass under seven of the ten bridges in the next twenty-two kilometres, most of them being 2.2 to 2.4 metres high. However, we had to join a parade of boats moving through one metre and lower lift bridges in Zwanshoek, Hilegom and Lisse.

As we passed through Lisse, Edi commented on a sign on a boatyard building. The name was familiar to us, but for a short while we couldn't think why. Then we remembered that Henk and Madij had bought our skûtsje, when she was named Nieuwe Zorg, in 1975 from Oldenhage in Lisse.

We continued through Lisse another four kilometres to Kagerplassen, which we crossed and entered the Rijn-Schiekanaal, which led us into Leiden. We passed the junction of Oude Rijn and then Nieuwe Rijn, where 200 metres beyond Wilhelminabrug, we saw a space just barely large enough for Zonder Zorg on a free mooring wharf on the right bank. We turned in the narrow canal and squeezed in with little more than a metre to spare fore and aft. It was 1445 and we had come 30.7 kilometres from Haarlem.

On Saturday morning we pedalled into the old city. We didn't find the charm we had enjoyed in Haarlem, possibly because here we were moored well beyond the old city. Itinerant moorage at the edge of the old walled city is crammed and even in the late morning as we arrived, we could see no available spaces. The moorage is mostly on finger floats and the arrangements appeared to be for boats under 12 metres in length. Further in, the all the canals in the centre of town have fixed bridges under 2 metres high, so this precludes use by most cruising boats.

In the afternoon we pedalled northward along the Rijn-Schiekanaal to a large marine supply store we had seen on our way by the previous day. We finally found two 20-litre jerry cans; we had been searching in vain for weeks. Marine fuelling stations in the Netherlands charge 15 to 25 cents more per litre for diesel than do the road filling stations. The explanation is that they have higher expenses. We have often seen road gas stations within a minute or so's walk of a suitable temporary

canal-side mooring, so our thought was to take advantage of these as we find them. Depending on the ease of the location, we can add two or more jugs to the tanks, saving €3 to €5 per jug.

We had found little in Leiden to cause us to want to stay longer, so shortly after noon on Sunday, 14 July we slipped from the free mooring and continued our journey. We passed back under Wilhelminabrug and then turned southeastward into Oude Rijn, which led us out through the suburbs of Leiderdorp.

Also along the way were many old windmills, including a rather large one at Alphen aan der Rijn. We are impressed with how well these antiques are maintained.

At Alphen, we turned southward to follow the Gouwe, which led past pastures of grazing cattle and fields of crops, mainly flowers.

With our low air draft we were able to glide under many of the bridges, having to wait for only two until we arrived at the edge of Gouda. There, we paused to be let under Steve Biko-brug, which with its 85 centimetre clearance was obviously too low. This was followed closely by De Kock van Leeuwensluis, which dropped us about 20 centimetres to the level of the canals of central Gouda.

While we were being lowered, the lock keeper gave us a booklet on the city of Gouda, and told us there was municipal moorage along the banks for the next few hundred metres just beyond the next bridge. As we exited the lock, Rabatbrug was lifted for us and we glided through.

At 1622 we secured in a tight space along Turfsingel with less than half a metre spare room fore and aft. As we arrived, the havenmeester pedalled-up on his bicycle and welcomed us. In response to our questions, he told us moorage would be €9.30 for one night, including water and electricity. He told us to take our time settling-in and that he would be by in the evening or possibly the next morning to collect the fees.

Before deciding on how long we wanted to stay, we decided to walk into the old city to see if there was much of interest to us. We were immediately charmed by what we saw. Just along the canal from Zonder Zorg is Molen de Roode Leeuw, the Red Lion Windmill, the oldest corn mill in the Netherlands. According to the plaque on its walls, it was a 1771 renovation of a stellingmolen built in 1727-28 to replace an older wipmolen that had stood there since 1619.

We turned and walked through two blocks of newer housing toward the centre of the old city, guided by the towering hexagonal tapered steeple of Gouwekerk. Quickly we arrived on the banks of the old Gouwe and followed it past the Visbanken, the ancient fish markets toward the spire of Sint Janskerk. A pleasant half kilometre walk from the boat had brought us into the Markt and its imposing fifteenth century Stadhuis. The City Hall was built between 1448 and 1450, and it is one of the oldest Gothic city halls in the Netherlands.

At the end of the eleventh century this area was a swampy peat marsh laced with small streams, such as the Gouwe, after which the city gets its name; in 1139, the name Gouda is first mentioned in a statement from the Bishop of Utrecht. The harvest of peat began along the stream banks and by 1225 the Gouwe was linked by canal to the Oude Rijn and its

169

mouth at the Hollandse IJssel was made a harbour. Kasteel Gouda was built to protect the harbour, which gave access to trade with Flanders and France and beyond across the Noordzee. In 1272 the Count of Holland granted Gouda its city rights.

Across the Market Square is De Waag, the Weigh House built in 1667. Now a National Monument, this building was formerly used for weighing goods, especially Gouda cheese, to levy taxes. Looking back from the front of De Waag, across the Markt and past the Stadhuis, we saw the western end of Sint Janskerk. At 123 metres, it is renowned as the longest church in the Netherlands; however, it is more famous for its stained glass windows, which were made between 1530 and 1603. These windows comprise the most significant stained glass collection in the Netherlands and they have been a popular tourist attraction since the seventeenth century.

Our whirlwind introductory tour of the old city of Gouda convinced us to stay for a while, so when the havenmeester came by Zonder Zorg in the evening, we asked to be charged for three nights. The total came to €13.85 with unlimited water and electricity. The total was about one-tenth the cost of a single night's moorage in Vancouver.

On Tuesday we explored the area around the Markt, and then in the afternoon we visited Sint Janskerk to admire the stained glass windows. The construction of the church was begun in 1280 and much of the present building dates from before the great fire of 1552.

It was built as a Roman Catholic church, but with the Reformation, it was assigned in 1573 to the Protestants. It continues today under the jurisdiction of the Dutch Reformed Church. The creation and installation of the famous windows ceased at the time of the Protestant takeover, and none was added for over twenty years.

Then from 1594 to 1603, the remaining windows were created. They have survived the wars and fires through the centuries and they now comprise half of all the sixteenth century stained glass surviving in the Netherlands. The windows are huge, many of them towering twenty metres and more in height.

The earlier windows depict typically Catholic themes, while later windows created under the Protestant control, include scenes with a more regional and national theme. Among the Old Testament scenes depicted is one of Judith Beheading Holofernes, another of the Queen of Sheba Visiting King Solomon and there is one on Rebuilding the Temple. Among the New Testament themes: John the Baptist Preaching, the Birth of Jesus, the First Preaching of Jesus and so on.

The number and scale of the windows are overwhelming and after two hours among them, we were just beginning to become aware of the magnitude of this treasure and its cultural and historic significance. Amazing to us is that the collection has managed to escape the ravages of fires and wars for centuries.

For unknown reasons, the windows of Sint Janskerk survived Beeldenstorm, the *Iconoclastic Fury*, which were outbreaks of

the destruction of religious images that spread across Europe in the late sixteenth century. During spates of iconoclasm, Catholic art, furnishings, fixtures and decoration were destroyed by mobs as part of the Protestant Reformation. Most of the destruction was of art in churches and public places.

The windows are monumental both in size and in artistic execution. The window above on the left depicts the Baptism of Jesus, and it was designed by Dirk Crabeth in 1555. He and his brother, Wouter designed some of the most magnificent windows in the church between 1555 and 1571. The one on the right shows the Beheading of Saint John the Baptist and it was created in 1570 by Willem Thybaut, toward the end of the church's Catholic era.

It remains a mystery today, not only why these stained glass windows were spared in the Beeldenstorm, but also why Wouter and Dirk Crabeth were allowed to continue their work after the changeover from a Catholic church to a Protestant one. The church has windows from deep enemies: Philip II of Spain and William of Orange, the founder of the Netherlands royal family.

After the Protestant takeover, Willem Thybaut also continued designing windows. In 1597 he created the window on the left, which depicts the Capture of Damietta, Haarlem in 1570. The window on the right is titled the *Meid van Dordrecht*, the Maid of Dordrecht and was created by Gerrit Gerritsz Cuyp in 1597. It is easy to see the change from Catholic to Protestant themes.

Shortly after the outbreak of World War II, workers quietly began removing the windows of the church and disassembling them as if for routine maintenance or restoration. They were all carefully packed into wooden crates and these were covertly removed to secret storage places, where they remained until after the Nazi surrender in 1945. Today, thanks to centuries of care, there are more than eighty windows in the church. It would take many hours over each of several days to even begin to gain a basic understanding of them.

We left Sint Janskerk with kinked necks and heads swimming with images. We took a slow meandering walk around the Markt, past the Stadhuis and De Waag and stopped in an Albert Hein to select some fresh fish, fresh produce and wine for dinner. As we walked along the canal back toward Zonder Zorg, we paused to think that here we were in Gouda, but we had not yet gotten to the cheese.

The following day we went exploring again on foot. We were so close to the heart of the old city that we were not tempted to take the bikes off the foredeck. We walked extensively through the streets and along the canals.

On one of our walks, the operator of Dirk Crabethbrug had arrived just before us and was cranking open the swing bridge, going along for the

ride in the process. The bridge is a rather new one, dating only to 1887, but it is named for one of the famous two brothers who created many of the oldest stained glass windows for Sint Janskerk. We did what the locals do; we paused to watch the bridge open. Then we watched as an antique tour boat slowly motored through with its load of sightseers, who watched us watching them.

On Wednesday we used our museum cards to gain free admission to Museum Gouda. The museum is housed in an interconnected group of buildings across the lane to the south of Sint Janskerk. One of the main buildings is the former Chapel of Saint Catharine's Hospital, which traces its origins to the fourteenth century, though much of the existing building is from the seventeenth century.

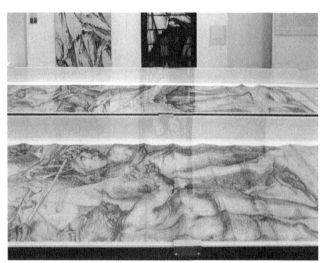

The first displays we saw were some of the original designs and cartoons for the famous stained glass windows in Sint Janskerk. Almost the entire collection of drawings has been saved and preserved, and they have been repeatedly used over the centuries to assist in the maintenance and repair of the windows. It is quite remarkable that not only the windows had survived, but so also had their initial artistic renderings.

The displays continued with paintings. Many of these are religious works that had been removed from the churches after 1572 when they ceased to be Catholic. One of these is a set of altar panels that had been commissioned to replace damage from the devastating fire of Sint Janskerk in 1552. The panels were done on oak planks by Gouda artist, Michiel Claesz. With the Protestant takeover in 1573, the panels were removed from the church and kept for centuries in the Orphanage of Gouda. The central panel depicts the flight of Joseph and Mary to Egypt.

Other religious paintings had been commissioned by various clandestine Catholic groups, such as this one done for the local Jesuits for their house chapel. It is the work of the well-known Antwerp painter, Cornelius Schut around 1630-35 and depicts the favourite theme of the Jesuits, the adoration and glorification of the Virgin Mary.

This painting of the Adoration of the Magi was done as part of a series painted by Wouter Crabeth the Younger in the 1630s and early 1640s. It was painted in 1631 as a commission for the clandestine conventicle of Sint Jan, a rather modest and inconspicuous building on the banks of the river Gouwe, where Father Petrus Purmerent conducted clandestine Catholic services.

Fortunately, not all the paintings in the museum are of a religious theme. There is a fine assortment of lighter themes, such as this one by Jan Steen titled *De Quack*, The Quack and it depicts a rather common scene from the seventeenth century; an open air play at an annual fair.

Of course, there is a collection of group portraits, which are mainly a Dutch invention of the seventeenth century. Early examples were often of civic and military officials in the stilted poses. They were popular among the many associations, boards of trustees and guilds. During the first half of the century, group portraits were very stiff and formal, everyone posed and looking at the viewer. More attention was given to details of a person's rank, social status and importance than was paid to the pose.

This painting is the first in a series in the collection done in 1616 by Jan Daemsz de Veth. It portrays the officers of the militia under the command of Colonel Gijsbert 't Hert. Interestingly, in this painting, rather than being placed in the conventional most prominent place in the group, the Colonel chose to be placed on the canvas where the best light would fall in the room where the painting was to be hung.

Among the group portraits is one of four deans of the Enkhuizen surgeons guild titled: *The Anatomical Lesson of Dr Zacheus de Jager*. It was painted by Christiaan Coevershof in 1640 and the deans are posed in the manner used by Rembrandt in his famous 1632 *The Anatomy Lesson of Dr. Nicolaes Tulp*. However; unlike Rembrandt, Coevershof did not portray an anatomy lesson, rather the painting served only as an historical record of the deans who are all stiffly positioned around the cadaver and staring straight ahead at the viewer. In Rembrandt's work, eyes and ears are intently on the lesson.

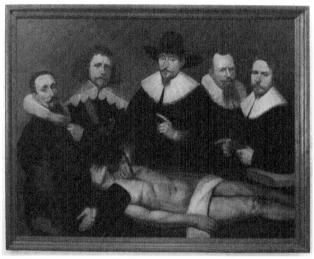

Among the displays is a reconstruction of the surgeons guild room, with its table and chairs and cabinets of seventeenth century surgical instruments. With the crude instruments fresh in our minds, we went down for a look at the dungeons, cells and torture chamber. The instruments we saw there were much more crude. It is definitely not a place we would want to have been when it was in use.

On a much lighter vein, there is a wonderful display of Gouda pottery. The museum has a collection of more than 5000 pieces and the displayed

pieces are frequently changed. Those not on display at the moment can be seen arrayed in large glass cabinets in an adjoining room. We thought this a wonderful use of the collection.

Desiderius Erasmus is one of the most famous sons of Gouda. Although he was born in Rotterdam and he died in Basel, the city of Gouda has adopted him. He is said to have been conceived in Gouda; his father was a Catholic priest and curate there and his mother is thought to have been the housekeeper. Erasmus spent his youth and had his early education in Gouda.

177

On Thursday morning we walked into the city centre. As we approached the Markt, the number of parked bicycles increased rapidly. At the rear of De Waag there was not a free spot to be found. We were pleased we had left our bikes aboard.

The reason for the crowd was the Thursday morning Gouda cheese market. From 1000 to shortly past noon teams from the guild of cheese-porters carry the farmers' cheese on handbarrows and lay them out in the Markt. Traditionally, buyers then sampled the cheeses and negotiated prices using a ritual system called handjeklap, in which buyers and sellers clap each other's hands and shout prices. Once a price was agreed, the porters would carry the cheese to De Waag for weighing and completion of the sale.

The first mention of the cheese of Gouda was in 1184 and it is one of the world's oldest cheeses still being made. These days most Gouda is produced industrially and the Gouda name *is not* protected internationally. However, there are still about 300 farmers in the area around Gouda who produce Boerenkaas, *Farmers Cheese*, which most definitely *is* a protected name of Gouda and it is made in the traditional manner, using unpasteurized milk.

Having filled ourselves with a sampling of the history and culture of Gouda, we were ready to stock up on Boerenkaas and continue our voyage. In the heart of the old city, just off the Markt, we found a shop, 't Kaaswinkeltje that specialises in the genuine Gouda. Inside we saw hundreds of cheeses on display. Next to several dozen of these were small dishes of samples.

We sampled and tasted and nibbled and enjoyed. The samples did their magic and prompted us to select several cheeses to have slabs and wedges cut for us. We were amazed with the low prices, generally in the range of €7 to €15 per kilo. With the dairy subsidy in Canada, we can barely find bulk factory plastic cheese at those prices. We left the shop with a wonderful variety of Boerenkaas that should last us well south in France and complement the cheeses we find there. The aged cheeses require no refrigeration, simply a stable temperature.

On Saturday morning I topped up our water tanks from the canalside hose bib as we prepared to head onward. While the tank filled, we reflected on the splendid time we had spent in Gouda. It is such a delightful city, so richly steeped in history and culture and it had caused our stay to expand from three days to six. The Havenmeester never came back to collect the additional three day's fees.

Chapter Twenty-Two

Utrecht, Gelderland & Noord Brabant

At 1105 we slipped from our mooring and continued along Turfsingel to Guldenbrug, which was soon opened for us. As we passed into the basin leading to Mallegatsluis, we passed three barges of fellow Barge Association members: Chouette, Esme and La Tulipe. We tooted and greeted them as we went by.

Mallegatsluis is a tidal lock, and once through it, we were out onto the tidal Hollands IJssel, which we followed a couple of kilometres eastward to Stolwijkersluis. This complex lock is only 20 metres long, but it has five pairs of doors. It divides the tidal waters from the canalized Hollandsche IJssel. During a few minutes of each rise and fall of the tides, the doors can all be opened to allow barges longer than 20 metres to pass directly through.

For the first day in nearly two weeks, it was overcast and there were occasional sprinkles of rain. We passed through placid rural settings and relaxed. Most of the bridges were high enough for us to slide under, but a few required lifting. At one of these near the town of Oudewater, a clog was swung out on a line to accept the posted €4.50 bruggeld.

Along the way, the water and banks were filled with waterfowl. At one point, we passed a marvelous little parade, mama duck and her ten fresh hatchlings, moving along in unison as if attached by lines.

In the mid-afternoon we arrived on the edge of Montfoort and decided to pause for the day. The free moorage at the approach to the town is in front of tidy homes, unlike the busier hustle and bustle we could see further along toward the town centre.

After we had secured, we walked the 200 metres along the canal to the bridge, which is at the central gate to the small town. We explored. the well-preserved historic town centre. Montfoort is a relatively new town, having received its city rights only in 1329.

After we has seen the sights, we found the local Albert Hein, where we bought fresh provisions for our evening's dinner. On our way back, the view of Zonder Zorg on her placid mooring convinced us we had chosen the better spot to moor. We much prefer the quiet places.

In the late evening light we enjoyed a splendid dinner in the cockpit with breaded kabeljauw, sautéed potatoes and green beans almandine, accompanied splendidly by a Touraine Sauvignon from Domaine de la Tour Ambroise. As we were dining, hot air balloons came over the trees and settled toward land.

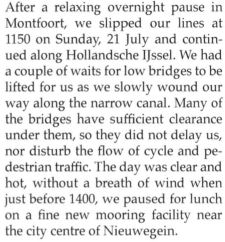

After a relaxing overnight pause in Montfoort, we slipped our lines at 1150 on Sunday, 21 July and continued along Hollandsche IJssel. We had a couple of waits for low bridges to be lifted for us as we slowly wound our way along the narrow canal. Many of the bridges have sufficient clearance under them, so they did not delay us, nor disturb the flow of cycle and pedestrian traffic. The day was clear and hot, without a breath of wind when just before 1400, we paused for lunch on a fine new mooring facility near the city centre of Nieuwegein.

After lunch we resumed our route, into the outskirts of the city of Utrecht. We quickly came to the end of Hollandsche IJssel and made a sharp turn to starboard into Schalkwijkse Wetering, which we followed south easterly for a kilometre or so before turning starboard again to follow the Meerwedekanaal southward. We joined the rear of a long line of pleasure craft that was just beginning to enter the lock. We paraded with them through the first set of lock gates and then through the second set. The locks here are complex to handle the differing levels of the connected rivers.

When we arrived in the second interconnected lock chamber, its sides were completely lined with boats, and they were rafted on each other three and four deep. We were the last boat in before the doors astern of us closed, so we simply sat in the middle of the chamber.

Gradually, the slowly swirling flow of the water entering the lock caused us to drift forward and to port, and we eventually were received alongside as the fifth-out in a raft.

Because of our position in the lock, we were among the first dozen of the thirty or so boats to untangle and thread our way out through the upstream doors and motor along the short arm from the lock to the Lek. The Lek is one of the major distributary branches of the Rijn and it flows to sea through Rotterdam. We were at the junction of some major east-west and north-south inland shipping routes.

At the river the parade split, with some boats turning starboard down the river toward Rotterdam. Others turned to port and headed up toward Arnhem or Nijmegen and about a dozen jogged slightly upstream, crossed the river and entered the continuation of Meerwedekanaal southward. We were in that group. After less than a kilometre we entered another lock where there was plenty of room for us to secure alongside for the short drop. Once we had been lowered from river level to canal level, the doors opened and the parade resumed.

The Meerwedekanaal is rather dull and boring compared to the other waterways we had been on thus far in the Netherlands. It is broad and it runs mainly through bland industrial areas, with warehouses and factories lining its banks. In many places along the banks were large barges. Some of these were really huge, like this one, which must be close to 200 metres in length. Fortunately, it was Sunday, and most commercial traffic seemed to be taking a day of rest.

We had a long pause waiting for a rail bridge to open for us. Apparently when our little flotilla arrived it was too close to the scheduled arrival of the next train.

In the early evening we arrived in the centre of the old city of Gorinchem, where just through Korenbrugsluis we found an eighteen metre gap among the moored boats. At 1848 we secured to a wooden pontoon alongside the old brick wall.

Once we had settled in, I put on my chef's toque and prepared chicken breasts in a crimini and oyster mushroom sauce served with basmati rice and butter-steamed carrots. With it we enjoyed a bottle of Farnese Primitivo and the wonderfully long and warm twilight.

During dinner the temperature finally dropped below 30°. Except for a few hours of overcast and drizzle on Saturday, we had been in two-week-long heatwave, with daily temperatures in the high 20s to mid 30s. Monday was again clear and by mid-morning it was already hot.

Gorinchem is one of the few cities in the Netherlands with its fortified walls preserved in their original state. Though obscured in history, it is thought that the community was established about a thousand years ago. Around 1250 Gorinchem became property of the Lords of Arkel and at the end of the thirteenth century earthen mounts reinforced with palisades were built around the settlement to protect it from domination by the neighbouring counties of Holland and Gelre. Otto van Arkel granted city rights in 1322 and in the following decades, city walls

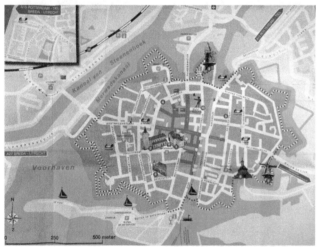

were built with seven gates and twenty-three watchtowers.

The ancient walled city is a compact oblong shape, measuring about 900 by 600 metres, much of it surrounded by rivers and the remainder with moats. The Linge flows through its centre and we were moored along it.

We walked along the side of the canal past Visbrug to Peterbrug, which we crossed into the centre of the medieval walled city. The city had been built on delta land between two rivers, the Linge and the Merwede at their junctions with the Waal, another major distributary of the Rhine that flows to sea on the southern edge of Rotterdam. With its water transportation corridors, Gorinchem became an important trading centre for fish, corn and grain.

We headed into the city centre and to the large squares there, Grotemarkt and Groenmarkt. Flanking the western side of Grotemarkt is the former city hall, which is now used as a museum and an art gallery. Beyond the museum is Grote Kerk with its leaning Grote Toren, which had shifted to about 3° out of plumb while still under construction in the 1840s as a replacement to the previous one that had been badly damaged decades earlier during the Napoleonic Wars.

We spent some time in the historic centre looking at the many old buildings. Ones we saw dated from the fifteenth century and we saw one portal dating to the fourteenth. From the centre we headed out toward the walls, where we found a walking trail that leads for about seven kilometres along the top of the walls, so we followed it around.

The south side of the city has the natural moat of the broad River Waal and the bars along its banks. This area now serves as the local beach, while offshore the large commercial barges ply back and forth between the coast and the heart of Europe.

Further around away from the river, moats were dug and the fortified walls had been built directly out of them to make access difficult for unwanted visitors.

Alongside the moat remain two of the many windmills that surrounded the old city. This one, Nooit Volmaakt stands next to the Linge as it enters the city from the north through Korenbrug. The second windmill, De Hoop is further around on the west side, just along from Dalempoort.

Dalempoort, dating from 1597 was the last of the city gates to be built. It is ornate with a watchtower and a clock, and it led into the city from the tiny, but at the time increasingly important salmon fishing port in the marshland just outside the walls.

We ended our circuit of the walls at Jachtensluis, the lock which takes pleasure boats out of the city and into the Waal. From there it was an easy stroll back along the banks of the Linge to Zonder Zorg.

Earlier on Tuesday we had cycled to the collection of big-box stores a kilometre or so up the Linge from our mooring. There we had put together bicycle panniers full of small hardware, paints, brushes, carving chisels, masking tape, sandpaper, wire brushes and, we hope, everything else that we need to finish decorating Zonder Zorg.

While were in the shopping centre, we finally found the ideal chairs for Zonder Zorg. We had been looking for seven weeks for chairs to serve both inside at the salon table and outside in the cockpit. From JYSK we bought some attractive and very comfortable hardwood chairs that both fold and recline. They are made from FSC Certified wood, ensuring responsible and sustainable forestry practices.

In the evening we relaxed with sautéed talapia filets served with butter-fried potatoes and green beans almandine. With it we enjoyed a bottle of Cava Portell Brut Nature.

Have I already mentioned that we love this cruising style?

Mid-afternoon on Wednesday, 24 July we slipped from our very pleasant moorings within the walled city of Gorinchem and continued downstream under Visbrug We continued under Peterbrug and paused on the bollards just short of the lock to wait for up-bound boats to be locked through.

When the door opened and discharged two small pleasure craft, we had our first glimpse into the tall, narrow chamber. There was room for us to squeeze in with about 10 centimetres clearance each side of our leeboards. With wiggle room at little more than one percent of our length, it was somewhat like threading a needle at arm's length.

We left the lock and entered the Waal, a major branch of the Rhine, which was full of large and very large barges plying their loads between the coast and Germany and further into Western Europe. The river is the boundary between Zuid Holland and Noord Brabant and just over three kilometres upstream it becomes the boundary between Gelderland and Noord Brabant. Fortunately, we didn't have to go that far in the current and the wakes of the heavy traffic; after only two kilometres on the Waal, we turned southeasterly and motored past the town of at Woudrichem on the Afgedamde Maas.

The Meuse rises in France and flows through Belgium into the Netherlands to become the Maas, which flows into the Noordzee south of Rotterdam. We passed through the lock and into the Afgedamde (Dammed) Maas. This is a fifteen kilometre canalised branch of an old bed of the river, which flows across to the Waal, a branch of the Rhine. Near its original split from the Maas, the old river bed became closed off from the river, and Heusdenskanaal was dug to rejoin the waters.

At less then two kilometres long, Heusdenskanaal is likely the shortest heavy traffic canal in the Netherlands. At its end, we passed through the large high-water gate and into the Bergsche Maas, the main stream of the river on its way seaward from France and Belgium. Also on their way seaward as well as heading inland, were very large barges.

Less than half a kilometre upstream, we turned into the Jachthaven of Heusden and at 1802 we secured to the first finger of the first pier in the harbour. It was late in the day and this was the only available space large enough to take Zonder Zorg. It was also the moorage furthest away from the Havenkantoor and access to land.

Edi's family name is Heusdens, which in the Dutch tradition, means from the city of Heusden. Her genealogy research showed her family had moved from the city by the end of the seventeenth century. She had never visited the city and she was eager to see it.

Late on Thursday morning, after a sleep-in and a leisurely breakfast, we threaded our way along the floats to the marina exit from where there is easy access to the city. We walked into the old city through Wijksepoort. The city of Heusden dates from the 13th century. It started with the construction of a fortification to replace a castle that had been destroyed when the Duke of Brabant captured the area in 1202. His new fortifications quickly expanded with water works and a donjon. Heusden received city rights in 1318 and the castle remained with the Dukes of Brabant until 1357 when it went to the Count of Holland.

Early in the Eighty Years War, 1568-1648, Heusden was occupied by the Spanish. However, in 1577, after the Pacification of Ghent, the people of Heusden chose to ally with Prince William of Orange. William decided to consolidate the town's strategic position on the Maas, and ordered fortification built. Moats were dug and the construction of bastions, walls, and ravelins was completed in 1597. With the new construction, the castle was enclosed by the city's fortifications and it lost its function as a stronghold. The donjon was converted to a munitions depot.

The castle of Heusden ended in sudden disaster; on 24 July 1680 during an intense thunderstorm, lightning struck the donjon. Sixty-thousand pounds of gunpowder and other ammunition exploded, and destroyed the castle, causing the economic demise of the city. Most of the citizens left. The original outlines of the main features were restored in 1987.

By early nineteenth century the defence works had fallen into disrepair and were dismantled. In 1968, however, extensive restoration works started, and fortifications were carefully rebuilt, based on a 1649 map of the city of Heusden by Johannes Blaeu, son of the famous Dutch cartographer Willem Blaeu. In 1980, the city of Heusden received the European restoration prize.

We wandered out through Vismarkt to Stadshaven, the small port that had been built in the thirteenth century with its narrow entry under a lift bridge. The inner basin is small, about sixty metres across, but even with the moored boats, there appears to be sufficient space for Zonder Zorg to enter and turn around. We talked of nosing Zonder Zorg in for a look when we depart on Friday.

There are many wonderful views along the city walls and in the city itself. Many of the buildings are restorations

or replicas of older structures, though we did see a few old date stones back to the beginning of the seventeenth century.

The city streets are mostly lined with tourist shops. In the bakery were loaves hanging around for the tourists to buy; there seemed to be no locals on the streets. The houses appear lifeless and we sensed no community vibrancy. The streets are filled with tourists and the shops are stocked with rather overpriced trinkets and snacks for visitors. In one small shop we looked at a thin selection of non-competitively priced fruit and vegetables, a small cooler with a few pieces of meat and shelves with packaged food. The place was obviously set-up for the desperate boater, camper or cyclist caught with an empty larder.

We retraced our way back to and through the marina to Zonder Zorg. By the time we arrived, most of the other itinerant boats had left and with very few of the day's replacements thus far arrived, she was in remote isolation. We relaxed onboard in the calmness of the hot afternoon.

We had arrived on the Maas, which rises as la Meuse in France and flows through Belgium into the Netherlands.

Chapter Twenty-Three

Onward to Maastricht

Shortly after noon on Friday, 26 July we slipped from alongside in the jachthaven and motored the short distance across to the entrance to Huesden Stadshaven.

We squeezed through the narrow entrance and into the tiny inner basin. Inside we found a vacant length of wharf with a few metres of spare room and maneuvered alongside.

After we had secured, we stepped ashore and did a quick circuit of the small harbour, shooting photos of Zonder Zorg lying in this restored

medieval harbour. Had there been room in Stadshaven when we had arrived on Wednesday we would have stayed there instead of outside in the modern jachthaven.

After we had satisfied our craving for a visit, we slipped our lines and turned in the very tight space to thread our way back through the old gate. We continued along the Maas for about ten kilometres, and then turned southeasterly along Zuid-Willemsvaart. Edi brought up a wonderful tray of food to nibble at along the way.

Shortly after leaving the river for the canal, we arrived at the first of thirteen locks that would take us cross-country while the Maas looped a much longer course to our north and east. Ahead of us at the lock were two large commercials, one of them a pair of dumb barges with a pusher that was together so long that in order to fit in the lock, it required decoupling the pusher.

We waited for two lock cycles before we were shown a green. On each of these, the lock was full with both up and down-bound commercials. We followed a freshly arrived commercial into the lock and rode up.

Further along, as we approached 's Hertogenbosch, we had to wait for down-bound commercials to make it through narrow lift bridge cuts. The delays at the locks and the bridges meant that our 20 kilometre trip to 's Hertogenbosch took over five hours, more than twice as long as anticipated, and all the mooring places were full when we arrived. In the Netherlands, it is prohibited to moor anywhere except where posted; whereas in France, it is permissible to moor everywhere except where prohibited.

We decided to continue on to Veghel, eighteen kilometres and three locks further along. We were the only boat in the locks along the way. At 2014 we arrived at Jachthaven Veghel, at the end of a kilometre-long blind branch through a heavy industrial area lined with wharehouses and commercial barges.

Edi's computer had crashed again, and she had booked the next available appointment with the Apple Genius in Amsterdam. It was for mid-afternoon on Sunday, so we decided to spend three days in the haven.

There is a very fine and rather compact shopping district centred about 300 metres from the haven and about half a kilometre from the boat was a large and well-stocked Albert Hein supermarket. We took advantage of these to refresh our supplies. Also, while Edi took the bus and train to Amsterdam, I lashed the two 20-litre diesel jerry cans to the trolley and walked a couple of loads from the Total station 400 metres down the street. The 80 litres cost €12 less than it would have at the last marine station we had seen.

This exercise gave me the opportunity to start calibrating the gauge on the interconnected pair of tanks. I shot a before photo and then as each 20 litre jug had been added. I then measured the outside dimensions of the port side tank, the starboard one being buried behind the house battery and the inverter and impossible to put a tape to. Both tanks appear to be of similar, if not identical size, so I calculated the volume of the slightly wedge-shaped port tank and doubled the results. My before and after photos appeared to confirm the math. A few more measurements will likely refine this and then some more permanent marks can be added to the gauge.

On Monday morning we headed back out the side branch and continued along Zuid-Willemsvaart, arriving almost immediately at the next lock. We could see the churn of water draining from the chamber as we arrived, and our wait on the mooring bollards was short. We were followed in by a rather erratically handled rental cruiser that bounced to a stop with several conflicting bursts of the engine and bow-thruster. After a short wait, we were joined by a 48 metre laden commercial.

The commercial waved us and the cruiser to exit ahead, since in its laden state it was restricted to 9 kph on this stretch. The cruiser roared past us immediately we had left the lock and sped on up the canal. We continued along more slowly, keeping safely ahead of the commercial and knowing we would be locking through the next locks with it, so there was no sense going faster and wasting fuel. We arrived at the next lock to see the cruiser impatiently waiting outside it for us. After it had bounced and jostled into place in the lock, I nestled in behind it and had the commercial come up our port side.

One more similar sequence brought us to the third lock of the day. Then fortunately, before the next lock, the erratic cruiser turned into the small canal leading to the northern side of Helmond and left the commercial and us at peace on the canal. Beyond the Helmond lock we turned back up the canal leading to the southern side of the city and took a peaceful canal-side mooring just short of the small lock that leads up into town.

The following morning we slipped just after 0930, turned in the narrow canal and headed back out into Zuid-Willemsvaart. As we entered the canal, we saw astern of us a parade of seven cruisers about a kilometre back, and we maintained speed to remain just ahead of them. At the next lock we entered first and took bollards on the starboard side at the top of the chamber. Two cruisers gently came to port side bollards beside us, then we heard a familiar roaring and thunking as the erratic cruiser bumbled in astern of us.

There were four of these up-bound locks and the routine was the same: We led the eight boat fleet out of the lock, along the pound and entered the next lock to watch the antics of the erratic cruiser.

In these locks, the lift requires changing the mooring lines up successive bollards in the chamber walls as the boat rises. In one of the locks I had to share a bollard with a bird nest, which had been built in the pocket I needed to use just above high water line. The birds had flown the coop, but I thought it would have been an interesting conflict of interest during incubation and rearing.

About five kilometres after the last of the up locks we came to a junction where Zuid-Willemsvaart turned to

the right toward Belgium, about twelve kilometres away. We continued straight on Kanaal Wessen-Nederweert for another fifteen kilometres until we came to the Panheelsluis, which took us down about ten metres to the level of the Maas. We turned starboard and headed upstream, shortly taking a branch off the river and into an area of marinas. At 1514 we secured alongside in Jachthaven Eurosports Wessem. It was cold and blustery and began raining as we arrived. We ducked inside and enjoyed our comforts through the increasing storm of an arriving frontal system.

Wednesday morning the front had passed and the day grew clear and warm. Mid-morning we offloaded our bicycles to go exploring and grocery shopping. We asked the haven-meester about the most convenient supermarket and he told us there was none worth looking at in Wessum, but that there was a good Spar in Thorn, about three kilometres away, next to the Belgique border.

A few days earlier, Edi had mentioned Thorn to me, calling it The White Village. I had looked it up on the Internet and was fascinated with what I found. First mentions of the area were as a marshy region near the Roman Road between Maastricht and Nijmegen. The marshes were later drained and around 975 Thorn Abbey, a Benedictine convent was built there by Count Ansfried and his wife Hilsondis.

In 995, after the death of his wife, the count became the Bishop of Utrecht. During the twelfth century, the abbey evolved from a religious to a secular order and it became a convent community for women without the strict laws of a religious order.

At its peak twenty ladies of noble birth lived there as canons. Admission required the women to prove that they had sixteen ancestors of noble birth, eight on each their father's and their mother's side.

The canons met in the Chapter Room under the leadership of the Abbess. Today on the walls of this room are hung portraits and pedigree documents of some of the twenty-nine Abbesses who led the community from 982 to 1795.

By the twelfth century, the abbey had developed into a complex of buildings covering an area of 250 by 250 metres. The Abdijkerk is the only building remaining today from that era.

During the twelfth century Thorn Abbey was deemed to be a sovereign principality, and its Abbess was the Princess. It became the smallest independent state in the Holy Roman Empire. Its imperial immediacy was confirmed in 1292 by King Adolf of Nassau and later Thorn was under the imperial protection of Emperor Maximilian I. Thorn minted its own coins of gold silver and bronze. Strangely, the coiners were reputed to be somewhat corrupt. Many of the coins they produced were underweight and were not well received by surrounding territories.

Following the French invasion in the winter of 1794–95, the formal abolition of the principality in 1797 meant the end of the abbey and Thorn became the first portion of the department of Meuse-Inférieure. With the Vienna Congress, Thorn became a municipality of the United Kingdom of the Netherlands. Now all that remains of the old principality is Abdijkerk, the Abbey Church, which had been enlarged and refined through the twelfth, thirteenth and fourteenth centuries.

Between 1780 and 1788 the interior of the abbey was radically altered, with all Romanesque and Gothic elements being removed and the walls fitted with neo-classical pillars and ornamentation. A marble floor was laid and the interior was completely painted in white. The crowning glory of the renovation was the altar. This Baroque masterpiece had been built for the Cartesian convent of Roermond, just downstream and across the Maas; however the Roermond convent went bankrupt and in 1785 the altar and other items were acquired by Thorn.

197

In the crypt under the altar, among the other relics, is a leaden coffin with the mortal remains of Hilsondis of Strijen, founder of the Abbey of Thorn. After her death, her husband, Count Ansfried of Teisterband became Boshop of Utrecht. Their daughter, Benedicta became the first Abbess of Thorn. For more than eight hundred years the Abbey of Thorn, a community led by women, had been a tiny hub of calmness and peace surrounded by the strife, turmoil and warfare of the rest of Europe.

Our museum passes had given us free access to Abdijkerk, and we emerged after more than an hour totally entranced. We walked along Wijngaard to the Gemeentemuseum Het Land Van Thorn, the community museum. Again, our museum passes gave us access. Now fully saturated, we pedalled along to the Spar supermarket, where we picked-up a few items to replenish our fridge, breadbox, wine cellar and pantry.

Back onboard Zonder Zorg we relaxed and puttered with chores for the remainder of the day. Edi continued carving the new name boards for Zonder Zorg's bows. We had gotten oak planks in Harlingen, wood chisels in Haarlem and she began carving in Gouda.

At 0930 on Thursday, the first day of August we slipped and motored along the kilometre or so to the bunker barge to take-on some diesel. I had been discussing the price of diesel fuel on the DBA Forum for the past few days, and the consensus was that the bunker barges at Wessen and Maasbracht had some of the best prices in the Netherlands. It was at €1.495 when we stopped, which is only €0.04 more than the road station from which I had hauled jugs in Veghel. We took on 160.55 litres and I continued the calibration of the gauge. A line-up of waiting boats built as we fuelled, showing the popularity of the barge.

As we made our way back out into the Maas and along it, Edi brought up a platter of open-face sandwiches, which we enjoyed as we passed through rather bland industrial areas. With little scenery of interest, after lunch Edi went below and began painting the Zonder Zorg name board that she had finished carving.

Shortly we came to the first lock of the day. This was one of the two smaller ones in a triple set, but it was still huge to us. We were pleased to see as we entered, that there are floating bollards in the walls. With the floating bollards, we simply secured Zonder Zorg between a pair of them and monitored the system to ensure that it didn't stick or jam. As the water rose, the bollard float-

ed up, maintaining the barge nicely alongside the wall. This was much simpler than the last several locks we had been through, where we had to keep moving the lines up the walls to successively higher bollards.

A dozen or so kilometres further along we came to the second lock, another set of three side-by-side chambers. The lights were red for all three of them, so we paused to see which one

would cycle for us. Shortly, the Oude Sluis gate opened and a parade of boats came out and we were given a green light. There is a caution sign at the entrance to the chamber mentioning turbulence toward the head of the lock. We secured to a pair of floating bollards about two-thirds of the way along the chamber, leaving room behind us for later arrivals. When the chamber began flooding, we experienced the largest and most violent churning I had ever seen in my many hundreds of locks during eight years of European canal boating. The floating bollards, and Zonder Zorg's shallow draft and flat bottom allowed us to comfortably ride the roiling water.

At 1630 we secured alongside a float in Pietersplas, a peaceful marina three kilometres south of Maastricht and just two kilometres from the Belgique border.

We enjoyed a wonderfully relaxing evening, with dinner in the cockpit and watching itinerant swans dropping by looking for orts.

In the warm, calm evening we sat well beyond sunset sharing memories of our superb experiences during our months in the Netherlands. Our

after-dinner Cognacs rendered the late twilight a tad blurry, even for the camera.

Chapter Twenty-Four

Barging Through Belgium

We had come 597 kilometres since leaving Harlingen, and added to our travels in 2012, we had travelled 895 kilometres through an extremely varied cross-section of a wonderfully boat-friendly country.

We paused in Maastricht to complete a short list of outstanding items, some of which were essential for our entry into Belgium. The guides, online forums and blogs all talk of the strict control by the Belgique authorities on arriving boats. There is mention of a checkpoint just inside the country where all arriving pleasure boaters must stop and have their papers, certificates, licenses and their boats inspected. Among the items we needed to complete was our new Zonder Zorg name boards. Edi continued chipping away at the task.

Mid-week Edi finished one of the names board and applied two layers of paint to match the artwork on the klick and the fries. While she was doing that, I repaired and restored a few spots on the fries and she repainted it and the klick. I also painted the spokes in the two leeboard winches and the newly installed anchor windlass.

It was not all work; we pedalled into Maastricht nearly every day to shop and to look around. It is an old city. Neanderthal remains have been found here and there are many Paleolithic remains from 8000 to 25,000 years ago. The Celts lived here 2500 years ago and by the first century it had become a Roman settlement.

We wandered the centre of the old city, pausing here and there to visit interesting looking buildings. Mostly, we were filling time while we waited.

We were waiting for my *International Certificate of Competence* with a *Code Européen des Voies de Navigation Interieur* endorsement. More easily stated as an ICC with CEVNI, which is the driver's license that I require to take Zonder Zorg through Belgium and

into France. I was still waiting for its arrival in the post. A dozen years ago I had entered our previous canal boat, Lady Jane into the Canada Ship Registry, and with that, my Canadian qualifications had been sufficient.

In early July this year I had received confirmation from the Royal Yachting Association that my 1972 *Canadian Navy Upper Deck Watchkeeping Certificate* and my 1975 *Canada Department of Transport Certificate of Service as Master Foreign-Going Steamship* were sufficient qualifications to waive having to pass courses and be examined for an ICC. While we were in Haarlem, I registered for an online CEVNI exam with Zeezeilschool Scheveningen in Den Haag and sent them the €45 fee. Although I was thoroughly familiar with the code, to refresh I

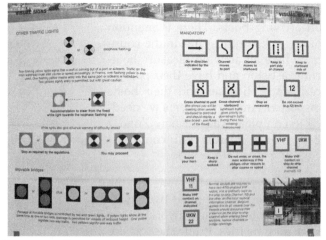

used the concise little booklet: "RYA European Waterways Regulations - The CEVNI Rules explained" by Tam Murrell, a fellow Barge Association member.

By the time we had reached Gouda, the school had received my payment, and the link to the exam had been activated. I sat in a cafe next to the cheese market and with their strong wifi, wrote both parts, scoring 100% on each.

I sent to the RYA in England my application and for the ICC with a reference to the pass on the CEVNI exam, asking them to send the licence to me in care of SRF in Harlingen. Since we were on the move with no planned itinerary, I thought this the easiest solution. Once we had a receiving address, I would have SRF forward the envelope to us.

I had received confirmation from the RYA that the certificate had been issued and sent to Harlingen on 24 July, so immediately we arrived at Pietersplas in Maastricht on 01 August, I emailed SRF in Harlingen to have the envelope forwarded to us. Then we waited.

Finally after five emails to SRF over the following week and more, the envelope arrived on in the Saturday afternoon mail on 10 August. Inside was my new membership card for the RYA. The ICC is free for members or £45 for non members, so since membership was £45, I applied for the free membership. I searched several times through the volume of flyers, leaflets and documents in the envelope, but could not find the ICC. It was mid-afternoon on Saturday and RYA offices were closed. I sent an email to my contact at the RYA offices telling her of the missing certificate and telling her we were moving on into Belgium and would send her a new address to which she could send the misplaced certificate, or a replacement.

Except for the certificate and having only one name board completed and mounted, we were ready to pass through the Belgique control point, so we decided to see if we could bluff our way past the authorities. The previous year we had spent six weeks without visas or cruising papers dodging and bluffing the authorities along the 3800 nautical miles of the Brazilian coast on our way back up from Cape Horn, so we figured that a Belgian check-point should be easy.

At 1020 on Sunday 11 August we slipped from our berth in Pietersplas, Maastricht and headed up the Maas. After less than two kilometres we crossed the Belgium border and shortly entered Toeleidingskanaal, which led us in about a kilometre to Sluizen Lanaye, the first lock in Belgium. We searched for a checkpoint or signs indicating where to check-in.

We joined four other boats in the chamber, one commercial and three pleasure, and rode up the 13.96 metres to the level of Canal Albert. Fortunately, there were floating bollards in the walls. Seeing no Belgique checkpoint, nor any signs indicating where it might be, we followed the parade of boats out of the lock and headed up-canal toward Liege, continuing to look for the checkpoint.

Seventeen kilometres further along Canal Albert through a dirty, drab and crumbling industrial canyon, we came to the next lock, écluse Monsin. There was still no indication of a checkpoint. After five kilometres we had rejoined the river, now called la Meuse, and arrived in Liege. The drab industrial canyon was replaced by walls of bland, modern apartment blocks, which had mostly replaced the old homes.

Some homeowners have managed to holdout against the rather unattractive and rampant development. There were breaks in the long screens of apartment blocks, where a few old buildings have so far escaped the destruction. Possibly further in from the waterfront there are areas of well preserved and restored old buildings, but what we saw did not invite us to pause in Liege to find out.

As we continued heading upstream on la Meuse, Edi brought up a platter of open face sandwiches. Besides giving us sustenance, this gave us something attractive to look at.

The scenery was mostly heavily industrial, with very few breaks of green or pleasant for the twelve kilometres from Liege to the next lock, écluse d'Ivoz-Ramet. Here we waited for the lock to cycle down.

The locks and approach facilities are set-up for huge commercial barges, and the temporary waiting arrangements show a lack of concern for pleasure boaters. This is likely why there are so few pleasure boats here. In the Netherlands we had seen excellent facilities for pleasure boaters, even on the busiest commercial waterways.

Above the lock, we continued through a seemingly endless industrial complex. Although there were a few breaks for more pastoral settings and small riverside villages, but they were very sparse and nowhere along the river did we lose sight of the factories and industrial plants. Many of these appear to be rendering the surrounding limestone hills into various elements and compounds. In front of many of them were huge barges loading bulk materials.

At 1735 we secured alongside the wall in the Port de Plaisance de Corphalie, across the river from the three nuclear power plants at Huy. We had come 53.7 kilometres into Belgium and had seen no sign of any checkpoint. When I registered at the Capitainerie, I was not asked for any papers, so it appeared to me that we were in Belgium. The inexpensive moorage included water and a wifi signal sufficiently strong for us to pick-up from our place in the basin.

The view upriver looked less industrial, and this coincided with what I had read: "La Meuse gradually becomes less industrial and more picturesque upstream from Huy". We were amazed by the dramatic decrease in pleasure boats and in the whole boating scene. In the small marina there were no boats over 10 metres in length, most being 5 or 6 metre runabouts.

At 1030 on Monday morning we warped Zonder Zorg back along the wall to the entrance, the basin being too narrow to allow us to turn around. Soon after regaining the river we arrived in Huy, a wonderful looking small town with many well preserved old buildings and gracefully curved stone bridges.

Looking down on this is the citadel and as we passed under its ramparts, we checked to see if its guns were pointed toward us as unauthorised visitors.

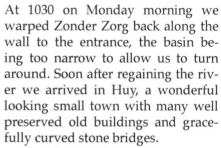

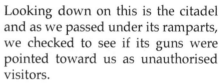

After the first lock in Belgium, we had been alone in the locks, whereas in the Netherlands we were often crammed in like sardines with six to over a dozen other boats. The boats we met heading downstream were almost all Dutch, and they appeared to be heading home.

In the early afternoon Edi made a platter of panini and we enjoyed them as we watched the scenery steadily improve. We had just finished lunch when we arrived at écluse d'Andenne-Seilles and secured outside its entrance to await the locking down of a commercial barge and a Dutch cruiser.

When we finally received a green light, entered the lock and were cycled up to the top, l'eclusier walked over to ask us the name of our boat, explaining he hadn't been able to see our name board as it was still below the lip of the chamber. We figured this was the end of our lawless run in Belgium. We told him Zonder Zorg, he jotted it down and walked back to his control tower. Shortly the upstream gate began dropping, and once it had bottomed, we were given a green.

We began breathing more regularly as we motored out. Upstream of the lock the scenery changed to a much more gentle nature. What factories existed were small and ancient, tucked in against the bases of the tall cliffs. There were wonderfully charming private estates tucked into the greenery along the river banks.

We passed through one more lock, écluse des Grands Malades and then entered Namur. Within two kilometres we came to the confluence of la Sambre and la Meuse and we kept to port to continue up la Meuse.

On the rocky spur above us was la Citadelle de Namur, overlooking the two rivers. Occupying over eighty hectares, it was once one of the largest fortresses in Europe.

Just above Pont de Jambes we secured Zonder Zorg to the wall and hopped on our bicycles to go across the bridge to the capitainerie at Port de Plaisance d'Amée. We were immediately taken by the lack of facilities for bicycles. Where in the Netherlands, the order of priority is pedestrian, cyclist, then automobile, here the order seemed to put the cyclist last. There is no bicycle lane on the bridge and we had to decide whether to handle the abuse from the drivers by using the roadway, or the gesticulations and harassment from pedestrians on the very narrow sidewalk.

From across the river, it had not appeared that the marina had facilities large enough to handle our barge. We were right. They told us the options, which were to leave Zonder Zorg where she was on the left bank, just below the Casino with no security, water or electricity for €8 per night, or head half a kilometre upstream, through écluse la Plante and continue another kilometre and a half to Port de Plaisance de Jambes. There they have security, water, electricity, wifi and no rowdies from the Casino, all for €17 per day or €85 per week. We pedalled back across the bridge to Zonder Zorg, struggling again to find a route in the very bicycle unfriendly environment. What a change from the Netherlands!

We ascended in the lock and at 1715 secured to the end of a pontoon in the marina. We had come another 36.1 kilometres into Belgium, a total of 89.8 kilometres without seeing a checkpoint, nor being asked for our papers. From here it is only 43.3 kilometres up la Meuse and into France.

Since we were two-thirds of the way through Belgium and had not yet been formally welcomed into the country, we decided to do it ourselves. For dinner we had panfried fresh Icelandic filet de fletan with sautéed Friesland potatoes, Belgian haricots fins almandine and sliced Roma tomatoes with shredded basil. To mark the welcoming ceremony, we accompanied dinner with a bottle of Cava Ferriol Brut.

One of the reasons that we had rushed to get to Namur was to be within an easy commute to Brussels International Airport. Dad had passed away in the Spring at ninety-nine and Mom a couple of years earlier at ninety-four. Their ashes still needed to be scattered and my extended family had agreed to come together on 18 August at the old family home at Shediac Cape, New Brunswick, Canada.

We booked flights departing Brussels at 1020 Thursday morning, 15 August to Montreal with a connection to Moncton. After six different transportation modes, we arrived in the wee hours of Friday morning. On Monday morning, family visits and duties completed, we headed back, arriving aboard Zonder Zorg twenty-five hours after we had popped out of bed. It was Tuesday and we were back in Belgium, relieved, though somewhat travel weary.

Early on Wednesday morning we slipped our lines and continued up la Meuse toward France. The scenery continued very pleasant with many fine buildings, some grouped in small villages and many standing as solitary riverside estates. Along the way we passed several impressive chateaux and some fortified hilltops.

There are nine locks between Namur and the French border, their chambers taking barges up to 98 metres long and 11.8 metres wide. The lifts vary from 1.7 to 2.89 metres, all but two of them being over 2 metres. The bollards along the tops of the chambers are broadly spaced for the large commercial barges, with no intermediate securing points for smaller craft.

Some overly zealous safety bureaucrat had caused protective fencing to be recently installed, making it impossible to toss lines over the bollards from our barge. Edi had to climb the slimy ladder up the chamber wall dragging the bow line with her, while I stabilised the barge in the chamber. After she had looped the bollard and passed me the end of the line to secure the bow, we moved aft and I tossed her the stern line to repeat the process.

This system worked satisfactorily; we had plenty of time to stabilise in the chamber before the operator began closing the downstream doors and then gradually opening the sluices to flood the lock. However; it was beginning to wear on Edi, who was nursing cracked ribs from being overeagerly hugged by my nephew as we were saying our farewells in New Brunswick.

As we were midway through the gates of écluse du Dinant, they began closing. We rushed to secure. There was no reachable bollard for our stern, so we did a long bow line and used it as a spring, motoring forward onto it as the lock keeper opened the upstream sluices all at once and sat back in lockside chairs with a buddy drinking beer and watching the antics of *les maudits plaisanciers hollandais*, the damned Dutch pleasure boaters. Fortunately, there were only three more Belgian locks before France.

We survived the abuse and motored into Dinant, which looks like a wonderful place to stop and spend some time exploring. However, we were by that time so turned-off by Belgium, that we continued without a pause.

We were still looking for the Belgique declaration station, when we passed a Douane sign. Just beyond it we saw a temporary building near the canal bank that could have been the reporting post, but its shutters were closed and it was very obviously not in use. Looking back from across the border, we could see no signs indicating boaters should stop. We suspect that the Walloons had decided to shutdown the reporting post, their attitude and infrastructure having scared away most of the pleasure boaters.

It no longer mattered; we had left Belgium and we were in France. Our experiences in Belgium were all in Wallonia, the southeastern portion of the country. From all that we had heard and read, pleasure boating in the northwestern part of the country, Flanders is much more pleasant. The topography there is similar to that of the Netherlands and they encourage pleasure boating and provide facilities. In Flanders an annual permit for Zonder Zorg would be €100, which by all reports is a very good value for the services received. On the other hand, there are no fees charged to pleasure boaters in Wallonia and the services provided seem worth that amount.

We shortly arrived at the next lock, the first one in France. L'eclusier took our lines with a hook on a long pole and placed them over the bollards for us. When we were secured he activated the lock and when we had reached the top, he motioned to me to come into the office. I took our thick portfolio of licenses, certificates, documents and other boat related papers. He didn't want to see any of it, he wanted only my name and the name of the barge to write in his log and he asked me whether we had a vignette. I told him that I had earlier bought the annual one for €534 and downloaded and printed it and that it was in the Zonder Zorg's window. He didn't want to see it

He gave me a remote-control clicker to activate the automatic locks in the Departement d'Ardennes, saying we would give it back at the final Ardennes lock.

We continued on to Givet, where shortly before 1800 we stopped for the day. To celebrate our arrival in France I sautéed some filet de fletan and we enjoyed it with mushrooms, fine green beans, pan-fried potatoes and sliced tomatoes with shredded basil.

We anticipated that the accompanying bottle of Champagne and the full moon were the first of many that we would be enjoying in France.

211

Chapter Twenty-Five

Into France

We had secured along the wall just above bridge in Givet. On Thursday morning we walked across the bridge to the town of Notre Dame and headed through the town and out beyond it following directions to the Brico-Marché, the French answer to Home-Depot. We needed a floodlight for the two tunnels that were just ahead of us at Ham and at Revin. The FluviaCarte states: "these tunnels have no illumination, so a floodlight is needed". We had found several great rechargeable lights at Canadian Tire the previous week in New Brunswick, but their transformers were all 120 volt only, not 120/240. After a three kilometre walk we arrived at the shopping plaza at noon to find that the BricoMarché was just closing for lunch. Back onboard, I dug out two LED flashlights and decided they were sufficient. The longer of the tunnels was only 500 metres.

At 1350 we slipped our lines and continued upriver under the ramparts of le fort de Charlemont. The fort was built by Charles V in 1555 during the invasion of France into the Spanish Netherlands as a means of securing the Meuse. Three thousand workers very quickly built defences that held up to attack when still unfinished. The works were subsequently added to by William of Orange, then the Spanish. In the seventeenth century the fort was remodelled by Vauban.

212

The size and complexity of the works tell of the strategic importance of the site. The Meuse has been a major trading route back into prehistory.

We arrived at the next lock, Les 3 Fontaines, which was manned, and again l'eclusier took our lines from the lip of the chamber with a hook. We were now in the Freycinet gauge locks, designed to take barges 38.5 metres long by 5.05 metres wide and 1.8 metres draft. Outside her fenders, Zonder Zorg has about half a metre of room on each side in the chambers of these locks.

Immediately out of the lock we came to Tunnel de Ham, and as we approached it, we could easily see the light at the far end of the tunnel. Having no floodlight seemed now to be of even less concern. I simply stood on the centreline with the tiller in the small of my back and aimed the mast at the light at the end of the tunnel. As long as I kept her relatively well centred, Zonder Zorg adjusted automatically to the water pressures from the sides and almost self-steered. After an easy 500 metres we were through.

Within another half kilometre we came to the next lock, which thankfully at 3.2 metres in height, was manned. Madame l'eclusier came out and took our mooring lines on a hook and placed them over bollards. We thanked her for her assistance as we were leaving the chamber. She confirmed that we had a remote-control, telling us that the next fifty or so locks are all automatic and unmanned.

We headed out of the lock and along the 800 metre derivation toward the river. The chart showed a *pont levis*

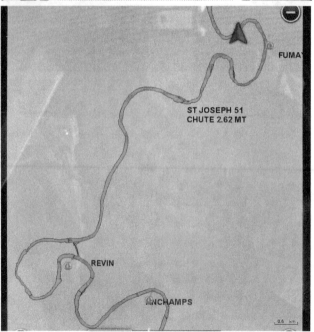

méchanisé, a mechanised lift bridge just before regaining the river, and I wondered whether the remote control worked for it. As we approached, I saw there was no concern; the bridge had been jerry-rigged in a partly open position to give the required 3.5 metre clearance. This clearance was one of the standards for the canals of France that was laid down by the 1879 Freycinet gauge.

Probably the vehicular use of the bridge is now so light that it makes more sense to keep it raised and rigged as a pedestrian crossing, and lower it only when required.

Once we were back out into la Meuse, Edi brought up a tray with a selection of salami, paté, pears, olives, cheeses and bread for us to nibble on as we continued upstream.

The waterway is mostly in the river, with short canals, called derivations leading to and from locks that step the water level past rapids or cataracts. Between the locks there is very little current. After twenty-four kilometres and six locks, at 1802 we stopped for the day at the Halte Nautique de Fumay.

On Friday morning, after a leisurely breakfast, we walked to the tourist information office and made use of their free wifi connection to catch-up. Then shortly before 1300 we slipped our lines and continued upstream. La Meuse describes a rather winding course through this area, and during the first four kilometres after leaving Fumay, we steered every point of the compass. At some bends, like at Ham and Revin. tunnels cut through a narrow neck to shorten the route.

After two locks we came to the Revin Tunnel, the second unlit tunnel for which we were warned to have a floodlight. Since the warning was written in the chartbook, lights have been installed, though likely these are to illuminate the cycle path that appears also to have new guardrails.

After we had cleared the tunnel and the lock following it, Edi went below and prepared a tray of nibblies for lunch and we enjoyed them as we made our way toward the next lock.

As we waited for ecluse Dames de Meuse to cycle, we were entertained by swans posing with an arched railway bridge as a backdrop.

At 1728 we secured alongside at the halte nautique de Laifour. It is a very small village, too small to have a bakery. Since everyone in France seems fixated on fresh bread every day, there was a placard next to the mooring informing visiting boaters that bakery goods be reserved the day before at the tabac. I walked up to small tabac across from the Mairie, which also had a *depot de pain* sign. I ordered four croissants and a baguette for the next morning and madame said they would be available from 0800.

We relaxed onboard in the peaceful little moorage, enjoying glasses of a beer we had picked-up in Namur: Blanche de Namur, biere sur lie, the 2012 winner of the title "World's Best White Beer".

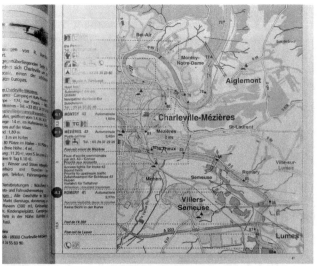

On Saturday morning it began raining just as I returned onboard with the bread and croissants. After slowly enjoying espressos and croissants in the dry of the cabin, we donned our rain gear and continued up river.

Our destination for the day was Charleville-Mézières, our first large community since Namur. Mézières was founded in the ninth century and half a century ago it amalgamated with the new town across the river, Charleville, which dates only to the seventeenth century. With la Meuse taking a very winding course through the city and offering over six kilometres of riverfront, we were looking forward to a pleasant scene. Among the places we wanted to see is Place Ducal, reputed to be one of the most beautiful squares in Europe.

Twenty-seven kilometres and four locks along from Laifour we began winding our way through industrial slums and crumbling canal-side infrastructure, which continued unrelieved

by any pleasant scenery for over four kilometres. Adding to the glumness was the persistent rain. We passed through ecluse Montcy and followed signs to le Port de Plaisance, the pleasure boat port and found the mooring places filled with residential barges. We continued along to the marina, where we saw only a dozen or so boats scattered around the eighty mooring pontoons. We also saw notice that the marina was restricted to boats under 14 metres in length.

We turned around just above the weir and found a spot on a concrete abutment on Ile du Vieux Moulin below a pedestrian bridge. There were already two boats on it and the remaining space was sufficiently long to take almost two-thirds of Zonder Zorg's length, leaving the stern hanging out. As we were securing, the heavy rain turned into an intense thunderstorm. During a break in the downpour, I took a short exploratory walk on the island, turning quickly back as the skies opened again. I saw little more than dense, wet vegetation. Thus far we had seen nothing of the city except crumbling industrial areas or a solid screen of unkempt heavily vegetated riverbank, beyond which we could see no attractive buildings nor any pleasantness. While we sat comfortably below in the torrential downpour, I searched the Barge Association forum and waterways guide for information on Charleville-Mézières. I found warnings of bicycle thefts from boat decks, of loud late night drunken partying by local youth in the park next to the moorage and of a barge having its moorings undone in the middle of the night and left to drift downstream toward the weir. Because of the heavy rain we felt safe from vandals, so we spent the night. Nonetheless, the uneasiness persisted and we decided to move on first thing the next morning.

216

At 0841 on Sunday, 25 August we slipped and continued up la Meuse, arriving after two more kilometres of bland scenery at écluse Mézières, just as the lock system was turned on for the day at 0900. The lock has a lift of 3.4 metres, and the flood wall at the top of the chamber adds a similar height. There are no bollards in the walls of the chamber, so while I stabilised the boat, Edi took the bow line up the slimy ladder, which had been soaking in the filled chamber overnight. The rungs were all bent and twisted out of shape, likely from barges using them to secure on the way up.

She secured the line to a bollard and then tried to find a way to take the stern line. The new lock house had been built directly on the edge of the chamber and safety fencing had been placed to make it safe for tourists, but dangerous for lock users and impossible for boaters to toss a line the six or more metres up to a bollard. Lying next to the lock house was a long pipe with a hook on its end, but it was too heavy for Edi to safely use. I resorted to using the ladder rungs to secure the stern, just as their distortions attest to many having done in the past.

When Edi had activated the chamber, all the sluices opened at once, sending great torrents of water flooding in. The lock seems to have been designed by non-boaters.

We continued along the river for another fifteen kilometres and two more locks, where at 1227 we passed through ecluse Meuse and entered le Canal des Ardenes. After one more lock, at 1330 we secured on the canal bank just beyond Pont-à-Bar. There are bollards along both sides of the canal for 250 to 300 metres, but they were filled with the fender-festooned boats of a rental base on the one side and half the other side was taken-up by a boat repair company's works-in-progress. The remainder of the bollards were occupied by long-term and semi-derelict boats. We dropped the spud pole to secure the bow and pounded a steel pin into the bank to take our stern line.

It appeared that many of the boats occupying the mooring bollards beyond the rental base and the service yard were lived-aboard by employees of the two companies.

In a light drizzle on Monday, we raised the spud pole, retrieved our mooring pin and at 0810 we headed up the canal, our departure timed to have us arrive at the first lock as it opened for navigation at 0900. As we motored, Edi went below to prepare some breakfast panini, which we enjoyed with cups of espresso.

While we ate we watched the passing scene as we glided through tranquil rural villages and past pastures of grazing cattle. The drizzle had abated to light mist and there was a growing warmth from the sun as it worked at burning through the dissipating clouds.

The first lock was followed immediately by a right-angled turn into a second lock, which led into a short tunnel leading through a narrow ridge. We had left la Meuse and entered Canal des Ardennes. On its way up it follows a small river, la Bar, which wanders off eastward in a long loop of a dozen or more kilometres around the end of the ridge. While it is doing that, the locks, tunnel and canal take about half a kilometre to make the same progress as the river.

218

Fourteen kilometres and two more locks brought us to ecluse Sauville, the final up lock on the canal. From this point, a 9.6 kilometre *bief de partage*, connecting reach or summit pound would take us to the beginning of a steep descent down into the vallée de l'Aisne.

At 1315 we secured to the wall at the halte nautique in Le Chesne. This consists of a 40 metre indentation in the stone walls on each side of the canal next to the narrow bridge opening. There is no fee and the moorage is supplied with free electrical outlets, water points, garbage bins and recycling containers. We decided to stay a couple of days, relaxing and getting ready for the twenty-eight locks in the next leg.

Chapter Twenty-six

Into the Champagne

For two days we enjoyed the free moorage in La Chesne taking advantage of the free shore power and water. Except for a series of thunderstorms rolling through on Tuesday, 27 August, the weather was generally fine. We had an artisanal bakery just across the street and a good 8 à Huite supermarket across the first bridge and along half a block.

The town is important enough to have two bridges across the canal, and on a couple of occasions we stood on the one above Zonder Zorg watching the passing commercial barges. There was a regular shuttle of barges past us, with the same half dozen coming and going every few hours, so we knew there was something going on not far along the canal.

We casually explored the small town and relaxed onboard. We often sat in the cockpit to snack or dine on the wonderful items we had found in the market.

We were gathering energy for the next leg of our journey. A kilometre along from us was the first of a series of 26 locks that would drop us in rapid succession more than 80 metres down to the Aisne. From there another two locks and 8 kilometres would take us to the village of Attigny, the next stopping place.

Wednesday, 28 August dawned clear and already warm. It looked like a splendid day to attack the series locks. At 0851 we slipped our lines and continued along the bief toward the first lock, arriving just after the system had been switched on for the day. This was our first down lock since we entered the Maas at Maasbracht in late July, and it was a joy to be able to simply drop the mooring lines over the bollards as we entered the chamber.

As we exited the lock, we saw the next one little more than a hundred metres further on. When we entered the second lock, we saw a commercial barge rising in the third. While we were being lowered, the commercial began leaving, and by the time our doors had opened, it was in the centre of the very short bief.

We slowly danced around each other and then headed into our respective locks.

These locks were built to the dimensions devised by Charles de Freycinet in 1879 when he was the French Minister of Public Works; he later served four times as Prime Minister of France. The chambers are 39 metres long, 5.2 metres wide and 2.2 metres deep to accommodate barges with a maximum size of 38.5 metres by 5.05 metres by 1.8 metres. Because the width and depth of a laden barge are within a few centimetres of the size of the lock, it takes much longer for it to pump its way into an up-bound lock or out of a down-bound one. It is like a piston in a cylinder. We had already settled into our lock and set it in motion while the commercial was still churning its way into its lock.

The fourth lock is only 600 metres from the first. We continued in rapid succession through locks 4, 5, 6, 7 and 8, admiring along the way the old lock houses. Now that the locks have been automated, there is no need for a resident lock keeper. Many of these houses have been rented out, but in remote areas, many remain vacant. The old lock house at écluse 8 iappears to be in good condition, but it is still waiting for a tennant.

We arrived at écluse 9 with the normal red and green lights showing, indicating that it was being prepared for us. We backed and filled in the approaches for ten minutes with no action from the lock. There are no mooring bollards in the waiting area, so I approached the grassy bank, dropped the spud pole and took a stern line to an old telephone pole across the towpath.

I walked up to the control building, pushed the intercom button and was immediately answered. I said: *"Nous descendons à l'écluse 9, mais il est en panne"*, We are descending at Lock 9, but it is not working. I received an immediate *"J'arrive"*, I am coming.

We had been at the lock for three-quarters of an hour by the time the roving lock keeper arrived. An up-bound commercial was by this time in écluse 10, so we needed to wait for it to finish there and then be lifted in écluse 9. Meanwhile a down-bound commercial had caught-up to us and was waiting just upstream. Since we move through the locks much more quickly than the Freycinet barges, we were asked to go ahead as soon as the up-bound cleared. We entered and watched the two commercials dance past each other astern of us in the narrow bend.

We continued along uneventfully, quickly passing through the locks. Increasingly the lock houses were lived-in and well cared for. At écluse 14 we had passed the midway point down the flight.

In the chamber I had selected a set of bollards that placed our stern rather close to the upstream gates. This would normally have been no problem, but the level of the upstream water was several centimetres higher than the gates and as we descended in the chamber, an increasingly high waterfall emerged, its spray wetting our cockpit and nicely cooling me in the heat of midday.

As we arrived in Éclise 15 we saw a sign on the downstream gates advising of *dragage dans la bief*, dredging in the pound. Below us we saw a Freycinet commercial alongside a scow with a mechanical shovel on it. The shovel appeared to be just finishing loading the barge with dredges from the canal bottom.

As we left the lock, the Freycinet slipped from the scow and headed upstream and we snaked a course leaving the Freycinet to port and the scow to starboard as we aimed for the next lock chamber.

I figured that we were now beyond the source of all the commercial activity we had seen upstream and that it was unlikely that we would be seeing any more commercial traffic for a while.

Shortly after 1400 we arrived at écluse 26, the last of the chain of automated locks.

At 1421 we had locked through and entered l'Aisne. It had taken us five and a half hours to transit the twenty-six locks and nine kilometres distance from Le Chesne, including nearly an hour and a half waiting at écluse 9. The FluviaCarte says: "It takes 7 hours to go down the automatic set and the next shops are at Attigny a day's navigation away". The phrasing of this was a bit confusing to me, but it was clarified when I saw Attigny was only ten kilometres along from the bottom of the set.

After less than a kilometre we passed through a low lock taking us from the river and back into la Canal des Ardennes. We hadn't eaten since breakfast, so after we had passed through, Edi prepared a platter of open face sandwiches; fresh lox and capers on chaource slathered multigrain baguette slices. We devoured these and dishes of olives as we followed the canal's meander through a lush forest.

At 1531 we secured alongside in the halte nautique d'Attigny. A quick visit to the supermarket two blocks away gave us the fresh ingredients for a delicious dinner. We relaxed onboard, pleased that the day had gone so easily.

On Thursday morning we slipped our lines at 0842 and continued downstream, arriving écluse Givry at 0900 as it was activated for the day. It was a slightly hazy day, which caused the sun to play wonderful light on the passing scene.

After we had passed through the lock, Edi went below and prepared a large pan of pain perdu au lardons for our breakfast. We enjoyed this with cups of espresso as we followed the winding canal along the 7.9 kilometres to the next lock.

The calmness of the day and the gentle morning sun offered wonderful scenes as we slowly made our way alone along the canal. We were surprised by, but delighted with the lack of traffic. We had the canal to ourselves, and except for the commercial activity around the dredging at Montgon, this has been the case since we left the Netherlands. We have shared only five locks and at our evenings' stops, there have rarely been more than two or three other boats, if any at all. Most of these have been Dutch flagged and heading back to the Netherlands.

Among the bushes along the banks we had spotted a cotoneaster plant filled with red berries, but we were well past it before Edi thought some branches would make a nice addition to the potted hydrangea we had in the bucket at the bow. I kept a sharp lookout for the next bush, and after a couple of kilometres, we found one to nose into.

A little further along the canal we spotted an apple tree heavily hung with reddening apples. I quickly reversed and manoeuvred the bow under the branches, and as we slowly drifted, we quickly picked all we could reach. Edi brought a boathook and we used it to bend a few more branches into reach. The apples were at a point of ripeness where they almost fell into our hands. We left with about ten kilos and continued along the canal.

The canal winds through mostly rural countryside, with a mix of pasture and forest along its banks. It is a very pleasant and peaceful route with an occasional tiny village, a distant steeple and a few impressive private estates. After four locks and 18.8 kilometres, at 1220 we secured to the wall in the halte nautique de Rethel. The moorage is clean and well organised, and it is only two hundred metres from a supermarket and the beginning of a rather large shopping district.

We walked through the town centre up the hill to église St Nicolas to admire the intricate stonework on its windows and doors, and on the way back stopped in the markets for fresh

supplies. After a leisurely breakfast the next morning, we slipped our lines at 0935 with our intended destination: Asfeld, a small village twenty-two kilometres and four locks further along.

We motored through pleasant forests with the calm water covered by dust and pollen. It gently moved aside as we glided through, leaving a beautiful pattern in our stern. The guide showed Asfeld as having a simple moorage, but when we arrived shortly after 1300, we found it rather grubby and barren, so we decided continue on. The next village that showed a mooring possibility was Guignicourt, sixteen kilometres and two locks further along. Within three kilometres we had passed through the last lock of the canal, écluse Vieux-les-Asfeld. We had come to the end of le Canal des Ardennes and entered le Canal Latéral à l'Aisne.

Edi brought up a tray of cheeses, breads, olives and sliced meats for us to nibble on as we made our way along the 6.8 kilometres to the next lock.

As we nibbled we were mesmerised by the reflections in the water as they made wonderful designs with the pilings along the canal banks. Shortly before 1600 we passed straight through Guignicourt, seeing no reason to stop there. The moorings are semi-derelict and are situated next to a sugar refinery and some huge grain silos. They offer no facilities and no charm. The town is a kilometre away and across two bridges. We continued on.

At 1602 we secured alongside the bank at the entrance to la Canal de l'Aisne à la Marne. We slipped in between a Frecinet péniche and a British cruiser with a metre or so to spare each end. There were other mooring places available, but they were all occupied by the complex sprawling of gear of a dozen or more anglers. I had long ago learned that you do not disturb the anglers; overnight vandalism to boats seems directly related.

About an hour after we arrived, Hensie, a deeply laden péniche arrived and asked the British boat to move, explaining it was in the only deep moorage available. The British boat skipper refused to move, indicating the commercial site further along, so Hensie's skipper gently rafted onto him, dropping his spud pole to secure the bow a quarter metre off.

His bow overlapped Zonder Zorg by about five metres, so he could use our uncluttered foredeck for easy access to and from the shore. We later learned that Hensie's load was for the industrial site about two hundred metres further along the canal with ample deep moorage, but the bargee said it was too dusty over there and mooring there would mean having to clean the barge.

At 0840 on Saturday morning we slipped our lines and backed out from under the bows of Hensie and around those of Medea, the péniche that was moored astern of us. A hundred metres along we came to the entrance to Canal de l'Aisne à la Marne. We could see no control device to activate the lock, which the FluviaCarte listed as automatic, nor could we see any indication there was a lock keeper.

After we had nosed up to the lock and had made it very obvious that we wanted to enter, the red light changed to red and green, indicating the lock was being prepared for us. We assumed that the lock keeper at écluse Berry, the next lock along Canal Latéral à l'Aisne only a hundred or so metres away, has controls for both locks.

The first lock house appeared to be abandoned, though it still seemed to be in reasonable condition. We were again in up-bound locks, so we changed our routine. As I slowed the barge in the chamber, I threw a stern line up the 2.5 metres to loop a bollard at the top of the wall, ran out three or four metres and secured the line to stop us. Leaving the engine in gear and pulling on the spring, I then climbed the ladder and went forward to take the bow line from Edi, who was still nursing broken ribs from a nephew's overzealous hug, and couldn't toss a line up to the bollard.

It was drizzling lightly as we worked our way up the canal and we seemed to be the only people around. Then around a bend came an unladen péniche. We waved acknowledgements as we passed. A couple of locks further on we had to wait while another down-bound commercial worked its way through the chamber.

We passed through a few small villages, but mostly the canal sides were agricultural land, predominantly wheat and sugar beet. From the fifth lock, we saw the lock houses had been rented out and they were very nicely maintained and decorated. The drizzle became intermittent and there was some detail coming to the bottoms of the clouds.

After nine locks and eighteen kilometres we came to the industrial outskirts of Reims. Five kilometres further along, we were still in unattractive surroundings as we approached the Relais Nautique de Vieux Port, the pleasure boat marina. Its maximum size is listed as 15 metres, too small for Zonder Zorg, so we continued past. Besides, it is very noisy and exhaust fumed with the Autoroute directly across the canal and busy stop-and-go urban traffic alongside the marina.

At 1352 we secured a kilometre further along on a stone wall with good bollards. Directly beside us was a very busy traffic lighted intersection, and as we sat there we could not relax. We decided to have lunch and then continue on up the canal.

Finally, after four more locks and another ten kilometres, we arrived in the town of Sillery, and at 1633 we secured to the wall directly in front of the Capitainerie in Relais Nautique de Sillery. The relais is a clean and rather new facility, with aluminium finger floats taking sixteen boats up to fifteen metres in length. Along the wall there is room for four or five barges of sixteen to thirty metres. We chose the place that was the closest to the wifi antenna.

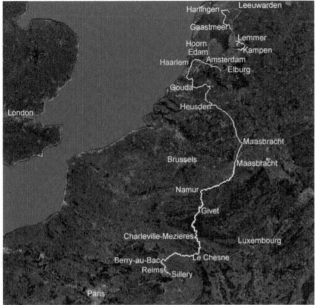

Sillery is located on the western slopes of Montaigne de Reims and is one of the seventeen Grand Cru villages of the Champagne viticultural area. Our winding route from Harlingen had taken us in ten weeks through 128 locks and along 996.2 kilometres of canals, rivers and lakes to cover a straight line distance of 452 kilometres.

After we had settled in, I visited the Capitainerie to check in and pay for a week's moorage and to get maps and information on the town, its surroundings and its facilities. There is a large, modern Intermarché supermarket just along the canal from the marina, and among the things I had learned during my decades as a wine importer and wine writer, is that where there is great wine, there is great food.

We easily found wonderful ingredients for a dinner to celebrate our arrival in Champagne. We were also celebrating that it was the last day of August; in the following days, France would go back to work after their *mois de congé*, their month of holiday, when much in France shuts down, or at least seems to.

Chapter Twenty-Seven

Enjoying Champagne

We relaxed onboard and tended to chores. We also went on walking explorations of the area. Just along from our moorage is one of the nineteen *nécroploes nationales*, French national military cemeteries, which occupy a total of thirty-five hectares in the area east of Montagne de Reims. They are the final resting places for 114,120 members of the French military during World War One. This was one of the major battlegrounds of the war from its beginning to its end. More than eight percent of the total French military dead from the Great War are buried here.

On Tuesday morning we caught the local bus into Reims. For €2.50 each we bought return tickets, which were good for an hour in each direction on all lines, including the new streetcar. Among other things, we wanted to visit Notre Dame. The current structure was begun in 1211 and it replaces a series churches on the site dating back to the late Roman era. In 496 Clovis, the first King of France was baptised in one of the former churches on the site. This led to twenty-five French kings, from Louis the Pious in 816 to Charles X in 1825 being crowned at Notre Dame de Reims.

The Cathedral is one of the finest examples of Gothic architecture, and its design uses flying buttresses to allow the huge windowed walls to soar to great heights. It was severely damaged during World War One and the restoration is ongoing. The more important pieces among the statuary in the entrance portals have been restored, including the Smiling Angel.

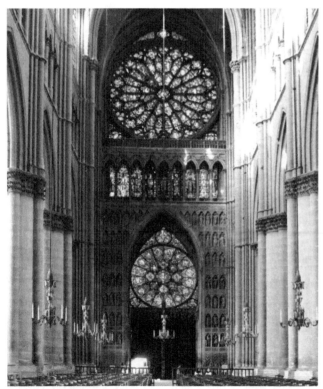

Most of the stained glass windows from the thirteenth century were destroyed by German artillery shelling; however some remain. The Rose Windows over the main portal are the most prominent of these. They are considered as superb examples of the stained glass art.

Also, high up in the nave and the choir some windows from the 1240s have survived.

Modern windows have gradually replaced temporary fillers. This trio by Marc Chagall, one of the great pioneers of Modernism, was completed in 1974.

The interior of the Cathedral is huge, and eight hundred years after it was built, it still ranks among the highest church naves in the world. The light strikes the interior in a seemingly endless variety of designs and the feeling inside is of a monument, rather than of a place of worship.

Outside, facing the Cathedral rides a bronze Jeanne d'Arc, the teenager who turned the tide for the French in the Hundred Year's War. She was condemned as a heretic and burned at the stake at the age of nineteen. The Church said "Oops" twenty-five years later and admitted a mistake. She was later canonised and is one of the Patron Saints of France.

A few blocks away is Eglise St Jacques, which was begun about 1190, two decades before Notre Dame. Its interior is wonderfully serene, and unlike Notre Dame, there is an overwhelming feeling of being in a spiritual place.

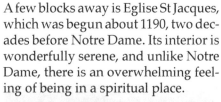

We were captivated by the peacefulness of the place.

On Wednesday morning I walked a few blocks to Case à Pain, broadly reputed as the best bakery in the region. We enjoyed a splendid breakfast of Brie de Meaux and Forme d'Ambert with fresh croissants and cups of espresso. The croissants proved to us that the high reputation of the baker is valid.

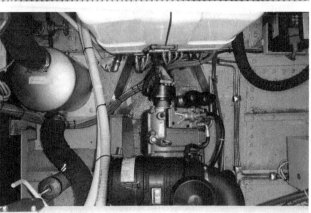

We relaxed and explored, but mostly relaxed and waited. We were waiting for a technician to arrive from the French distributor of our Perkins engine. Since our first outing from Harlingen in early June, we had experienced a problem with leaking of diesel oil and coolant from the engine as well as some oil from the transmission. We had Dutch technicians come to us from Harlingen when we were in Winsum, Workum, Lemmer, Ens, Elburg and Haarlem. Then we had them come from the distributor in Utrecht while we were in Gouda and Gorenchem. Now in Sillery we were waiting for the first French technician to arrive.

We continued to celebrate our arrival in Champagne with more Champagne. For dinner I prepared pan-seared coquilles St Jacques, basmati rice and green beans amandine and we enjoyed these with a bottle of Champagne Canard Duchesne.

As we were savouring our way through the bottle I thought of my friend and former business partner, Philip Holzberg, who in the 1980s and early 90s had done a splendid job of representing and promoting Canard Duchesne in Canada. He had gone on to own a vineyard in the Burgundy and a wine chateau in Bordeaux, before his tragic death a couple of years ago. Cheers, Philip!

Late on Friday morning Julien arrived after a two hour drive from Beauvais, and from the series of photos I had emailed, he quickly found a faulty connection on one of the fuel injector lines. He had brought spares and he had soon fixed the fuel leak for the ninth time. From stains, he tracked down the coolant leak to a faulty connection in the return line to the coolant reservoir. He had no spares to for this, but was able to cobble together a temporary remedy with a piece of hose and some clamps. After engine run-ups and testing, he cleaned a couple of litres of fluids from the bilges and took them for disposal.

He left mid-afternoon, telling us he would have the proper parts ordered and would return to install them the next week, wherever we happened to be along the canals. We needed to keep heading south; we still had a long way to go to reach our winter moorage in Carcassonne.

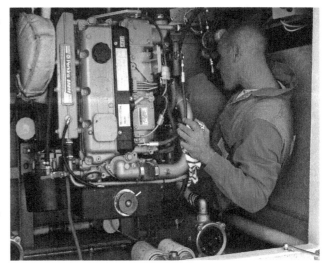

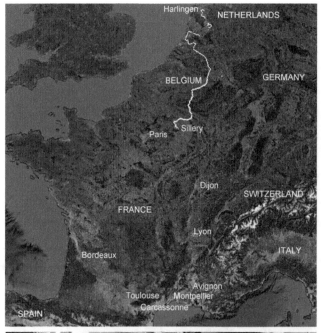

We still had over a thousand kilometres to go to get to Carcassonne and a little over two months to do it before scheduled work on the Canal du Midi would hamper and possibly prevent our progress. Because of timing, we decided to give Paris a miss on this trip and to head southeastward from the Champagne, taking the Canal Lateral à la Marne and the Canal entre Champagne et Bourgogne to the Saône. Not only was this shorter, but it entailed fewer locks.

However; we still had some more of the Champagne to explore before we left, so we decided that the following morning we would continue around the Montaigne de Reims and head a bit west to Épernay, the Capitol of the Champagne.

On Saturday morning, 7 September I walked over to Case à Pain for some pain chocolat and croissants, which we then enjoyed in the cockpit with cups of espresso. As we relaxed over breakfast, the sky slowly filled with cloud and the forecast rain showers began. We had the patio umbrella up, so we continued our late breakfast.

At 1015 we slipped from the wall in Relais Nautique de Sillery and continued up the canal. We glided along through wheat fields with a backdrop of Champagne villages nestled among their vineyards on Montagne de Reims.

It was drizzling lightly, but this did not deter the serious fishermen, nor joggers nor even a young woman on her horse, all of whom used the old tow path beside the canal. Along our planned route for the day were three locks leading up to the *bief de partage*, the summit pound, in the middle of which is Souterrain de Mont-de-Billy, a 2302-metre-long tunnel under a rib of Montagne de Reims. From the tunnel, the waterway leads down eight locks to the end of the canal. The lock houses we saw on the way up were occupied and well-maintained.

The intermittent drizzle had turned to persistent light rain by the time we arrived at the entrance to the tunnel. Its signal light was red and we could see the interior lighting was on, indicating a boat was inside. We didn't know whether the boat was coming or going. If it was going we had a long wait; if it was coming the wait was much less.

There are no bollards along the new concrete wall in the tunnel approach, so we eased over and dropped the spud pole. Within a few minutes faint details emerged in the shadowy darkness of the tunnel mouth. The details filled and soon became the bows of a commercial péniche completing its transit.

Immediately the commercial barge had passed the sensors at the mouth of the tunnel, the traffic light switched from red to green. Then as its stern cleared the mouth, the tunnel's interior lights went out. We waited for the suck and turbulence of the passing barge to subside, and then raising the spud pole, we headed toward the entrance.

As our bows crossed through the beam of the sensors, the interior lights came on. Faintly in the distance we could see the point of light at the far end of the tunnel, 2.3 kilometres away. The towpath beside the canal continued into the tunnel.

The entire interior of the tunnel is lined with stones laid in a graceful barrel vault and the construction was completed in time for the opening of the canal in 1866. During World War One, after the Germans artillery had disabled the canal, the French used the tunnel to hide barges loaded with artillery pieces. Looking back we could see the entrance slowly getting smaller. The interior was dry, with none of the commonly found dripping from the tunnel roof.

We took advantage of the respite from the rain. Edi went below and quickly put together a tray of bread, cheeses and olives for us to enjoy during the twenty-odd minute passage through the tunnel. It was not her usual fancy spread; the table top was wet from the rain and would have soaked a tablecloth and our dry time was not anticipated to be sufficiently long to allow her to do a fancy arrangement. Lunch was wonderful, made even more so by the setting.

Zonder Zorg handled superbly through the tunnel, balanced between the effects off each wall and easily seeking the centre. A little bit of guidance with the tiller from time to time was all that was required. After twenty minutes we were at the end of the tunnel and ready to head back out into the rain.

We started down the six-kilometre-long series of eight down-bound locks and about halfway along we came to a malfunctioning one. As we approached, we had as usual turned the control rod dangling over the canal. It lit the orange flashing light at the gate and turned the signal from red to red and green. It did everything that was automated to happen except filling the lock and opening the gates for us. We secured to a bollard on the bank and I called Ch22 on the VHF. Mme. l'éclusier said: "J'arrive".

The next lock malfunctioned also. It had allowed us in, but after I had lifted the activation bar the doors would not close. Again I signalled the lock keeper and she quickly came to set things in motion again. She seemed to know exactly what to do, as if these were regular occurrences, which I suspect they were so late in the season. They are likely on the VNF list of winter maintenance.

At 1607 we finally made it down to the end of Canal de l'Aisne à la Marne, a T-junction with Canal Latéral à la Marne. We turned to starboard and headed downstream. The first lock along the canal, the one in Tours-sur-Marne malfunctioned, so I needed to call VNF again. It took nearly half an hour for a different lock keeper to arrive and lock us through, and by this time it was getting very tight for us to make it through l'écluse de Mareiul before it closed for the day at 1700. Slowing us along the way was the second movable bridge we had seen since the Netherlands, but it responded quickly to our twist of the

dangling wand and we needed to pause for only short while.

We arrived at the signalling wand for l'écluse de Mareiul at 1650 and watched as our twist was acknowledged by a flashing orange light. However, the red light went out and stayed out; we got no red and green to show the lock was being prepared for us. We later learned that, even though the system is listed as operating until 1700, any new locking-through is switched off ten minutes before that; we likely missed it by seconds.

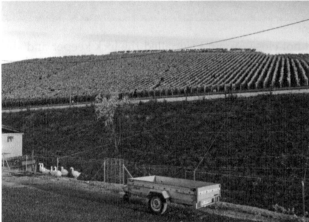

We secured to the bollards on the quai at the approaches to the lock and shut down for the day. We were in the countryside a kilometre short of the village of Mareiul-sur-Ay and four kilometres short of the town of Ay. When I checked the engine after our day's run, I again saw diesel oil and coolant puddles in the bilge. I was not happy.

Sunday morning we arose to a world covered in heavy dew and the sun rising mists off the canal. Beside us, next to the lock house the geese were warming themselves in the first rays of the sun, and above them on the slopes the grapes began another day of ripening. With only about two weeks until harvest, they need all the sun they can get.

Edi had the diced bacon smelling wonderfully and was just about to add the eggs to the pan when Mme.l'éclusier arrived to ask us if we wanted to lock through. I told her we were getting ready for breakfast and were thinking of going through in half an hour. She said the lock wasn't working properly and it needed help, but that she would be away for over an hour. I told Edi to turn the bacon off and hold the eggs. Within two minutes we were entering the lock.

We passed through Mareiul-sur-Ay, and not tempted by the rather Dogpatch-looking moorings, we decided to continue on to Ay. From my visit here in 2004 in Lady Jane, I remembered a long quai in the centre of town, though I did recall very shallow water alongside. The new FluviaCarte showed the quai, but did not mention of the shallowness alongside. They left it to us to discover with our 0.95 metre draft. Fortunately, Zonder Zorg's skeg is about 10 centimetres deeper than the tips of her propeller blades.

I easily poled off with a boathook, and we continued along to écluse de Ay, which we passed through without any need of assistance. This automatic lock was working, though with its very slow emptying, we suspect there is a problem with the upstream paddles. We secured alongside the wall on the bollards just below the lock. Edi reheated the bacon and put on the eggs while I pulled some espressos. We had arrived in Ay.

For the first time since Namur, Belgium we dug the bicycles out of the forepeak. We needed fresh produce and meat or fish for dinner, so we crossed the canal bridge and continued along about three hundred metres to the Leclerc supermarket, which I recalled from our previous visit here a decade ago. The store was still there, but it is closed on Sundays. We turned around and headed the three kilometres into Magenta, across the Marne from Epernay, where we found the Leader Price open. It is located in a cheap neighbourhood and

has very low quality produce and meats to suit its main clientele. Nonetheless, we did manage to put together a small basket to see us through until the better markets open on Monday.

After lunch we walked into Ay to explore. At the entrance to the town is the wine-country-mandatory decorated wine barrel. Ay is one of the best of the Grand Cru villages of the Champagne and its specialty is growing the two red grapes of the region: Pinot Noir and Pinot Meunier.

Ay is home to over forty Champagne producers. Signposts throughout the town point directions to those nearby. It is a small town, so most of the signposts show half to three-quarters of the producers.

The town is long and narrow, ranging along a strip between the canal and the base of the slopes of Montagne de Reims. We walked the three blocks through to the beginnings of the vineyards. The grapes were in good tight clusters and most had taken on the deep blue-purple colour of maturity.

Some bunches in less sunny exposures were still in the process of changing colour. Still others had not yet begun ripening. It has been a rather patchy growing year, with frost, rain and hail disrupting the flowering, fruit set and the ripening.

This is not unusual for the Champagne, a region that lies at the northern extreme of the viticulture zone. The vines are tough and resilient and over my four and a half decades of visiting the region, I have seen that the growers and producers are even tougher and more resilient.

We walked along, passing the bottoms of the corduroy slopes of Montaigne de Reims and back in among the buildings that abut the vineyards.

We passed a wonderful series of open gates giving glimpses into the domains and lives of *les viticulteurs*, the grape growers. During my decades in the wine trade, I consistently saw that the art and science of grape growing are the most important aspects in the production of fine wine. Wine of fine quality cannot be made without fine quality grapes. The winemaker can do nothing to improve the quality that comes from the grower; rather, the winemaker's task is to prevent as much as possible any lessening of the quality, shepherding the natural processes as the grapes become wine.

242

We walked along streets that seemed completely lined with Champagne producers, some large, some small, some famous, others near unknown outside their own small circles. It was Sunday and everything was closed. Edi and I seemed to be the only activity in town.

We headed back down into the centre of town, past the church as darkening clouds threatened more rain. As we scurried to beat the rain back to Zonder Zorg, we hurried through an older section with many half-timbered buildings from a few centuries back. We promised ourselves to take more time in the following few days to further explore Ay and its surroundings.

Back onboard, the rain passed and we relaxed. Within a week we had seen the temperatures plunge from a daytime high of 38° when we were in Sillery to 19° this week. Autumn was closing in on us and the tree above us sent a continuous rain of reminders onto our decks.

We had a private visit scheduled with Champagne de Venoge in Épernay on Wednesday, and our thoughts had been to head down the canal four kilometres, pass through the lock at Dizy and then head a little over five kilometres up the branch of the Marne to Port de Plaisance d'Épernay. This would entail about two and a half hours of motoring. Moorage in Épernay was listed as €2 per metre per day, so €34 a day on top of the €14 for the ten litres of diesel consumed getting there and back to our free moorage in Ay. Edi suggested that for the €48 we stay in Ay, take taxis to and from Épernay and buy a bottle of Champagne with the change.

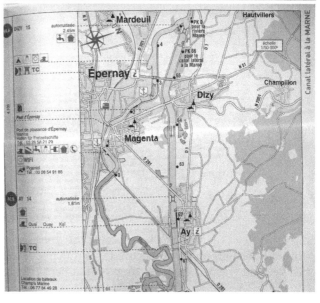

With the trees above us accelerating their defoliation, we decided to move Zonder Zorg back up through the lock to the quai above it. It has no overhanging trees. We watched as a Freycinet gauge peniche filled the lock. These barges are within a few centimetres of the same dimensions as those of the chamber, and we watched as the skipper put the twin rudders hard over so that the lock doors astern could swing past them and close.

When the lock was clear we slipped our lines and I headed down canal about 200 metres to a point where the canal is about 20 metres wide, sufficient for me to wind Zonder Zorg around and in the process, twist the lock signalling wand. Meanwhile, Edi had walked up to the lock to receive the lines when I entered. In short order we had made it through the lock and were secured in a much less leafy place. We swept away the thick layer of leaves and washed the boat, then settled back into relaxing and enjoying Ay.

On Wednesday morning I phoned to reserve a taxi for 1440 to take us from Zonder Zorg to Epernay. This timing was calculated to get us there about five minutes before our 1500 appointment with Champagne de Venoge. The taxi arrived at the barge twenty minutes early, so we arrived at the doors of de Venoge nearly half an hour ahead of schedule. This left us with too little time to take a meaningful walkabout. Besides, it was threatening to rain again, so I rang the bell.

Our hostess and guide, Emma Dawe-Coz found no problem with our earliness. She is a lively young woman, born in French Guyana of a British mother and French father, and is nearing completion of her wine degree in Reims. Part of these studies is serving an internship in the export marketing offices of a Champagne house.

As we walked through the tank rooms, she explained the background of the house of de Venoge. It was founded by Henri-Marc de Venoge, a Swiss who had earlier travelled to Italy and discovered wine. In 1825 he settled in the Champagne in Mareuil-sur-Ay, where he set-up in the wine trade. In 1837 his business became Champagne de Venoge. His wines very quickly rose to prominence and he played a dominant role in the rapid expansion of the Champagne business. He experimented with disgorgement and the refinement of other steps in the Champagne process. In 1864 de Venoge launched Cordon Blue, a symbol of nobility since the sixteenth century, and which has since become the synonym of refinement and of the art of living. De Venoge is credited as the originator of the illustrated label, a departure from standard at the time; black lettering on white paper.

From the fermenting rooms we descended deep into the chalk strata that underlie much of the central Champagne region. The chalk holds moisture well and maintains a humidity of around 70% in the cellars and the temperature remains a rather constant 11° to 13° year round. These conditions are ideal for the secondary fermentation of the wine and for its ageing on lees. The network of chalk tunnels beneath de Venoge extend about a kilometre and a half. De Venoge is considered a medium-sized house, annually producing about 800,000 bottles. Although it is one of the Grands Marques, its wines are not found in supermarkets. The house prefers to sell to restaurants, hotels and wine shops.

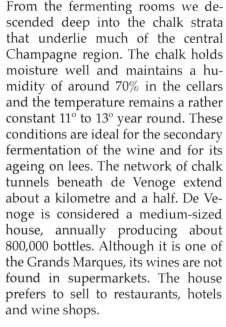

We walked past lines of *pupitres*, the riddling racks that are used to move the sediment from the side of a bottles to its neck. The sediment is mainly dead yeast cells from the second fermentation, the fermentation in the bottle that gives Champagne its bubbles. At de Venoge, hand riddling is still done on its cuvées prestiges and its vintage wines.

We then came to the reserves of older vintages. There are variously sized stacks of the what appeared to me to be the whole gamut of the house's vintage-dated brands: Louis XV, Grand Vin des Princes, Blanc de Blanc, Blanc de Noirs, Brut Rose and Cordon Blue, and these were in varying size formats.

I found a bin of 1961, among my favourite vintages. The scrawled label on the stack showed that only forty-five bottles remained.

A bit further along was a barred gate, much like the image of a prison door. Emma told us the room beyond held the older vintages, but it was too dark inside to see anything but forms. I thrust my camera through at full arm's reach and shot some random flash photos. One of the photos showed some stacks around the corner to the right and across on the opposite wall. The labels that are readable show bottles from 1921, 1911 and 1893, two of the vintages younger than our skûtsje Zonder Zorg and one older.

We continued our circuit of the caves, slowly making our way back to the staircase and then back up them to the bottling, disgorging and labelling lines. We continued to the tasting room.

While we looked at the displays of current and past packaging, Emma prepared a tasting for us. She offered us a range of their Champagnes, beginning with the Cordon Blue Extra Brut and progressing through to the Rosé Brut Réserve. Our favourites were the Blanc de Noirs Marquis and the Rosé Brut Réserve. We particularly liked the Rosé, with its hints of strawberries on the nose, delicate cranberry-strawberry palate and long, elegant fruity finish. This is finest non-vintage rosé that I can recall tasting in my many dozens of cellar visits in the Champagne since my first visit here in 1967. At about €35, it is definitely on our buy list.

We emerged from De Venoge after a splendid two hours and walked into the centre of Épernay to continue our search for proper Champagne glasses. Aboard our sailboat, Sequitur we had used some of our hand-blown hollow-stem crystal from home, and thinking we would quick-

ly find similar ones in Europe, we hadn't brought any with us to Zonder Zorg. Now in the capitol of Champagne, we thought that we would surely find some. Before we left De Venoge, we had asked where we would best look and we visited the all shops recommended, and finding no stems even close, we asked for further recommendations. They yielded nothing better than the supermarket stems we had bought in the Netherlands. Empty handed, we continued on to the huge Carrefour supermarket, where we filled our huge bags to overflowing and took a taxi back to Zonder Zorg.

On Friday the thirteenth of September, my sixty-ninth birthday, we were interrupted mid-breakfast by the arrival of Julien, the technician from the Perkins distributor. The parts he had ordered had arrived and he did the two hour drive from Beauvais in a little over ninety minutes to come and install them and to thoroughly clean the mess in the bilges, which had come from the various leaks.

After he had replaced the jerry rigged coolant return line with the proper part, Julien tracked-down the new coolant leak that I had reported after our trip from Sillery to Ay. The coolant reservoir overflow had simply spilled over the engine and into the bilges. He added a line to the overflow spigot and led it to a plastic bottle he strapped to the raw water inlet at the bottom of the bilge. This is not as elegant as an expansion tank, but at least now any overflow will have a better place to go.

After Julien had finished the installations and cleaning of the bilges, he did a long engine run, both free turning and under load at low, medium and high revolutions to see if there were any more problems.

Finally, with the repairs, cleanup, testing and warranty servicing paperwork done, Julien headed back toward Beauvais and we began retracing our route back up the Canal Latéral à la Marne. As we again passed the halte nautique of Mareiul-sur-Ay, it looked even more unattractive than it had the previous week on our way down.

Of more interest to us were the vineyards planted to the brink of the chalk cliffs above the town of Mareiul. In years past I had marvelled at vine roots poking out of the cliff face six and more metres below the vineyards. I had several times used this exact location to bring my small groups to discuss Champagne viticulture as I conducted wine tours through France.

After two locks, we came again to Condé-sur-Marne, where instead of heading back up the Canal Aisne à la Marne, we continued straight along Canal Latéral à la Marne. We had come to the end of the Champagne viticulture area; the land around us was now flat and the vineyards had been replaced with fields of wheat and sugar beets. Though we were still in the Champagne-Ardennes Region, we had left what oenophiles think of as The Champagne.

The lock controls along this section of the canal continue with the dangling wand. By this time Edi was an expert at grasping and twisting the wand as we passed by.

From four kilometres back we had seen a large white object at the entrance to the lock, and as we approached, it had become clear that it was a very poorly designed overflow sluice. It was directing a large volume of foaming water across the canal just before the entrance to the lock chamber. As we neared, I tried to assess the strength of the crosscurrent so that I could compensate. Previous experience told me that as our bow reached the narrow current, it would swing to port, but to not correct; the stern would be almost equally swung as it met the current.

The trick is to correctly estimate the amount the barge would be offset and to then compensate by steering that amount off centre on the approach. At this lock, with the sluice so close to the entrance and with its stream so strong, there was little margin for error. To approach too slowly would place us too long in the current; to approach too quickly would risk serious collision damage to the barge if the estimate of the current's effects were wrong.

My estimates were close, and with some heavy engine, tiller and bow-thruster work, we ran through the current and its resultant eddies and countercurrents and made it into the chamber with only a few fender bounces. Once inside we saw that the lock had another trick to play on us. The mooring bollards are set in small concrete bays, with only about fifteen centimetres space to allow a tossed line to fall into place. Complicating this, the safety geeks had placed railings to protect the public and to further hamper the boater in looping the bollards. To make the situation even

less comfortable, it began to rain again.

After two more locks and a total of 35.8 kilometres, at 1630 we backed onto a five metre finger pontoon in the halte publique in Châlons-en-Champagne and dropped the spud pole to secure the bow. When I did my post-run engine room check, I was disappointed to see a small puddle of fluid in the bottom of the bilge. Hoping that it was merely residue from the previous leaks that had finally made its way down from puddles in the engine's nooks and crevices, I decided to let it be for the moment, and monitor it in the coming days.

To cheer things up, in the evening I prepared seared St-Jacques and served them with mushrooms sautéed in butter and Armagnac over basmati rice with haricots verts fins amandine and roma tomatoes. We celebrated my sixty-ninth birthday with a bottle of Champagne Canard Duchêne and bid a formal farewell to The Champagne.

Chapter Twenty-Eight

From the Champagne to the Burgundy

It was raining on Saturday morning as we raised the spud pole, slipped our lines and continued up canal. It continued to rain, varying from heavy drizzle to heavy downpour as we worked our way up eight locks and along 34.1 kilometres of canal to Vitry-le-François.

For the first while we passed rather bland canalside scenery, much of it grain elevators; this area is the bread-basket of France, with huge fields of grains, mostly wheat. Along the way there were remnants and ruins of industrial efforts from the early nineteenth century as France emerged from the turmoil of the Revolution and the Napoleonic era.

The rain had eased to a fine drizzle at 1600 when we reached the end of the Canal Latéral à la Marne. At the T-junction we turned right and started along Canal entre Champagne et Bourgogne. As we motored, we saw the banks on both sides of the canal lined with commercial péniches, with not a single space available. Within a kilometre we arrived at the Port de Plaisance de Vitry le François, where fortunately, one of only two spots in the port capable of taking Zonder Zorg was empty, so we quickly manoeuvred to fill it.

We wore around, backed into the space and secured alongside at 1620. According to the sign on the gate, the Capitainerie closes at 1600 and is closed on Sundays, so we had no way to pay for our overnight moorage unless we stayed until Monday. Memories of the town from a previous visit in 2003 in Lady Jane, plus the fact that everything would be closed on Sunday, quickly ruled out a two day stop.

In a steady light rain on Sunday morning, 15 September we slipped our lines from the bollards and turned to starboard to continue up Canal entre Champagne et Bourgogne. Ahead of us was a climb of 239 metres with 71 locks in 155 kilometres. This would take us to the summit pound and a 4.8 kilometre tunnel through the top of the pass, before starting our descent of 156 metres over 43 locks and 64 kilometres to the Saône at Heuilley. We were hoping that, once we reached the summit and started down into the Burgundy, the near-steady rain of the past week would have stopped.

Within a few hundred metres we were out of the rain under the broad railway bridge, waiting for the first of 71 up locks to be prepared for us. After we had entered, Mme l'éclusier took our lines with a hooked pole and placed them over bollards at the top of the wall 3.5 metres above us. When we had risen to the top, she gave us a *telecommand*, a remote control device to activate 51 of the locks and half a dozen of the lift bridges along our way to the summit. She also gave us brochures explaining the automated locks and the operation of the nineteen manual locks and seven manual lift and swing bridges on the way up, as well as details on the 43 locks down the other side.

We headed out of the lock as the skies began to clear for the first time in many days. Our remote worked as advertised at the next lock and we managed to loop the bollards at the top of the lock wall. The first dozen and a half locks have a lift of a few centimetres either side of 3.15 metres, so with Zonder Zorg's deck half a metre above water, the tops of the bollards are not much more than a metre above our heads, making it rather easy to toss a loop of line around them.

The locks in this section of the canal fill right to the brim, lowering the height of the line toss, but making fenders useless in protecting the hull from the masonry of the lock's rim. It is not so bad going up; the loss of fender protection is only for the last few minutes while waiting for the gates to open and then motoring out of the lock. I remember these locks from our trip down them in 2003. Entering them required precise manoeuvring, and with a lightly gusting wind, it became nearly impossible to enter without some scrapes. Lady Jane received a few paint blemishes at waterline during that descent.

Our remote control functioned well until we came to a lock without the "Click Here" sign three hundred or so metres before it. I had noticed that directional signs along the towpath had been turned around, apparently as a juvenile prank and the missing transponder post was likely another. I let Edi off on the bank and she went walking back along the towpath, clicking as she went. The pranksters must have pulled out the signpost and its transceiver and threw it into the bushes; however, Edi's persistent clicking of the remote finally elicited a response from the signal lights at the lock. They turned from Red to Red and White. It appeared that the pranksters had also smashed the green lens.

A few locks further along, our twelfth of the day, the remote refused to activate the lock as we repeatedly clicked at the sign on our way by. I dropped Edi off at a mooring dolphin and she

254

went back along the towpath again, but even standing beside the sign, she could get no response from the lock's signal lights. I called the VNF on the cell phone and reported the situation, adding that I suspected the batteries were dead in our remote control. We secured to the dolphin and waited. In about twenty minutes a VNF van arrived with a fresh remote control, and it easily triggered the lock to cycle for us.

It was 1730 by the time we had made it through the lock and into the town of St-Dizier and we moved quickly along the 1.8 kilometre bief to make it through écluse St-Dizier before it closed for the day. The lock functioned flawlessly and were quickly locked through. Our guide shows a mooring quai immediately beyond the lock, and we had been planning on using it for the night; however, the neighbourhood looked seedy to us and there were scattered groups of young men lolling about and appearing to be looking for mischief. Knowing that this is an economically depressed area, our long experience and our guts told us rather forcefully to continue along the canal.

After three kilometres we arrived at Pont Levis de Marnaval and glided through the narrow gut. This is actually two bridges in series, the first a swing bridge, which is normally open and it is immediately followed by a bascule lift bridge. Beyond these bridges is écluse Marnaval, on which the signal lights were out as we arrived, indicating it was closed for the day.

We secured to the spud pole and a pin pounded into the bank in a serene rural setting just downstream of the lock. On Monday morning Edi walked our gangway to the bank and started back down the canal toward the signal sign. She cheered as she was immediately successful at triggering the lock.

We were running low on both water and diesel oil and needed to replenish. On our FluviaCarte I had
highlighted the places that showed
these were available. The next water
shown was in écluse Chamouilley,
three locks and five kilometres further along. An hour and a half later
when we arrived at Chamouilley,
there was a VNF éclusier there to take
our lines and explain to us that the
automatic mechanism was not working correctly and that he would manually bypass the system to lock us
through. I asked about water, and he
said he had never seen any available
at this lock. We both then searched
and proved the FluviaCarte wrong.

He told us there was water at the lift
bridge house at Bayard, three locks
further along, and that he would be
accompanying us along the way to
assist with two lift bridges and a lock
on which the automatic systems were
not fully functioning.

While we motored in the steady rain,
l'éclusier rode the towpath on his
Moped, passing us to open the bridge or
work the recalcitrant lock mechanisms.

At 1315 we secured to spud pole and
a pin pounded into the bank, just
downstream from the manual lift
bridge in Bayard and its bridge keeper's house. Once we had secured,
l'éclusier led me to the water he had
promised. It was a simple faucet in
the utility sink in the room he used
as his waiting place while tending
his series of locks and bridges. It had
no threads and I thought of jury-rig-
ging a cuff adaptor, but we weren't
that needy of water. He suggested we
simply fill-up some bottles; I told him
we needed close to a thousand litres.

The good news was that there is a gas station in the supermarket lot just 300 metres from Zonder Zorg's mooring. The gauge level had been down below the sight glass, and I estimated about 30 litres remaining. It was below the level of the intake for the hot water and

central heating system. Hot water was not a problem, since the engine heated the tank when we motored and gave more than a day's supply; however with the persistent rain and cool weather, interior heating would be welcomed. I made four trips with our two jerry cans on the trolley and added 160 litres to the tanks.

At 0955 on Tuesday we raised our spud pole and retrieved the mooring pin from the bank. We had told l'éclusier that we intended continuing up canal at 1000, and he had arrived a few minutes early to push the buttons to halt traffic and lift the bridge for us. He then scooted up the towpath and hand cranked the next lift bridge for our arrival.

Then he continued along to the next lock to take our lines as we entered and to override the controls on the malfunctioning automated system. He scooted on past us after we had left the lock and opened the manual lift bridge half a kilometre further along. He bade us farewell as we passed through the bridge, telling us that the all the locks and bridges from écluse 51 through 23 were automatic and, as far as he knew, properly functioning.

A few hundred metres further along as we entered Joinville, we passed a quai overflowing with boats, including two British barges. One was a replica luxemotor, the other a replica narrowboat. We continued on past about a quarter kilometre to an empty place on a public quai, where we had been told there was free water. At 1355 we stopped to fill our tanks, which took over an hour. By the time we were watered, it was past mid-afternoon, and since we had already

done 15.9 kilometres, 7 locks and 6 lift bridges, we decided to pause for the night.

Not long after we had stopped for water, the two couples from the British boats walked along and saw the free quai and quickly moved their boats along to moor astern of us. They had been on a quai with charges for mooring and for water. With our tanks full of water and more readily available, I flashed-up the generator and we ran three loads of laundry through the washer and dryer.

At 1020 on Wednesday we slipped our lines and continued up canal. The two British boats had departed before us, so unless there were down-bound boats, all the locks would be filled when we arrived and we would need to wait for them to cycle down. At the next few locks, we again saw the marvels of incompetent lock design, with overflow sluices dumping a gushing crosscurrent just short of the lock entrances. Also here we saw locks overflowing their rims when filled. We are amazed that nearly a century and a half after these locks were designed and built that these flaws still remain.

The chambers of the locks are deeper along this section, and instead of the 2.85 to 3.15 heights we had been seeing, the walls were now 3.4 to 3.85 metres high. This made it rather difficult to throw a line up from our low decks to ring an unseen bollard whose position is marked with a faded paint stripe at the top of the wall. At the next of these higher locks, while we waited for it to prepare for us, I nosed into the bank and Edi hopped ashore with a boathook and walked to the lock to take the lines.

By the time we reached écluse 41 it had begun raining again, making it our twelfth consecutive day with rain. The guide showed a water faucet at the lock, but we could see no sign of any. Immediately upon heading upstream from this lock, the canal crosses a bridge over the Marne and then immediately passes a lift bridge. Over much of its length to the summit of the pass near the source of the Marne, the canal follows the general course of the river using its waters to fill the locks and pounds.

We arrived in Donjeux relieved to see that the two British boats had decided to stop. This meant that our progress would be quicker with the locks empty from the passage of a down-bound commercial barge that we had just met. We continued up canal.

About half of the lock houses along this stretch of canal appeared to be occupied. Some were completely plain, with no apparent effort to dress-up the setting. Others were well decorated and the one at écluse 38 was a screaming example of kitsch run wild. There was a small replica of Michelangelo's David mixed in with gaudy gnomes, storks, pink flamingos, some Bambi characters, Grecian urns, squirrels, frogs, snails and so on.

At least two of the gnomes were a tad risqué. We wondered at the taste of the tenant and pondered her sanity as we watched her watching our reactions from the upper window.

In the early afternoon we paused before a lock to wait for a barge to cycle down, which meant the following locks would be in our favour as we approached them.

Then at 1540 we secured alongside in the halte nautique of Froncles, which is part motor-camper parking and part boat moorage. We had come another 23.6 kilometres and had worked through nine more locks. A short while after our arrival, the capitain came by and collected our €4 fee for moorage. Since we had paid for it, we plugged into the shore power and topped off our water tanks.

During a lull in the rain in the late afternoon I walked through the small town in search of the reported supermarket. The town had certainly seen better days, but it appeared that the metalworks, Les Forges had been on hard times for a long while. There had been an attempt to bring some commerce to the old area by the chateau, but most of the spaces look to have been vacant for a long time. I found the supermarket just as the skies opened for another downpour, so I took my time shopping, giving the rain plenty of time to abate.

At 0910 on Thursday we slipped and continued up canal, me in Zonder Zorg and Edi on bicycle. We had decided that it would be easier to handle the lines from the top, and instead of dropping her off before each lock, it seemed easier for her to pedal between the locks, which are spaced here at an average of about two kilometres apart. The speed limit in the canal is eight kilometres per hour, so she had no problem arriving at the lock in advance of Zonder Zorg.

Along the way we passed one of the few fishermen we had thus far seen in France that was not enraged that we had disturbed his fishing by having the audacity to use a boat on the canal. To us it seems that many of the canalside fishermen think that the canals had been built for fishing, not boating, and that boaters have no right to disturb their lines. This wooden man was an exception.

The locks were in our favour, and we moved along smoothly, with Edi using a large carabiner on the end of a line to haul up the mooring lines and drop them over the bollards.

Our eleventh lock of the day, écluse 26 at Condes was a complex one. Almost immediately out of the lock is a tunnel. Then directly from the tunnel the canal crosses on a viaduct over the Marne and at the end of the viaduct there is a lift bridge.

At 1406, having done 25.8 kilometres, twelve locks, three lift bridges and one tunnel, we secured alongside at Port de la Maladière in Chaumont. Shortly after having arrived, we pedalled across the bridge and back down the canal a kilometre to the huge new Leclerc supermarket to restock our supplies.

In the late afternoon we were visited by the VNF area manager, who asked whether we were leaving the next day, and if so, when and how far we wanted to go. The two locks after Chaumont are automatic, but from there the following nineteen are manual and we needed to be accompanied by an éclusier. We told him we would be at the first manual lock for its opening at 0900.

Shortly after 0800 on Friday we slipped and followed a tiny Belgique boat with four huge people aboard. The boat was no more than eight metres long and barely more than two metres of beam and it listed almost dangerously when any of the crew moved to one side or the other.

We followed the little boat into the first lock, just a few hundred metres along from our mooring place. There we were amused with their coordinated balancing act as they kept the boat more-or-less upright while getting their lines to the lock bollards. We learned that the two couples had been boating together as friends for a dozen years and we tried to imagine the boat's cramped interior arrangements to accommodate their four very ample bodies.

The second automatic lock followed within a kilometre and a half, after which there was a three kilometre pound to the first manual lock. During the motor between the first two locks, Edi had laid-out everything for breakfast, and then as we left the second lock, she began cooking. Very shortly she emerged into the cockpit with my plate of pain perdu à jambon garnished with sliced tomatoes and avocadoes. A minute later she brought up a hot cup of espresso.

We finished our breakfasts shortly before we arrived at the third lock, where we were met by a tiny elderly woman. She hand cranked the gates closed behind us, closed their paddles, went to the upstream gates and cranked open the paddles there to flood the lock.

As Zonder Zorg's foredeck reached the lock rim, we had offloaded Edi's bicycle. Once we had reached the top of the lock, I cranked open one of the upstream gates as madame l'éclusier did the other, then after I had motored out, I watched as she closed the gates and dropped their paddles. She soon drove past on the towpath toward the next lock.

Edi was in hot pursuit on her bicycle along the towpath to take our lines as we arrived in the locks. This process worked well for us, for the two couples in the Belgian boat, and because Edi helped crank the gates, also for madame l'éclusier. Besides the handwork on the locks, there was a vertical lift bridge that needed cranking up. Here Edi could do nothing but watch as the bridge opened and we passed under.

At our first lock after noon, madame l'éclusier was replaced by a young man, who continued the process she had commenced. Thus we worked our way up the canal for 29.6 kilometres and through fifteen locks and one lift bridge, until at 1440 we came to our spud pole and a pin pounded into the bank in Rolapmont. The rain had stopped a little before we arrived and the skies looked more promising for clearing than we had seen in two weeks. This was our thirteenth consecutive day with rain.

Moored astern of us was the 13.5 metre Lemsteraak, Nettie. She had been built in 1911 not far from where Zonder Zorg had been three years earlier and she still had her traditional sailing rig. Aboard was a young Dutch couple, at least younger than us. They were on their way back to Amsterdam, which they had left in April to navigate up the Rhine and the Main, then across the canal to the Danube and down it to the Black Sea. They then sailed to Istanbul, through the Bosporus and the Greek Islands, around the Agean coast and around the Mediterranean coasts of Italy and France. From there they motored up the Rhône and the Saône and over the Plateau de Langres to here.

On Saturday morning the sky was the clearest we had seen it in two weeks. We bade farewell and success with the remainder of their voyage as Nettie continued down canal and we continued up.

We had organised with l'éclusier to have the next lock ready for us at 0900. There were five more manual locks and a manual swing bridge that needed to be worked for us. Following us into the locks was a French couple from St-Jean-de-Losne. He is an electrician for one of the boatyards there, and because his expertise is in too much demand during August when nearly everyone in France takes their holidays, he and his wife take their major annual boating trip in September.

By 1100 we had smoothly made our way up the first four manual locks and then through the swing bridge at Jourquenay and were in the final manual lock. As we were locking up, I asked l'éclusier what the traffic was like at the Balesmes Tunnel, and he phoned the control point to find out. There was a péniche chargée on its way up from the other side that we would need to wait for, likely for up to two hours.

We thanked l'éclusier for his work and we headed off to do the final three locks to the summit pound. These are all automatic, they all worked properly and shortly past noon we were at écluse 1, the seventy-first and final up lock of the canal. In seven days we had come 152 kilometres and up 239 metres through 71 locks 15 movable bridges and a tunnel. From here there is a 10.1 kilometre summit pound with two tunnels, the first being only about 150 metres long. The second tunnel is 4820 metres long, nearly five kilometres, and it passes nearly beneath the source of the River Marne.

As we motored along the bief the two kilometres to the first tunnel, we passed below the ramparts of the citadel of Langres 130 metres above us. The ramparts are nearly three kilometres long as they encircle the ancient city that dates at least to the Roman era. As we motored, the clouds thickened and it looked like we would have our fourteenth consecutive day with rain.

At 1241 we arrived at the traffic control displays at the entrance to the Balesmes Tunnel. They were very confusing; the gate was up, the panel was alternating between *Tunnel Open 243 Go, Tunnel Ouvert 243 Passez* and *Tunnel Offen 243 Durchfahrt*. However; the light was red. I radioed the control centre for clarification, and was told to ignore the open gate and the multilingual signs telling us to go. They are wrong and we must wait for the green light.

With a port stern line, I looped a bollard on a duc d'albe as we slowly passed, then swung in toward bank on it out of the channel, stopped and dropped the spud pole and tightened in the stern line. Our wait extended beyond the two hour estimate, then grew to two and a half hours. At two and three-quarter hours we were still waiting, then the light went green.

We had a green light, an open gate and a panel telling us in three languages that the tunnel was open and to proceed. We waited and wondered about communications and safety.

As our wait neared three hours, the faint blur we had seen deep in the tunnel had grown into a barge. We continued to wait as it painfully slowly pumped its way out of the tunnel and along the narrow cut. It was a deeply laden Freycinet gauge barge that was making about 1.5 kilometres per hour. I kept the spud pole down and the line attached to the dolphin as the barge approached and passed us. Even at its extremely slow speed, its propeller was churning a huge suction to overcome the thin slice of water beneath its deeply immersed flat bottom.

Finally, at 1546 we raised the spud pole, slipped our line and started into the narrow channel leading to the tunnels. The first one was quick and easy, almost like training wheels for the real thing.

As we entered Balesmes at 1600, we saw that the towpath had been blocked-off with a locked door and hoardings to keep out anyone but the authorised. We were relieved to see a series of green lights running down the length of the tunnel as far as we could see. Also, we could see no navigation lights of boats coming toward us down the tunnel.

Faintly in the distance we could see the light at the end of the tunnel, nearly five kilometres ahead. The speed limit in the tunnel is 4 kilometres per hour, but Zonder Zorg does not naturally move that slowly. At idle she moves along at somewhere around 5.5 kilometres per hour and I decided to avoid the hassle of shifting in and out of gear to stay at 4, and I simply ran at idle.

The oval of light at the end of the tunnel gradually grew as I watched the distance markers along the tunnel wall. Every hundred metres there is a plaque affixed to the wall giving the distance from the southern entrance in decimetres, so watching them was a welcome distraction from tedium of steering a course centred between the walls. It also helped prevent auto hypnosis.

The tunnel is 8 metres wide and running alongside the channel is a towpath of 1.5 metres. This gives a navigable width of 6.5 metres, so we had a tad above a metre each side for wiggle room. After 45 minutes the oval of light had morphed into an ellipse, the bottom half being the reflection in the water of the upper half.

At 1651 we emerged into daylight again. We had done the transit in 51 minutes, averaging 5.67 kilometres per hour, about 40% over the speed limit. We were relieved to see no flashing blue lights of traffic police as we motored out.

At the end of the summit pound, within two kilometres of the tunnel, the route begins a steep descent, with eight locks of 5.13 to 5.28 metres height in about three kilometres. It is an automatic series, with each lock triggering the next. I calculated that we had enough time remaining before lock closure to run the series, so we set off. At 1840 we were in écluse Percey, the eighth and last of the series, and from there we motored the two kilometre bief to Villegusien-le-Lac. At 1855 we secured to bollards on the bank just short of the next lock. It had been a long day, with 17 locks, 2 tunnels and 1 lift bridge.

Sunday dawned totally clear, and after a leisurely breakfast, at 0956 we slipped from the bollards and continued down the canal and through écluse Villegusien, lock 9 of the 43 that would take us down to the Saône.

The day remained clear and warm as we enjoyed the play of light through the trees and the reflections off the water. Shortly after noon we came to écluse Choilley, number 16 in the series to find it refusing to open for us. I called the VNF office on the radio and received the familiar response: "*Quelquen arrive*", someone will arrive. Someone did eventually arrive, and after a 37 minute wait, we finally were allowed into the lock.

We continued without problem from there, working our way down through another fourteen locks to écluse Pouilly, lock 28 of the 43 to the Saône. At lock 24 we had passed signs indicating we had entered the Burgundy. As we left the Pouilly lock, its traffic lights went out, indicating the system was closed for the day.

We continued along the 2.7 kilometre bief to just above écluse St-Seine, lock 29 where at 1829 we secured the stern to a bollard on a tiny concrete jetty and dropped our spud pole to hold the bow off the rubble bank. We had come another 30.6 kilometres and 21 locks.

At 0958 on Monday morning I raised the spud pole, slipped our line and headed toward the St-Seine lock. It looked to be another fine day, already with a dome of blue having burnt through the top of the morning mists. The automatic eye caught our approach and the lock functioned flawlessly. We continued down the flight of locks, ten of them in eleven kilometres without problem, then at the eleventh lock of the day, the automatic system refused to function.

After a pause to wait for the arrival of the itinerant éclusier from VNF, we continued along. Two more locks malfunctioned and we got to see more of the roving éclusier. In the early afternoon we passed under the impressive stone viaduct at Oisilly. It was built in 1866-67 to carry the railway 4820 metres across the valley of le Vingeannot, the river that the canal follows down from the Plateau de Langres.

Two more locks malfunctioned on our way down to the Saône. On one, the hydraulic ram to one of the downstream doors appeared seized, and it needed to be detached and the door hand cranked. It was getting late in the season, and the locks were obviously begging for some winter maintenance.

After another lift bridge and three more locks, we came to the final lock of the canal. We deposited our telecommande in the slot and once it was digested by the automated system, the lock cycled down and let us out into the kilometre-long bief to the end of the canal.

At 1531 we arrived at the Saône and joined the line behind a rental boat, waiting for our first lock on the river. In nine days we had worked our way through 114 locks, 71 up and another 43 down to cover the 224 kilometre length of the Canal entre Champagne et Bourgogne. Along the entire route, we had seen no rental boats; I knew that was about to dramatically change.

.

Chapter Twenty-Nine

Down the Saône

As we waited for the lock, astern we could see a steady parade of bumper boats zigzagging downstream toward us. We had entered an area of easier navigation and the realm of the rental boats. These get their well-deserved labels of *bangy boats* or *bumper boats* by their manoeuvring antics in and out of locks and moorings. They require no license or qualifications to drive and are amusing to watch, but because of their unpredictability, they are dangerous to be near. Unfortunately, they constitute the vast majority of the pleasure boats in the Burgundy.

Once we had locked through, we headed down the Saône, which varies between 60 and 100 metres wide along this section. Its current was rather gentle; even after all the recent rains, it was only about two kilometres per hour, but it helped us along.

All the mooring space was occupied as we passed Pontailler-sur-Saône and Lamarche-sur-Saône, so we continued down river. Actually, there was plenty of room for ten or more additional boats to moor, but the rentals had spaced themselves out eight to a dozen metres apart, with no gap long enough to squeeze-in Zonder Zorg. Experience told me that getting one or two of them to move and make space is nearly impossible. It was early evening by the time we reached Auxonne and we found the same gap-toothed boat arrangement on the public moorings there, so we went into the commercial marina of Port Royal.

We were a tad tired from the 49.1 kilometres and 17 locks, so we slept-in a while on Tuesday. Then at 1040 we slipped from the marina float and continued downstream through the next lock and arrived at St-Jean-de-Losne at 1300. The public moorings on the Quai National were full, so we motored past.

St-Jean-de-Losne is considered as the hub of the French canal system; from here boaters can head out in six directions. It is on the Saône, which can be followed south to the Rhône and Mediterranean and across the Midi to the Atlantic, or followed north through to the Lorraine and the Moselle into Germany or Belgium, or across to the Champagne and Paris or onward to Belgium. The town is at the junction with the Canal de Bourgogne, which can be followed across to the Seine and down to Paris. Four kilometres upstream of the town is the junction with Canal du Rhône au Rhin, the canal up over the Vosges and into the Alsace and the Rhine. Downstream about 55 kilometres is

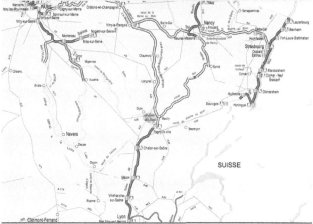

the junction with Canal du Centre, which can be followed westward across to the Loire and then northward to Paris. We had based Lady Jane here for four of our six years a decade ago.

We turned off the river toward the entrance to Canal du Bourgogne and continued to starboard beneath the bridge and into the basin.

At 1315 we secured to a visitor's float at Blanquart. We chose it because both the guide and the advertising in the guide note that it has wifi, and we had not found an Internet connection in nearly two weeks. The signal is very weak and the few times we managed to connect, there was no bandwidth to even load emails.

We stayed for two days, replenishing our larders from the two nearby supermarkets. I also spent some time pumping-out the oil from the bottom of the bilge and cleaning the area. I pumped out one-third of a litre of lubricating oil using our Pela oil change extractor and then set

about trying to find its source. I had suspected the PRM gearbox, since the initial drops of oil were beneath it and there were stains on its bottom. The level on the gearbox dipstick was a bit below the low mark, so I topped it up. After I searched in vain for any sign of where the leak might have been, I thoroughly wiped-down the entire engine and gearbox and laid absorbent pads beneath them to quickly show any new leakage.

Midmorning on Thursday we motored out to the fuel float and took on 300 litres of diesel. Before fuelling, the gauge showed that we had about 80 litres of diesel remaining in the tanks and after fuelling the accuracy of my calculated marks was proven. A winter project now is to add more permanent and more easily readable markings.

After fuelling we continued down the Saône aided along by the current. An hour and a half later we came to our first big lock since Belgium. It is 185 metres long and 12 metres wide and is one of

five similar sized locks that will take us down to the Rhône at Lyon. Four kilometres before the lock I contacted l'éclusier on VHF and announced our arrival in twenty minutes. He said he would have the lock ready for us when we arrived. With drops of 2.5 to 4 metres, they are not high, but they are equipped with intermediate bollards in the walls to make locking easy. We were quickly through.

As we headed downstream we passed many birds along the river banks. There were grey herons watching the water for their next meal and white ibis doing the same. Swans were rooting around in the shallows and sharing the water with thirsty cattle.

Mid-afternoon we left the Saône and motored up the Doubs to look for a mooring for the night in Verdun-sur-les-Doubs, a kilometre upstream. When we arrived at the port we saw it was arranged as a sort of modified Mediterranean moorage, stern ties without the bow anchor or buoy. With our rudder extending a metre beyond the stern, I did not fancy backing in. I thought of nosing in, then thinking of

having nothing but 8 to 12 metre bangy boats to hold our 17 metres and 18 tonnes vertical to the quai and broadside to the river current, I decided to move on.

We headed back out into the Saône and continued downstream. Shortly after passing through a second lock, we saw space on a float in front of a restaurant in Gergy. As we approached, we saw a body hanging on a scaffold above the float. On closer examination it was a sculpture of a curvaceous female pirate climbing the rigging of a non-existent ship, apparently as part of the decoration theme of the restaurant. The restaurant and float are part of a camper

facility, which was closed for the season. At 1549 we secured, having come 43.4 kilometres. We walked the short kilometre up the hill to downtown Gergy for some fresh provisions for dinner.

Later, just as I was turning the cutlets over in the pan for their final three minutes, the flames on the stove went out. Our propane tank, which we had started when we arrived aboard on

3 June, had finally run out. It had lasted us seventeen and a half weeks. I went forward to change bottles, having had the forethought to buy a spare tank while we were in Sillery. I had chosen one of the new transparent fiberglass Butagaz Viseo tanks. These hold only 10 kilograms of fuel, rather than the 13 of the aluminium tanks. Their full weight of 16.5 kilos compared to the 26 of the aluminium, makes them much easier to strap on a bike for an exchange. Being able to see the level of the remaining fuel is a huge plus.

Our regulator didn't fit the new bottle. The sautéed potatoes were done, as were the Brussels sprouts and mushrooms, but the cutlets were raw on one side. I put them on a covered plate and zapped them for a minute in the microwave and plated a very nice dinner.

Late morning on Friday we slipped and continued down the river. Along the way we were over-taken by large commercial barges and we met others heading upriver. Also, there were many bangy boats. These are most readily identified from afar by the ridiculous number of fenders attempting to protect their sides from the results of erratic boat handling. This one, if there is the same arrangement on the other side, has thirty-two fenders, including three across the stern.

At noon we passed the entrance to Canal du Centre, which heads west-ward to the Loire across the bottom of Burgundy's Côte d'Or. We contin-ued down to the city of Chalon-sur-Saône and under its fifteenth century Pont St-Laurent.

At 1222 we secured to the visitor's float in the port de plaisance. We were met by a staff member, whom I told we needed to buy some parts for our gaz system. He told us that a two hour stop is without fee, but for more than that it would be €9 for up to six hours and a ridiculous amount for overnight. I said we'd be less than two hours.

I quickly went ashore with our boat's regulator and searched among the gaz fittings in the hardware section of the huge Carrefour supermarket. I found nothing compatible. I found an Internet connection, surfed to the Butagaz website, found their new Viseo fibreglass tank, looked at the photos and saw that it comes with a special regulator. Apparently the woman in the Intermarché in Sillery had omitted to include ours when I had bought the tank. I walked over to the fuel pump check-out booth in the supermarket parking lot, which is the most common place to exchange gaz bottles, and told the clerk that the Viseo regulator had been forgotten when I had bought a new tank.

With no questions asked, she gave me a regulator. Back onboard, I connected it to our line, clipped it to the bottle and Edi put the kettle on for tea. At 1426 we slipped and continued past the swans and back out into the Saône.

As we approached the commercial port, a 190 metre barge was winding around and was perpendicular to the canal bank. I could see its bow was moving left, but as a courtesy I called it on VHF Ch 10 and asked permission to cross its bows. I received a friendly affirmative.

Within minutes the deeply laden barge had completed its turn and was beginning to overtake us. In a few more minutes it was past us and moving at double our speed down the river.

We met other large barges heading upriver, both deeply laden and empty. In the late afternoon we locked through écluse Ormes, which because of our radio call was ready for us when we arrived.

At 1800 we secured to the wall on mooring rings, just upstream of the Pont de Tournus. Because of the current, we had passed under the bridge, then turned around and stemmed the current back upstream to the quai.

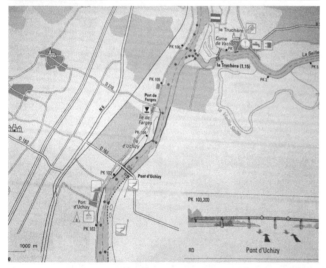

Saturday is market morning in Tournus, so soon after rising we took advantage of it and shopped the stalls for breakfast goods and some fresh items for dinner.

We found some wonderful multigrain bread at a small stall. Avocados, green beans and tomatoes were bought at another. A fishmonger sold us a thick dos de cabillaud and so on.

At 1022 we slipped, turned in the stream and continued downriver. Moored toward the southern end of the city centre was a huge cruise barge of rather graceless design, built more to cram into the 195 by 12 metre locks than it was for looks.

An hour later we were passing the place where in 1984 we had rescued an unfortunate couple from their sailboat. They were headed to the Mediterranean in their new twelve-or-so metre boat on their maiden voyage and they had found a shoal in a bend. They had apparently misinterpreted the channel markers in a narrowing.

It had been April and the river current was strong. When we had arrived on the scene, the boat was heeled over beyond its gunwales by the current and it was hard against the bank of the shoal. We passed a towline and tried to pull the boat off, but the current was far too strong for that. We took their anchor and set it at full rode length out into the channel, but their windlass was not strong enough. Finally, as the boat began flooding, we took them and a few of

their valuables off. At their request, we had landed them on a ramp just upstream at Port d'Uchizy, where they said they would phone for assistance. We told them we would report the incident when we reached Macon. As we had passed back downstream, we had seen the boat awash and rolled onto its side well onto the shoal from the channel.

Back to the present, we continued through Macon and at 1614 we secured to a float in Montmerle-sur-Saône. We had come another 59.9 kilometres and had passed through another lock. About an hour after we had arrived, the Capitain de Port came by to collect €10 for moorage, which included water and electricity, so we filled our tanks and plugged in.

Around midnight there was the noise of heavy machinery outside, and powerful searchlights illuminating us and the river bank. I looked out through our windows to see a solid wall of windows slowly gliding past. A lock-filling cruise barge was gradually coming to a set of dolphins and a landing stage just upstream of us.

In the morning I headed ashore to the market just after busloads of cruisers had been whisked away to their daily tours. It was raining as I walked the short distance to the covered market to see what there was to entice me. I found nothing that I hadn't seen better the previous evening in the supermarket across the street, so I crossed the street.

At 1110 we slipped from the float, turned and continued downstream. We passed under some wonderful old suspension bridges, dating to the first half of the nineteenth century, like this one at Beauregard.

Passerelle de Trévoux is particularly attractive. It crosses the river at what was once the capitol of the independent principality of Dombes, which had broken away from the kingdom of Arles in the eleventh century and had its own parliament until 1762.

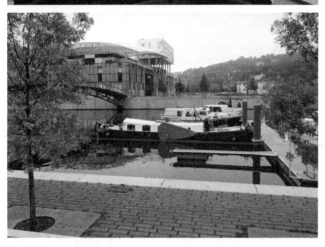

In a steady rain we continued down the Saône and into the suburbs of Lyon, the third largest city in France. We wound our way around the bends and under the bridges in the strengthening current as we neared the confluence with the Rhône. As advised by the guidebook and riverside signs, we closely monitored VHF Channel 18 to listen to other boats reporting their progress up and down the river.

By 1600 the heavy rain had eased to a light sprinkle as we passed under Basilique Nôtre Dame de Fourvière and began passing the downtown core of Lyon. At 1636 we secured to a stub of a finger float in the newly renovated Place Nautique du Confluence at Kilometre 1 of the Saône. The construction was so new that the capitainerie was still not finished, so it was housed temporarily in a utility trailer. I walked up to pay our fees, which were €22 per night, including all services. I asked for the wifi code and was told that, while the wifi worked well throughout the marina, the connection to the Internet did not. The connection varied from very poor none at all. We have continued to see this in France; they appear to have a major problem with connectivity.

Nonetheless, I paid for two days, primarily since we needed a break. In four days we had come 214 kilometres from St-Jean-de-Losne and we were just one kilometre from end of the Saône. Besides, just across the passerelle above Zonder Zorg's stern is a vast new shopping mall anchored by a huge Carrefour. In addition to the break, we needed a shopping fix.

Chapter Thirty

Down the Rhône to Avignon

After a two day break in Lyon, at 1049 on Tuesday the first of October we slipped from the float in Place Nautique du Confluence and re-entered the Saône to run its final kilometre to the Rhône. The architecture along the final kilometre is a cross between creative, experimental and wild. An orange building has as its exterior curtain wall a coarse filigree of metal plates, and in one corner there is a five storey high crater that seems to be the shockwave impact from an asteroid that appears to be just about to collide with it. The architect likely has a more artful explanation of the design

Looking back upstream we saw the shopping centre next to the port, with a Novotel occupying the upper floors of the complex. It and the building next to it would be considered radical designs were it not for the orange creation next along and the others just beyond it

To add to the wild, just along from the orange building is a green one with two huge craters in its riverside façade. Next to it is a four storey black shoebox-shaped structure rather daringly cantilevered way out over the river from a base of ten or twelve metres height.

Next to the shoebox is an adolescent's rendition of a space station. It is difficult to get a scale, but I estimate the building to be 40 metres high. It is still under construction.

From the signs on the riverside hoardings, the building is the new site of the Musée des Confluences. It is sited appropriately, on the narrow point of land between the Saône and the Rhône.

At 1109 we passed the bifurcation buoys and entered the Rhône. The current seemed to be about 5 kilometres per hour as we moved along at 14 with turns for 9. With this much current, when heading downstream there is little margin for error in the bends and through the bridge holes. Fortunately the channel is generally wide and the bends are mostly gentle.

In less than four kilometres we came to our first Rhône lock, écluse Benite. It was ready for us as we approached, I having used the VHF to advise l'éclusier of our arrival from twenty minutes back. L'éclusier took our details over the radio: name of boat, flag, length, beam and draft, number on board, departure port and destination. There are fourteen locks along the river to the Mediterranean and we need to pass through twelve of them.

At 190 metres, they are 5 metres longer than those on the Saône, but at 11.4 metres width, they are 60 centimetres narrower. The big difference; however, comes with their height. Where the Saône locks range from 2.5 to 4 metres, the twelve locks on the Rhône average 11.9 metres in height and they range up to 22.5 metres.

Fortunately, all these locks have floating bollards in their walls, so it is easy to secure the barge for the ride. In fact, these huge locks are easier to negotiate than are the smaller, Freycinet gauge ones of which we had done some 250 during our first six weeks in France. One thing I always do with a floating bollard, once I have a line around it, is put some of my weight on its top to see if it moves easily. If it is stuck or jammed with detritus in its guide rails, it is difficult to scramble along to a working bollard after the water has begun moving in the lock chamber.

We were lowered nine metres very smoothly and effortlessly; it was our easiest lock since the Netherlands. We paused a while after the giant sluice gate had opened before we headed out, giving it the opportunity to drip off much of its water before we passed under it.

Outside and back into the river we were again being swept along with the current. It was a bit slower in this stretch and we moved along at a rate of 12 to 13 kilometres per hour. The river is managed by La Compagnie Nationale du Rhône, La CNR, which was set-up in 1933 with three main objectives: improvement of the navigation conditions; creation of irrigation canals and the installation of a series of hydroelectric power stations to utilise the strong flow of the river. On the riverbanks are vineyards in terraces climbing the steep hillsides.

We were entering the wine growing region of the Northern Rhône. The hillsides above the riverside roads and behind the dotting of little villages are covered in terraced vines wherever the slopes face an adequate portion of the day's sun and are not too steep. On many of the hilltops are ruins.

281

Our next lock, écluse Vaugris was ready for us as we arrived, and again it was a very simple procedure locking down. As we left the lock and moved back out into the current beneath the dam, we were alongside the vineyards of la Côte Rôtie, which translates to the Roasted Hillside. These vineyards are reputed to be among the oldest in France, with wine known to have been grown here at least since Roman times and likely earlier.

Among the more famous vineyards here are Côte Blonde and Côte Brune on the steep hillsides above the village of Ampuis. The story goes that a wealthy vineyard owner gave his two finest plots to his two daughters, one a blond and the other a brunette.

Four kilometres downstream from Ampuis begins a pair of sharp bends in the river at the town of Condrieu. Before the serious works done by the La CNR to reduce the current, this was a major navigational hazard. In the middle of the bends were les Roches de Condrieu, the rocks which brought to grief many boats.

On the steep slopes above the town are the terraced vineyards of Condrieu. The Viognier vine is at home here, making some of the world's finest examples of that variety. The vines are believed to have been brought to the area by the Greeks in the sixth century before Christ.

We passed under le Pont de Condrieu, which bridges the narrows, and we headed around the next sharp bend. Navigation has been made so much easier through this once fearsome place.

In the middle of the bend, above the suburb of la Maladière, are the vineyards of Château Grillet, often erroneously called the smallest Appelation d'Origine Contrôlée in France.

At the next lock, écluse Sablons we had to wait while a lock-filling cruise barge was lifted and headed upstream past us. We have been seeing three or four of these each day on the rivers since we passed downstream from Chalon-sur-Saône. If we see that many in the distance we cover in a day's cruise, there must be several times that many on the Saône-Rhône system. It was into October and the 180-metre floating resorts all seemed to be filled with passengers.

We entered our third lock of the day, and again had a very easy descent. This one has a 12.2 metre drop, which shows how much the engineers had raised the water level through the bends and past les Roches de Condrieu.

Downstream about four kilometres from écluse Sablons, on the riverbank in front of the village of Champagne, is an old and now retired cable ferry pylon. For centuries before the bridges were built, lines were stretched across the river between anchors such as this. A ferry was attached to a pulley on the line and, by using a rudder to angle the side of the ferry to the river, the current pushed the ferry across the river.

In the old pylon at Champagne we saw a staircase of projecting stones winding its way up the tower. These stone steps were used to reach the top of the tower to string and adjust the cable. They reminded us of the steps we had used on our climb of Wayna Picchu from Machu Picchu in 2010 during our three-year sail around the South American coasts.

Three kilometres downstream from the pylon at Champagne is le Pont d'Andance, the oldest suspension bridge still in use in France. It was built in 1827, engineered by Marc Séguin, renowned as a pioneer in wire rope design and fabrication. To test his cable strength theories, he built a small suspension bridge over La Cance, a narrow tributary downstream a few kilometres.

In 1825 he built his first major suspension bridge across the Rhône, joining the towns of Tain l'Hermitage and Tournon. That bridge was partly destroyed in 1944. Le Pont d'Andance was his second bridge across the Rhône and it still carries regular traffic.

Six kilometres further along, at 1800 we secured to float just upstream of Pont St-Vallier. It has no facilities, but it is a solid new pontoon of about 30 metres length in a very quiet area. It is so new that it does not appear in the latest edition of Du Breil Guide Fluvial from 2011. We had come 76.1 kilometres and had passed through three locks.

On Wednesday morning we slipped at 1030, turned in the current and continued down river. Half a dozen kilometres down we passed beneath the ruins of Tour d'Arras and its surrounding vineyards. We were four kilometres from the next lock, écluse Gervans and I radioed l'éclusier to inform her of our arrival in twenty minutes.

She told us there was a commercial following us down the river and that it would arrive a few minutes after us. We were to wait for it to enter and then follow it in. We arrived at the lock and slowed to drift along as we waited for the barge to overtake us.

As we approached the commercial mooring dolphins, we saw people with luggage waiting on the catwalk. They motioned to us and we quickly understood that the barge was going to pause on the dolphins to pick them up. We accelerated and moved further along and out of the way of the barge.

We had dawdled because the waiting float for pleasure craft had a bangy boat plunked exactly in its middle, leaving insufficient room for anyone else us at either end. We moved along to it and asked the skipper to move either forward or astern to allow us to moor. He seemed afraid to move, likely having bounced around and struggled to get there. He folded his arms, thrust out his chin and refused to move his 10 metre boat from the centre of the 25 metre float.

We motored forward and came to rest against the crash barriers, hoping the huge barge didn't need their assistance with his manoeuvring into the lock. There were no horizontal beams to take our fenders, nor was there anything we could use as a temporary bollard. We hung onto the pilings to stabilise Zonder Zorg against the suction and wake of the passing barge. The skipper appeared to have properly appraised the situation and he motored dead slow past us and into the lock chamber.

After the barge had entered, we had the amusement of the bangy boat bouncing around in the chamber trying to moor as two more pleasure boats, which had been following the barge, joined us. One was a Belgique cruiser, the other another bangy, which offered us further entertainment.

After the lock had taken us easily down 11.5 metres, we all paraded out and continued down river. Within five kilometres we swept around a bend and headed east past the town of Tournon on the Right Bank.

Linking Tournon with its neighbour Tain-l'Hermitage across the river, is la Passerelle de Tournon, built in 1825 by Marc Séguin as his first suspension bridge across the Rhône. After its near destruction during World War Two, it was rebuilt and is now used for foot traffic only.

Across the bridge and above the town of Tain-l'Hermitage, on steeply terraced slopes are the famous vineyards of Hermitage. Because of the bend in the river, the vineyards face south for the maximum daily sun. This, added to the fact that slope of the hill is almost perpendicular to the summer sun, the vineyards receive as much direct sunlight during the growing season as is possible here at 45° North.

The Syrah is the grape planted here, and the conditions allow it to show at its finest, making some of the greatest Syrah wines in the world. So renowned were the wines from Hermitage, that the Australians and other New World wine producers called their Syrah grapes Hermitage. After nearly two centuries of name abuse, trade laws have now finally stopped that practice.

As we swept around the next bend, which is just over two kilometres along, and again headed south, we looked back at hill of Hermitage. It is such a small area for such a famous wine.

Another dozen kilometres brought us to écluse Bourg-lès-Valence. The same four pleasure boats paraded in astern the commercial, with us last. We quickly secured and watched the remainder of the bouncing acts. After another easy 11.7 metre drop we all paraded out and downriver for five kilometres through Valence.

In the centre of Valence, under Pont Frédérique Mistral, a huge barge was sunk pointed downstream against the wall on the Left Bank. The bridge is at the end of a sweeping 45° bend to starboard, and it appears the skipper misjudged the current and was swept to port and ended up on the wrong side of the channel beacon and the bridge pier it marked.

There was a work scow with a pollution boom moored alongside on spud poles. It appeared to have been a very recent accident. As we motored in the erratic wakes of the bangy boats, we hoped that the skipper of the sunken barge hadn't been trying to avoid a meandering rental boat.

On the southern side of the city the two bangy boats dropped-out of the parade and entered le Port de Plaisance de Valence-Épervière. The remainder of the parade continued down river, along the way meeting another huge river cruise ship.

Another hour and a dozen kilometres brought us to écluse Beauchastel, where we and the Belgian boat followed Camaël into the lock. After an 11.82 metre drop we headed out and continued down the river following Camaël, while the Belgian boat stopped on the waiting float at the downstream side of the lock.

A short distance along we met a large unladen barge putting up a very large wake as it headed upstream against the current. A few minutes later we passed under Pont de la Voulte and looked at the mooring that is indicated in the guide. I did not like the openness of the wall and the way the wake of the barges ahead and astern of us rolled along it. It looked like a rough place to stop, so we continued along.

We met another floating resort as we made our way along the eighteen kilometres to the next lock. It was a long bief, and ahead we could see Camaël slowly pulling away from us, until even in the long strait sections we could no longer see her. We knew that we had fallen too far behind her to have her wait for us at the next lock.

At écluse Logis Neuf we had the chamber all to ourselves, which really gave the space an added feeling of size. The drop of 11.7 metres went quickly and without hitch, and we motored out to run the three kilometres to our prime mooring spot for the day at Cruas. The little port is designed for small boats and has a tricky crosscurrent entrance past shoals, but it has space for three boats of fifteen metres length, which we might squeeze onto. As we arrived, I could see all the larger spaces were occupied, so we continued along.

Just downstream is la Centrale Nucléaire de Cruas, which looked benign in the early dusk. We continued along in the fading light looking for a place to stop for the night. With the current running at five kilometres per hour, and with the uncharted waters beyond the channel markers, we could not simply approach a bank and moor.

Five kilometres downstream, as we approached the eleven kilometre derivation leading to the next lock, I looked at the possibility of mooring at the canoe haul-out in the short arm above the Barrage de Rochemaure. However, prudence and poor chart symbols in the guide made me continue on past.

The sun set, but I was not concerned about navigating in the dark. We had our Navionics charts on my iPad and with its built-in GPS, we had an accurate plot of our position and track. The track was following perfectly our path along the derivation, which leads eleven kilometres to écluse Chateauneuf. I switched on our navigation lights and we continued along confidently.

In the fading light we met a lock-filling barge convoy on its way up river. We crept along the final half kilometre to the lock, using primarily the iPad to help pick out shapes around us. Most of the locks we had been in thus far on the Rhône have had a similar layout in their upstream approaches, so we knew what to look for. We found the pleasure boat float, but plunked exactly in its centre was a boat of about nine metres length. There was nobody aboard, and not wanting the liability of moving the boat along so we could share the float with it, at 1958, after adjusting our fenders, we rafted onto it and shut down for the day. We had come 88.5 kilometres and had passed through another four locks.

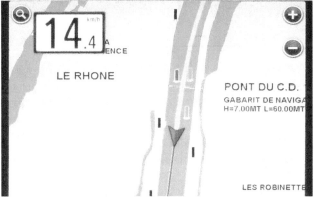

We were awakened shortly after 0800 on Thursday morning by an irate man who was demanding to know why we had rafted onto his boat. He could not understand that he was hogging the entire float and leaving no space for others. I told him we would be ready to move in about fifteen minutes and he fumed.

As we slipped at 0815, we saw that the small boat was a CNR company launch, which as a commercial boat is not allowed to use the pleasure boat floats. Besides, La CNR has its own boat moorage on the other side of the lock entrance. The lock had been ready and waiting for the launch, so we motored directly into the chamber from our raft and secured to a bollard near the front to allow plenty of room for other boats astern. The CNR launch chose to a bollard at the rear of the lock.

After a 16.5 metre drop, we waited for the gate to lift and the barriers to open. When the light turned green, we slowly motored out, as is required by regulations. The CNR boat was impatiently nipping at our stern all the way out. Once we were clear of the lock entrance, it sped past us, cut across our bows and went across to the pleasure boat float. We continued downstream.

We were a little over a kilometre further downstream when the launch came speeding down toward us and cut across our stern. As the skipper saw me aiming my camera, he put his hand up in an apparent attempt to block the shot. It appears we had discovered a CNR employee with a company boat and an attitude problem.

A short while later we watched as two huge cruise barges danced around each other changing mooring places. These cruise ships operate on fixed schedules, and with the rapid increase in their numbers in recent years, it appears that available moorage facilities have not followed apace. This juggling looked like the rearrangement of a raft to prepare for departure.

Soon we entered le Défilé de Donzère, the Donzere Gorge, a deep and narrow corridor through limestone hills. Because of the force of the water through the defile, the early boaters called it Robinet de Donzère, the Donzere Faucet and it was one of the most respected stretches of water along the old Rhone. It is crossed by Pont de Robinet, a wonderful old suspension bridge that was built to a Marc Seguin design in 1847.

Within a kilometre downstream we came to a more modern structure, la barrage du garde at the beginning of the 28 kilometre derivation canal that takes traffic around a series of the former navigational hazards, including Le passage de Pradelle, Le Banc Rouge, La Désirade and Pont Saint-Esprit. These hazards were finally bypassed in 1952 with the opening of écluse Bollène, which with its 22.5 metre drop is the highest lock in Europe. Bollène even tamed the waters in Le Robinet.

A short distance into the derivation there are crossover signs on the canal banks, indicating that boats must cross to the other side of the channel. This is to assist large barges in manoeuvring through a pair of 80° bends. As I crossed over to the port side of the channel, I was hoping there wasn't a bangy boat coming upstream unaware of the meaning of the signs. Fortunately, the only traffic was a large pushed convoy, and we met green to green as required.

When I contacted l'éclusier at Bollène, I was told there was an up-bound commercial in the lock and a down-bound waiting for it. We could join the commercial in the lock. As we approached the lock we met the up-bound Cartoon, and saw ahead of us Bonova, the barge that we would follow into the chamber. The timing was such that we had to slow only at the last minute to allow Bonova to settle into position. We quickly came to a bollard and were ready for a 22.5 metre descent.

As the walls grew around us we marvelled at the engineering that had gone into taming the Rhône and making it much more safely navigable. I thought of boats that, before the taming of the river, had to run through a series of rapids, rocks and bends as the river dropped thirty metres in thirty kilometres. We reached bottom, the gate opened and Bonova headed out. We were left in the cavernous space by ourselves, which added to its sensation of size.

As we motored out, the enormity of the lock continued to impress us. The hydroelectric generating complex at Bollène is huge, particularly when viewed from the downstream side. La CNR manages thirty-three power stations, which together generate 16 billion Kilowatt hours of electricity, about four percent of the French consumption.

We passed under the ramparts of medieval fortified castles at Montfaucon and Roquemaure. Along the way we met a steady stream of commercial barges heading upstream.

Some graciously posed for us beneath the ruins of Château de l'Hers. Château de l'Hers dates to the twelfth century and sits on a small rocky outcrop on the Left Bank of the river. It once regulated navigation on the Rhône, but today the commercial barges and pleasure boats pass by giving it only admiring looks, rather than taxes and tolls.

Beyond Château de l'Hers on a narrow ridge a few kilometres east of the river sit the ruins of Châteauneuf-du-Pape, the Pope's New Castle. The château was built as a residence in the fourteenth century by Pope Jean XXII, the second pope of Avignon. The vineyards that he had planted around the château are today the centre of the famous Châteauneuf-du-Pape wine growing area. The intensity of the wines come from the fist-sized stones throughout the coarse gravel and clay of the ridge, which hold

the sun's heat well into the evening and continue to warm the vines into the night.

Edi created a wonderful platter of open-face sandwiches for lunch and we ate along the way.

Eight kilometres downstream we came to écluse d'Avignon. At 9.5 height metres it is a very large lock, but rather diminished in our eyes after having so recently come through the one at Bollène.

We were quickly down and passing through the suburbs of Avignon. At Villeneuve-lès-Avignon we passed beneath the ruins of Tour Philippe-le-Bel, which was once part of the western access control to the twelfth century Pont Saint-Bénezet, the famous Pont d'Avignon.

We continued down to the junction of the two branches of the Rhône, turned in the current and headed up the eastern branch into the centre of Avignon. On the quai, just short of the Palais des Papes was a line of moored cruise barges.

Ahead of us was Pont Saint-Bénezet and on our starboard bow were Nôtre-Dame des Doms and Palais des Papes. The Palais, which was built in the fourteenth century as the papal residence, is the largest Gothic palace in Europe.

We continued around the end of the remains of le Pont d'Avignon and half a kilometre upstream of it, at 1605 we secured to mooring rings on Quai de la Ligne. We had come another 75.5 kilometres and had descended through four more locks.

In three days we had come just over 240 kilometres from Lyon through swiftly flowing current and busy commercial traffic. We needed a break.

Chapter Thirty-One

Exploring Avignon

Late on Friday morning, after a sleep-in and a leisurely breakfast, we walked through the wall at Port de la Ligne and into the old city. We wound our way through a maze of streets, many just barely wide enough for small cars and others too narrow even for that. We were headed for Les Halles, the covered market.

Inside we found a huge selection of stalls, offering the full range of fresh items that would be found in a huge supermarket. There are fruit and vegetable stalls, one of these with a great selection of specialty mushrooms: chanterelles, cèpes, trompettes, morilles, pied de mouton, girolles and so on. There are several butchers and charcuteries and there is a line of fishmongers along the side of the hall. There is a stall with a vast selection of fresh and dried herbs, nuts, legumes, dried fruit, candied fruit, salts and peppers. Of course there are the cheese stands and the bakers and the wine vendors. We chose some fish and some produce, including a selection of wild mushrooms for the evening's dinner.

After we had dropped-off our purchases onboard Zonder Zorg, we headed back through the old city to le Palais des Papes, the fourteenth century seat of the Catholic Church.

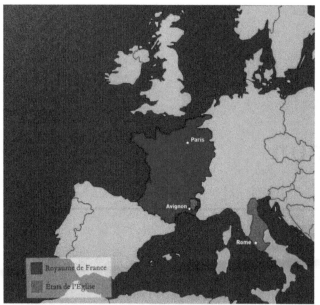

In the thirteenth century, the papal court was itinerant, rarely staying in Rome and residing in several cities in its states. At the beginning of the fourteenth century, bitter disagreements between King Philip the Fair of France and Pope Boniface VIII culminated in 1303 with an attack against the Pope in his palace at Anagni. In 1305 the archbishop of Bordeaux was elected pope as Clément V. He remained in France, primarily to adjudicate the fate of the Knights Templar, whom the King of France, being in deep financial debt to them, had capriciously accused of heresy. In 1309, still with no fixed address, the Pope stayed in Avignon and in Comtat Venaissin. He systematically promoted French bishops to cardinal, and by the time of his death in 1314, he had created a small French majority in the Sacred College, ending the Italian domination. The next six popes elected were consequently French and they chose Avignon as their permanent seat and built the Palais des Papes.

Avignon was the property of Charles II of Anjou, Count of Provence, King of Naples and Sicily and therefore vassal of the Pope, to whom he offered support. Avignon was also next to Comtat Venaissin, a Church possession since the late thirteenth century. This was a peaceful and stable territory at the confluence of the Rhône and Durance rivers and close to the Kingdom of France, to which it was linked by Pont Saint-Bénezet, the famous Pont d'Avignon. Lying at the crossroads of major land and water routes, Avignon was ideally located in the heart of Christian Europe.

For two years after the death of Pope Clément V, the College deliberated on choosing the next pope. Finally, after intense negotiations, in 1316 they chose the seventy-two year old Jean XXII, intending him as a transitional pope in view of his advanced age. He lived for another eighteen years and transformed Avignon into the capitol of Christendom. During his reign, the Curia increased from 200 to 500 and an additional 1000 lay officials were working in its support.

We paid our admission and entered the huge complex of buildings. The construction of the palace had been the largest building project in the Christian world in the fourteenth century. Work was begun in 1335 under Pope Benoît XII, and by the time of his death in 1342, the Old Palace had been built.

Huge additions, called the New Palace, were begun under his successor, Clément VI. Construction paused for a four year break because of the Great Plague of 1348. It was then mostly completed in 1352. It was then and is still now the largest Gothic palace in Europe.

The construction accounted for approximately one quarter of the annual expenditure of the Pontifical treasury and involved monthly salaries for a workforce of 850. Locally quarried limestone was used and its purchase and transport accounted for sixty-five percent of the cost. Reinforcing the vast complex are ten tons of iron embedded in the masonry in an innovative technique. In the complex are 15,000 square metres of floor space.

Inside the first courtyard, le Cours d'Honneur, we saw continuing excavation of the grounds, with seemingly the same temporary scaffolding I had seen on a previous visit in the mid-80s. Either there is some serious archeological work being done, or this thirty year dig is simply an example of the speed of French public works.

We strolled around the huge courtyard getting a feeling of the scale of the place and marvelling at how well

preserved much of it is after two-thirds of a millennium. It has survived not only time, but also the ravages of political and religious wars, revolution and the confiscation and destruction of Church properties.

The architecture is rather bland and slab-sided, typical of the Gothic style, but there are some very pleasing features. We headed inside, following the clearly laid-out tour route and on our handheld audio guides listening to commentary about what we were seeing.

In the lower kitchen we saw across the entire end of the large room a fireplace, in which food was cooked. Set in one end of it was a much smaller domed oven, reminiscent of the ones we had seen in the sixteenth century Monestario Santa Catalina in Arequipa, Peru on our wanderings there.

On the second floor of la Tour du Pape, the Pope's Tower, is le Trésor Bas, the Lower Treasury. There we saw stones in the floor lifted to reveal hidden vaults. These vaults, one in each corner of the room, were discovered as recently as the mid-1980s. According to documents, the vaults had held Church archives transferred from Rome to Avignon by Pope Benoît XII. Also concealed below the stones in ironclad chests with multiple locks, would have been gold and silverware and sacks of gold and silver coins. Only the Pope, the Chamberlain and the Treasurer could enter the heavily guarded treasury.

On display nearby were examples of the silver coins that had been struck by eight of the Avignon popes: Clément V, Jean XXII, Clément VI, Innocent VI, Urbain V, Grégoire XI, Clément VII and Benoît XIII. Only one of the Avignon popes did not strike any coins; Benoît XII considered that his predecessor had issued a more than sufficient quantity.

The coins on display were either gros d'argent or demi-gros d'argent, which translate to bigs of silver and half bigs of silver. The gros d'argent pictured here had been issued by Clément VI.

In le Trésor Haut, the Upper Treasury, recent restoration work has uncovered original painted ceilings and upper walls from the fourteenth century. The high room apparently had dropped ceilings installed over the centuries, likely to make the room easier to heat.

The tour led out into the gardens behind la Tour du Pape. In these gardens the popes had a menagerie of exotic birds and animals and plantations of imported trees. The animals and trees are gone, but from the space we could look up at the Pope's Tower in the Old Palace, completed by 1342.

Along to the right is the New Palace, which was completed in 1352. We walked along the base of its walls and went back inside to continue the tour.

We climbed a long circular staircase. This was part of the new kitchen tower built in 1342 by Clément VI, which featured several stories for storing and preserving provisions.

At the top of the tower is the Upper Kitchen. This has an eighteen metre high pyramidal chimney above its centre. Beneath the chimney had been the hearth surrounded by a large rectangular structure with several levels of spits, on which large quantities of food could be simultaneously cooked. Dishes were then taken directly along to the Grand Tinel for final preparation in the Dressoir. The Grand Tinel was the papal banqueting hall. Its interior had been decorated with frescoes in 1345 by Matteo Giovannetti. The Pope held sumptuous receptions there, sitting separately along the south wall on a cathedra that was bedecked with multicoloured fabrics and surmounted by a canopy. He dined off priceless crockery, gold and silverware and looked out over the guests seated at tables around the walls.

In 1413 the Grand Tinel was gutted by fire and for a long time it was known as the burnt room. Its roofs and terraces were rebuilt between 1414 to 1419. From the Grand Tinel we made our way up onto roof edge walk, from where we looked across Cour Benoît XII to the bell tower on Palais Vieux.

From another portion of the roof edge walks we had a fine view across the courtyard of the tower of the Old Palace.

Back inside we looked at displays of some of the original hand-painted floor tiles. These had been found during excavations and restorations both here in the Palais des Papes and also at Châteauneuf-du-Pape, the Pope's new castle about fifteen kilometres north of Avignon.

We came to a room that had been richly decorated with frescoes depicting outdoor scenes. Most impressive to me is the wall with a hunting scene featuring a falconer with his two dogs.

Another impressive frescoed wall depicts a scene of people using various nets and lines to catch fish in a pool. The colours are still vibrant after more than six hundred and fifty years.

The colours on the painted ceiling are also bright, so I suspect that it and the walls must have been protected behind covers of some sort as the palace went through a number of uses after Benoît XIII, the last Avignon pope left the palace in 1403.

Photography is forbidden in the room, likely to prevent accidental flash use damaging the frescoes. The room is guarded, so I had gone to the next room and set-up my camera to shoot inconspicuously in front of the guards. Back in the room, I managed to get a few acceptable shots.

We entered the fifty-two metre long Grand Chapel, which at the time of our visit was spoiled by an exhibition of horribly garish modern attempts at art. Even with the distraction, we were able to appreciate the scale and grandeur of the vast room.

From there we went up and out onto another set of roof edge walks. This one, above la Cour d'Honneur offered a great view across the courtyard to la Tour du Pape. We went back inside and down to the huge Tribunal de la Rota, which is at ground level, beneath the Grand Chapel. It was here that Tribunal of the Apostolic Causes met to deliberate. Their judgments were without appeal. On the walls and vaults above where the Tribunal sat, Matteo Giovanetti in the 1350s had painted a series of frescoes depicting the Last Judgment.

There are still vestiges of frescoes on the walls and in one vault there remains a bright fresco depicting a series of saints.

From the 1403, when the past pope left, until the French Revolution, legates and then vice-legates governed Avignon and the Comtat Venaissin on behalf of the Pope. They altered and redecorated apartments in the palace, destroying certain elements. In 1791 the people of Avignon expelled the Pope's last representative in Avignon and Comtat Venaissin became a part of France. Palais des Papes remained vacant for almost two decades, and then from 1810 to 1906 it served as a military barracks, a horse stable and a prison.

As we walked back to Zonder Zorg for a very belated lunch, we were amazed that the palace has survived as well as it has.

After our lunch, in the late afternoon we walked along the riverfront to Pont Saint Bénezet, le Pont d'Avignon of history, fable and song. The fable goes that bridge was the inspiration of a young shepherd named Bénezet who came from Burzet, a hamlet in Ardeche. In 1177 he arrived

in Avignon as an adolescent, claiming he had been told by God to build a bridge across the Rhône. The young teen was a leader of men; his words stirred crowds and he encouraged the people of the town to build the bridge. He organised fund raising and travelled broadly collecting alms and donations.

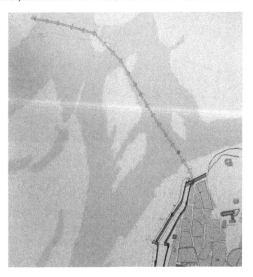

The bridge, which was completed in 1185, was an extraordinary undertaking for the time. It spanned 915 metres with twenty-two arches and in doing so, it crossed the fastest and most powerful river in France. The course of the Rhône at Avignon has been constantly changing, with bars and islands appearing and disappearing. The spring thaws bring catastrophic flooding. Huge bridge-destroying trees are washed downriver in spates and after storms.

All that remains of the bridge today is four arches with a chapel in the pillar between the second and third arches. It has a long history of political and environmental destructions and subsequent rebuilding. In 1226 the King of France in a bitter dispute destroyed all but two arches of the bridge, from the French end all the way to the Bénezet Chapel, all that he claimed belonged to him. It was likely quickly rebuilt, since the records show that people of Avignon were officially rebuked by the Pope in 1237 for having done the work despite Royal prohibitions. In the fourteenth century, the Avignon Popes strongly supported the maintenance of the bridge. Finally, at the end of the seventeenth century, the repeated reconstruction of the bridge was abandoned.

We put our passes from Palais des Papes into the turnstile slot and were allowed in. A bridge led across from the Avignon ramparts to the toll tower.

The construction of the ramparts of Avignon had been begun by Pope Innocent VI in 1355 to strengthen defences and they remain well preserved today. Over four kilometres around, they enclose an area that made Avignon at the time the second largest town after Paris. At the toll gate, fees were collected for use of the bridge, the amount depending on whether it was foot traffic, horse and rider, hand cart, wagon or herd of livestock. Our fees had already been collected, so we continued through the toll tower and across the drawbridge onto the bridge. At the third pillar we descended a flight of stone steps on its side and arrived at the chapel.

Across from the simple stone chapel is a balcony on top of the downstream buttress of the pillar. These triangular buttresses had been built on both the upstream and downstream sides of the pillar cribbings to break the river's current. Research has determined that the method of bridge construction was to prepare a stone casing on a large wooden raft, float it into position and begin overloading the casing with stones until it sank. Under the weight of the masonry, the wood remained on the bottom.

Looking back along the bridge to Avignon, we see Palais des Papes just inside the ramparts beyond the end of the bridge. The popes there ran through the process of canonising the teenaged Bénezet for his miraculous bridge.

In 1965, during restoration work, Compagnie Nationale du Rhône discovered wooden planks and beams beneath the four remaining cribbings. Their thickness varied from 20 centi-

metres to 1 metre 10 and the wood was carbon-dated between 290 and 530 AD. Across the river at the Villeneuve end of the bridge, the cribbings include fir beams dating between the ninth and eleventh centuries. There were bridges here before the young Bénezet came to town and the fable of Saint Bénezet has a few more holes in it.

As we strolled back in along the bridge, looking upstream at Zonder Zorg, we pondered what we had seen and learned during this very full day in Avignon.

Chapter Thirty-two

Onward to the Midi

At 1008 on Saturday, 5 October we slipped our lines from the rings on the wall of Quai de la Ligne, turned in the current and headed back down river. The skies were clearing from an overnight shower as we glided past les Roches du Dom and headed around the stub of Pont St-Bénezet.

Le Pont d'Avignon posed gracefully for us in the midmorning sun as we approached. It then took on an ominous appearance as we passed round its end and fell under the eye of le Palais des Papes and ghosts of popes past. They probably sensed our thoughts on their impoverishing the guilt-ridden people so that they and their vast court could live in sumptuous splendour, gaiety and decadence.

Just downstream we began passing the long line of cruise barges that lined the quais. As we passed we wondered whether the German couple had found their barge before it had left. They had stopped us to ask where the boats were. We told them to head out through the gate and follow the river downstream. They asked what is downstream. When we told them it was the direction the water is flowing, they wanted to know how to tell. We gave up. As we passed the barges, the current swept us along, adding about six kilometres per hour to our speed.

We rejoined the main branch of the Rhône and continued downstream, having no problem determining which way it was. We passed under the impressive Pont TGV Méditerranée, the twin bridges that carry the high speed train to and from the Mediterranean coast.

Below the mouth of the Durance we met an upbound laden barge pushing a huge wall of water as it bucked the current, which was sweeping us along at above 16 kilometres per hour. I had the engine turning at 1400 rpm to give us nine kilometres per hour through the water so we could maintain proper steerage.

Because of our radio call, l'éclusier had prepared the lock for us by the time we arrived at écluse Vallabrègues. This was our last Rhône lock, and as with all the previous ones, the ride down was easy.

After a descent of 11.7 metres we emerged and waved a farewell to l'éclusier. Except for the rude and aggressive CNR launch operator at écluse Châteauneuf, all the staff at the locks had been very professional, polite and friendly.

Almost immediately out of the lock, we began seeing Château de Beaucaire ahead on the Right Bank, and across the river from it in Tarascon, Château du Roi René.

Château du Roi René is a superb fifteenth century structure commenced in 1400 and completed in 1435. It was built by Duke Louis II d'Anjou to replace the fort built earlier by Duke Charles I d'Anjou on the site of an ancient Roman castrum.

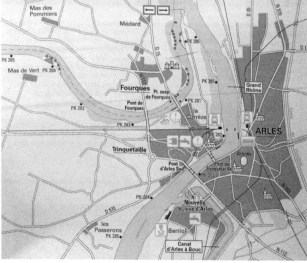

In the early afternoon a southerly wind picked-up, and blowing upstream against the swift current, it kicked-up a short, steep chop. We butted into the chop, making tall spouts of spray. Further downstream we passed a dredge and barge. It was working at a necessarily ongoing operation along the channels of the river. The changing currents constantly move banks and shoals and even add new ones.

We met what appeared to be a low-budget cruise barge. It was one of the earlier ones from a couple or more decades ago, from a less popular time before huge and garish had become the fashion.

As we approached the junction with le Petit Rhône, we were still making about nine kilometres per hour through the water and the current was moving us along over the bottom at above sixteen. In a current like this it is important to be aware of drift in the river bends. As we neared the junction I made sure we were properly lined-up well in advance.

There was no problem; we easily made it into the small branch of the river. We had left the domaine of La CNR and had again entered waterways run by VNF. As we left the main stream of the Rhône and entered le Petit Rhône, our speed began dropping. Within a few hundred metres we were down to about ten kilometres per hour and into considerably easier steering. Our intention was to stop on a quai that is marked on the charts in both the FluviaCarte and the Guide Fluvial. It is shown just downstream of le Pont suspendu de Fourques in the Arles suburb of la Corrèze.

For us it was an ideal place to stop overnight and visit Arles, a town which dates to Greek settlements in the sixth century BC. I slowed as we approached, in preparation for manoeuvring alongside the quai and as we passed under the bridge, the only thing that looked like a moorage was a two-metre-long stage on two pilings with another piling three metres further along. The current from the bridge abutments was swirling in eddies in front of the tiny landing. We decided to visit Arles another time.

We continued down le Petit Rhône, paying close attention to the channel beacons. Some marked clearly visible rocks or patches of crud, others marked shoals made obvious only by the dead trees lodged on them, but most marked unseen shallows.

Instead of our thoughts of pausing for lunch on the quai, Edi brought up a platter of open-face sandwiches for me to enjoy at the tiller, while she ate hers in her lounge chair on the fore-deck.

Mid-afternoon we came to the junction of le Petit Rhône and le Canal du Rhône à Sète. We took the righthand fork and left the river for the canal.

Barely a hundred metres down the canal we came to écluse St-Gilles, which was ready for us because of my earlier radio contact. The lock is large, 80 metres long by 12 metres wide, but the guides give no height. When I asked l'éclusier, he told me it was a drop of 44 centimetres. This is a long way from the 22.5 metre drop we had at Bolène.

Immediately out of the lock we began seeing derelict boats hauled-out onto the canal banks. It appears that the VNF have been doing some clean-up of sunken, derelict and abandoned boats.

As we made our way along the edge of the Camargue, the vast delta formed over the ages by the various river courses at mouth of the Rhône, we began seeing chevaux camarguais, the famous Camargue horses. Today, most of the wild horses in the delta have been captured, and in the area bordering the 85,000 hectare parc naturel régional de Camargue, breeding Camargue horses has become an important industry.

As we continued along the canal, we saw so many derelict boats and barges that we thought we were going through a boat graveyard. We could not believe that so many had been allowed to deteriorate to such a degree without intervention of the authorities. The canals seemed lined with derelicts, both afloat, sunk and appearing ready to sink. The sheen of oil on the water marked the recent sinkings; around the long sunk, the slicks had mostly dissipated. These derelicts are a hazard to both the environment and navigation.

We continued along the canal, taking in the late afternoon the branch leading into Aigues-Mortes. At 1800 we came to the spud pole and a pounded pin on a grassy bank about 700 metres short of the centre of town. We had passed a supermarket next to the canal and we had stopped about a hundred metres beyond it, in the first available place. From Avignon, we had come 83.7 kilometres and had passed through two locks. While Edi straightened-up Zonder Zorg, I walked back to the supermarket for fresh provisions for dinner.

At 1000 on Sunday morning we raised the spud pole, recovered our pin and continued along the canal into Aigues-Mortes. The town had been built by King Louis IX in the thirteenth century to give France a Mediterranean port. In the main square is a statue of the King, later canonised as Saint Louis, setting out on the Crusades.

Dominating the town is tour de Constance. Its six metre thick walls were once used to imprison religious and political dissidents. It now houses the tourist office. Around the corner to starboard is a low railway bridge, with a clearance of only a metre beneath it. It is normally open, unless there is a train scheduled, when it closes ten minutes before the scheduled time. We hoped none was due.

We were in luck, and we passed through the open bridge and headed up the branch leading back to le Canal du Rhône à Sète. Since it was Sunday, a common change-over day for the bangy boats, we met a mix of wildly zigzagging novices having just picked-up their boats and more stable skippers with a week of practice.

After about nine kilometres we began a section of the canal that runs along a narrow sandbar with the Mediterranean on one side and the étangs on the other. The étangs here are slightly salty ponds isolated from the sea by bars and low dunes generally rimmed with salt marshes. Pink flamingos are a common sight here, as are, unfortunately, derelict campers, huts and hovels.

We continued to pass derelict boats moored along the canal banks. Amazingly, the boat pictured here had not been abandoned; we saw people living aboard. To us they appeared to have fallen a little behind on their maintenance and they have an rather strange sense of tidiness.

As we passed the rental base in Carnon, we were relieved to see so many bangy boats moored. The marina appeared full and they were rafted two deep along tha canal, meaning that only a small portion of their fleet was out jeopardising other boat traffic.

Five kilometres further along, at 1250 we secured with spud pole and a stern line to a bollard in le halte nautique les Quatre Canaux. After we had secured, we pedalled the kilometre

into Palavas-les-Flots, a Mediterranean beach resort, where we found it a dead post-season community that likely would not have enthused us even in high season, so we pedalled back to relax aboard Zonder Zorg.

Shortly after 1000 on Monday we raised the spud pole, slipped and continued along the canal. A short distance along, we passed a long line of outboard skiffs, mostly 5 to 6 metres in length, which were moored in front of small houses on the thin bank between canal and étang. This was the étang fishing fleet.

Not far beyond the tiny community, the bank separating the canal from the étang narrowed to a metre or less, and in some places had disappeared altogether.

Over its top we could see nets hung on pilings and frames, and here and there, a fisherman in a skiff working trapped fish out of the nets. Herons and gulls dot the banks using a more basic method of fishing.

Across the canal, on the Mediterranean side is a towpath. This is well used by hikers and cyclists, including some that pause to try their luck at catching any fish that had escaped the nets and birds.

We passed another tiny fishing community, a few houses on a fattening of the bank. These communities are on narrow islands of canal bank and their only method of access is by boat. All the way along the canal we had seen the banks have been eroding and gradually disappearing.

The speed limit is 8 km/h and this is prominently posted frequently along the canal. The local fishermen, whose homes and livelihoods depend on the banks, speed by in their runabouts at 20, 25 and more km/h, putting up huge wakes. They all seem to be in a great rush to get to and from their nets before their banks erode.

At 1200 we secured to bollards on the quai just downstream of the lift bridge in Frontignan. The mechanism of the lift bridge is in deteriorated condition, so it is opened only twice a day, ten minutes each at 0830 and at 1600. We had decided to arrive early, do some provisioning and top off our water tanks. Under a hinged cover in the quai, I found the water tap shown in the guides. It was dusty and covered in cobwebs, and when I put a wrench to the seized faucet, nothing came out.

We walked across the bridge and along to the moorings on its upstream side. There we found modern electrical and water pylons along the quay. A minute before 1600, nearly all the boats on both sides of the bridge had engines running in anticipation of the opening. Not far behind schedule, the bridge opened and the boats swapped sides. We secured to the quai and found the modern pylons not working. The water and electrical outlets worked on tokens, and the token machine was out of order. A phone call to the Capitainerie in the commercial port brought a man who switched on the pylons, bypassing the need for tokens, and we all enjoyed free water and shore power.

Frontignan is famous for its sweet white wine: Muscat de Frontignan, a vin doux naturel made from the Muscat Blanc à Petits Grains in a technique that dates to the thirteenth century.

At 1000 on Tuesday, 8 October we slipped our lines and continued up canal. The sky was completely clear, there was not a breath of wind and the temperature was already approaching 25°. On our way out of Frontignan, we motored slowly past several more boats threatening to sink. One wooden one was so nail sick that I was expecting planks to fall off as we slowly passed.

314

Very shortly we came to the end of le Canal du Rhône à Sète and entered le Bassin des Eaux Blanches, a lobe of l'Étang de Thau. Thau is a shallow lake of brackish water about seventeen kilometres long. Filling nearly half its area are oyster farms. These are on the northern side of the lake and a buoyed navigational channel runs across their southern edge. As well, there are navigational channels through the oyster farms to the three towns on the north shore: Bouzigues, Mèze and Marseillan.

I headed on a course to take us between the cardinal buoys at the narrows. Once we had put them in our stern, I steered on a lump of land that was just rising over the horizon. From the chartlet in the Guide Fluvial and the chart on the Navionics app on my iPad, I determined this was the hill behind Pointe des Onglous, which is at the entrance to le Canal du Midi. We cut across the lake, ignoring the dogleg of the buoyed channel and saving a bit of time exposed to the building wind.

About an hour and three-quarters into the crossing our course brought us to the channel along the edge of the oyster farms. The annual harvest from these is around 20,000 tonnes, about ten percent of total annual consumption of oysters in France.

Shortly after reaching the buoyed channel, we passed the entrance to the fishing port of Marsiellan across from a channel out to the Mediterranean. With its access from the sea, Marsiellan is a popular yachting port and its mooring fees reflect this. The fees listed in the guide made our decision not to stop an easy one.

As we approached the lighthouse on the breakwater at Point des Onglous, the steep wind chop gradually abated and then we found lee.

At 1225 we left the waters of Étang de Thau and immediately began motoring past a long line of derelict boats. Many of these appeared to have been abandoned and many were sunk at their moorings.

The majority of the sunken vessels were sailboats, mostly small sloops under eight metres in length. With the proximity to the sailing waters of Étang de Thau and the Mediterranean, these boats were likely seeking the free and apparently unregulated moorage of the canal. This is the beginning of the Canal du Midi.

None of the sinkings appeared to have been recent occurrences. We were amazed that they remained untouched by the VNF, with seemingly no concern for the pollution of the water nor of the view. Most had been stripped of all their rig and gear, but one still had a cradled mast.

Not all the derelict, abandoned and sunk craft were sailboats. As we moved beyond the easy reach of the sea and the étang, the sailboats had left space for power boats to be abandoned. Among the derelicts were also cheap and graceless liveaboard conversions that are prime candidates for future dereliction.

Four and a half kilometres along the canal from Étang de Thau, we came to the first lock. It was closed for lunch until 1330, so we paused for a bite to eat ourselves, hoping that as we continued beyond the lock we would see a more pristine Canal du Midi.

Chapter Thirty-Three

The Canal du Midi

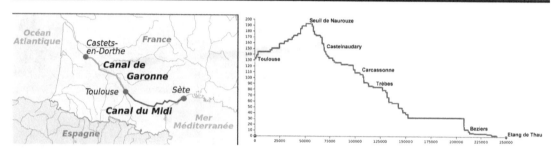

The Canal du Midi connects the Étang de Thau on the Mediterranean to Toulouse. In doing this, it rises 189.4 metres through 74 locks over a distance of 183.5 kilometres to a 5 kilometre summit pound. From there it descends 57.18 metres through 17 locks in 51.6 kilometres to Toulouse, where it connects to the Canal de Garonne, which leads past Bordeaux to the Atlantic.

Construction of the canal was begun in 1666 and it was completed in 1681. The inspiration and driving force behind its construction was Pierre-Paul Riquet. At the time it was widely praised as one of the great achievements of the seventeenth century. Initially it was named Canal royal en Languedoc, but with the Revolution in 1789 it was renamed Canal du Midi. In 1996 it was

named as a UNESCO World Heritage Site, described as: "one of the most remarkable feats of civil engineering in modern times".

While Edi prepared a quick lunch for us, I walked up to the lock to look at the bollard arrangement and to plan our passage through it. Most of the locks on the canal have curved sided chambers, though a few have been rebuilt with parallel sides. The original dimensions of the chambers are 29.2 metres long with a maximum width of 11 metres at the centres. The entrances past the doors are 5.8 metres wide, the design principal being to allow two 20-metre barges of 5 metres width to easily fit into the lock simultaneously. The average height change of the locks is 2.1 metres.

Shortly after 1330, madame l'éclusier finished her lunch break and pushed the appropriate buttons on her portable box to open the gates and allow us in. The rise of this lock is only 1.51 metres, so looping the bollards was easy, though with a broken mid-point bollard not replaced, we were rather strung-out with our lines. We made it through our first curved lock unscathed and motored out with a better idea of what to expect.

Very soon out of the lock we passed through a section of canal where all the plane trees had been cut down. In 2006 the first outbreaks of coloured canker were detected. This disease is caused by a microscopic fungus, now believed to have come to France during World War Two in the wood of US Army ammunition boxes. The number of infected trees reach 83 in 2008 and 153 in 2009.

Selective tree-felling campaigns have been conducted to try to stop the spread but with no effect. In addition there is no effective treatment against the disease. By 2011, a total of 1,338 diseased trees had been identified in 211 separate areas.

There is now a fifteen-year program to remove all 42,000 plane trees along the Canal du Midi and replace them with other species. Costs will run to a quarter billion Euros. They had been planted in the 1830s to help stabilize the canal banks and the plane had been selected because its roots grow in dense tangles and don't mind wet feet.

As we approached écluse de Garde de Prades we finally came to a section of canal with seemingly healthy trees; at least they were all standing and all still had leaves. The écluse de garde serves as a flood gate and is normally open unless l'Hérault is in flood. We passed through and out onto the river, which for a short stretch serves as as the navigational channel. After about a kilometre we turned off into an arm leading to l'écluse ronde d'Agde.

This lock was built in 1680 with a perfectly round chamber to allow barges to enter and choose to be lifted and go straight ahead into the continuation of the Canal du Midi, or to be lowered and turn left into the river Hérault below the weir. It was a wonderful piece of seventeenth century ingenuity and engineering. Unfortunately, its beauty and symmetry were destroyed in 1984 when it was modified to allow Freycinet gauge grain barges to use it.

About a kilometre and a half after the lock we came to one of the more famous bridges along the canal. Le Pont des Trois Yeux, the Bridge with Three Eyes. This is one of the 126 stone bridges that had been built across the canal, many of which are still in use today. The bridge gracefully spans a wider section of the canal, providing one arch for navigation, one for the towpath and one to allow better water flow.

Four kilometres further along we came to a complex structure, l'ouvrages du Libron, the works of Libron. This unique structure allows the canal to traverse the Libron River. Where the canal and river intersect, the Libron is at sea-level and the Canal du Midi is very slightly above, so a traditional aqueduct was not an option.

The problem was further exacerbated by the Libron's propensity to flash flood up to twenty times a year. The problem was originally solved by the building of a pontoon aqueduct known as the Libron Raft which utilised a flush-decked barge to fill and protect the canal channel in times of flooding, allowing the river and its debris to flow over the barge.

Because the raft blocked the canal, navigation was closed until the flooding subsided and the barge could be removed. To replace the barge, in 1855 the works were built to better allow the two streams to coexist. The structure was designed to allow the river to be directed to enable a canal boat to safely pass, while limiting the mud and debris being deposited into the canal by the flooding river.

The works allows the river path nearest an approaching boat to be stopped for sufficient time to allow the boat to cross through that area and rest for a time in the "protected area" between the two paths. The river path behind the boat is then returned to flow and the path in front of the boat is halted, allowing the boat to cross this second path without interference. This *new* solution, which is barely over a hundred fifty years old, elegantly solves the problem.

After we had uneventfully passed through écluse Portiragnes and under another graceful stone bridge, at 1640 we secured to bollards on a quai just downstream from the lock in Ville-neuve-lès-Béziers. We had come 49.9 kilometres and had passed through three locks since leaving Frontignan mid-morning.

321

At 0855 on Wednesday morning we slipped and headed up toward the next lock a hundred metres along. There was no delay in passing through it, nor with the next one a kilometre further up canal. Four kilometres further along we pulled over and secured to bollards to wait for three boats to be cycled down in écluse Béziers.

While we were waiting we were entertained by the manoeuvring antics of a bangy boat attempting to moor on the canal bank astern of us.

We watched as it somehow got perpendicular to the Left Bank. With no wind and with negligible current in the canal, we could not figure out how the skipper managed to do it. Then, as if to reverse the error, the boat somehow managed to do a 180° turn and ended up with its bow on the Right Bank.

The boat was sufficiently far away from us that we thought it safe to divert our attention and watch the parade of boats coming out of the lock. They were all rentals, and offered a more immediate threat. By the time they were safely past us, the bangy astern had finally managed to secure parallel to the bank.

Écluse Béziers is a modern parallel-sided lock built to replace the original curved-sided double lock. Because it replaces two locks, it is double height. At 4.24 metres, it would be nearly impossible for an up-bound boat to loop the bollards at the top, so the chamber has mooring rods set in indents in the walls. The looped mooring lines slide up these as the water rises.

The next lock, écluse Orb is only 375 metres further along and appears to replace an original multiple set of locks that brought traffic back up from the River Orb. It has parallel sides, is 6.19 metres high and has the same system of mooring rods. Locking through both of these was easy.

From écluse Orb we motored across le pont-canal de Béziers. This superb bridge was built in 1856 to finally end the need for barges to descend to the Orb, cross it and lock back up the other side. It is 198 metres long supported on arches of seventeen metre span and it is considered to be by far the most attractive of the nineteenth century stone canal bridges.

A kilometre further along we came to the traffic light controlling the entrance to l'échelle de Fonserannes. We were delighted that it was green as we approached; passage is tightly scheduled. Up-bound traffic this time of year is between 1000 and 1215 and then 1600 and 1815 and the passage takes 30 to 45 minutes. L'écluse de Fonserannes, which is also called les neuf écluses, is a staircase lock that now consists of seven interconnected ovoid lock chambers. There were originally two additional locks that connected the bottom of the staircase to the river, but since the 1856 opening of the aqueduct over the river, these are no longer used and the entrance to the system is now in the side of the seventh chamber.

I dropped Edi off on the quai at the entrance and then continued into the chamber, while she climbed the stone steps to the top of the first lock to take the lines. We settled into place and the gates closed behind us.

323

The sluices were opened to flood our chamber from the next one up the ladder. When the next chamber above us had drained into our chamber, our upstream doors were opened and the sluices in the next set of doors were opened to continue filling the two chambers. The initial surge of water was a bit frightening to see coming down the chamber toward our bows like a tidal bore. However, Zonder Zorg was well-positioned and the brunt of the wall of water passed down our port side making it rather easy tending the bow line to keep us against the wall.

We had the stern line led aft to a bollard as a spring and I was motoring forward on it with the tiller lashed to keep the stern in. I monitored this from the bow and had to tie-off the bow line and go aft only once or twice per lock to adjust the stern line or the tiller.

Once the water level in our chamber had reached the proper depth above the gate cill, l'éclusier motioned us to move forward into the next chamber. As we waited for the next buttons to be pressed by l'éclusier, we had the entertainment of watching the bangy boat bounce its way in and bumble alongside the other wall. Finally the gates were closed astern of us and the process repeated.

Les neuf écluses, was built to take barges 21.5 metres up and down the steep embankment above the valley of the Orb. It was one of the major engineering accomplishments on the canal. Pierre-Paul Riquet had planned and engineered and lobbied for thirty years before King Louis XIV approved the construction of the canal in 1666. Among his planning was a visit to the Canal de Briare, where he studied les Septs Écluses, the flight of seven locks there. The Briare had been completed in 1642 to connect the Loire to the Seine, its 57 kilometre length and 36 locks taking barge traffic up 41 metres from the Loire Valley and then down 85 metres on the other side toward the Seine. It was the first summit level canal in Europe and Riquet gathered ideas from it for the Canal du Midi.

The building of a canal to link the Atlantic to the Mediterranean was an old idea with many projects being previously devised. Leaders such as Augustus, Nero, Charlemagne, François I, Charles IX and Henry IV had dreamed of it for its political and economic benefits. François I even brought Leonardo da Vinci to France in 1516 and commissioned him to survey a route for the section from Toulouse to Carcassonne.

We quickly progressed up the staircase of locks and a little over twenty-five minutes after we had entered the first chamber, we were looking into the final one. Then a couple of minutes later we were in it and rising to its top. L'échelle de Fonserannes is one of the three most popular tourist destinations in the Midi, along with Pont de Gard and Carcassonne and we were closely watched all the way up. Too closely! The tourists obliviously interfered with our attempts to get mooring lines onto bollards and they very dangerously and obviously ignorantly stood in line bights.

The view back down the flight is superb, and it is made all the more so by having just spent half an hour getting to know it intimately.

At 1211, thirty-one minutes after we had entered the first chamber, we exited the final one. L'éclusier could take an extra four minutes for lunch. From the top of l'échelle de Fonserannes begins the longest bief of the canal. For 54.2 kilometres there are no locks as the canal winds around the sides of low hills and ridges at 33 metres above sea level.

We motored out and soon came upon a logging scene, as crews worked at removing infected plane trees from the canal banks. At 1303 we came to the spud pole and a pin pounded in the bank just upstream of Pont de Colombiers. We had initially stopped for lunch, but found the place so pleasant and restful that we decided to stop for the day. We had come 14.2 kilometres and up 11 locks.

Astern of us was a bangy boat flying a huge Canadian flag. We chatted for a while with the two couples from Vancouver who were aboard; they were near the end of a two week rental. As we chatted, we watched a prime candidate for the ugliest boat design award motor past.

After a very peaceful night, at 1055 on Thursday we raised the spud pole, retrieved our mooring pin and continued up the canal. Within a kilometre and a half we came to the entrance to le tunnel de Malpas, which was the the first canal tunnel built in Europe. As we approached, we acknowledged the canalside signage by blowing our air horn to signal our presence to any oncoming traffic. We were hoping that any oncoming bangy boat skippers were aware of the meaning of our signal and knew to blow their own horn.

We received no response from our toot, so we continued into the one-way tunnel. The interior is lined with a vault of cut stone and there is a narrow towpath along the Left Bank side. About midway through, the cut stone vaulting gives way to a coarse spongelike surface, which some sources call sprayed concrete and others eroded limestone. It looks like a combination of the two.

Just beyond the exit were two bangy boats waiting for us to complete the passage. They had obviously heard our horn signal and stopped. Because they were down-bound vessels, they had priority, but this fact and the requirement to blow a sound signal seemed not to have been part of their few minutes of pre-rental instruction.

At 1252 we secured to bollards on the bank about twenty metres short of the new bridge in Capestang. We had come only 11.8 kilometres and it was still early, but this looked to be a very pleasant place, so we decided to pause for a while.

Beside us was the wifi antenna we had read about and there were also shore power and water outlets. A German man came from the boat moored 50 metres astern of us to take our lines, but we were secured by the time he arrived. We asked if he had the wifi code and he told us the system had never worked since he arrived two years previously. Rather than paying €18 per day for moorage with no wifi, we moved back down the canal to the first available free spot. There was no water or electricity there, but our battery was fully charged and we still had over 500 litres in our water tanks.

Nor were there any bollards, so we secured to a pair of mooring pins we pounded into the bank.

Moored ahead of us was Vrouwe Antje, a 1902 Dutch klipper with a youngish British couple, John and Jane and their 3-year-old daughter, Sophie. We spoke with them and learned they have been cruising and sailing their antique klipper through Europe since 2006. John is a pilot for British Airways, and he commutes from wherever the barge is to London to fly his monthly allotted schedule. Because he usually has this compressed into a single run of days, this arrangement leaves him with about two-thirds of every month to enjoy the barge.

The old town of Capestang lies on the slopes below the canal and from the banks beside us we had a fine view across the roofs to the massive bulk of thirteenth century Collegiate church of St Etienne.

The church, intended to be the largest in the region, was begun on the remains of an eleventh century church, but never completed. The nave and transept were built, but funding ran out before a choir, apse or ambulatory were started, thus the strange shape.

We spent a restful few days in Capestang. Among our daily walks was one down the hill for breakfast croissants or a multigrain baguette from the artisan baker in the square across from the church. There is a large Intermarché at the edge of town, less than half a kilometre from our mooring, so we had plenty of fresh provisions.

Sunday morning is market day in Capestang. The set-up is in the square by the church and a visit to the stalls provided us with some more fresh produce and some local cheese, and on the way back, bread from the baker.

Shortly after 1100 on Sunday we recovered our mooring pins and motored the hundred metres or so to a set of bollards under the bridge and connected our hose to the water outlet there. With our water tanks again full, we slipped just after noon and continued up the canal. The banks were lined with moored boats, a few itinerants, but mostly boats and barges buttoned-up for the winter.

We shortly arrived at le Pont de Capestang, the infamous wrecker of boat and barge superstructures. While not the lowest bridge on the Canal du Midi, its somewhat irregular arch has low shoulders that have rearranged many barge wheelhouses.

As we neared, we could see the obvious chipped masonry where centuries of barges have inadvertently enlarged the opening. We saw no need to lower our mast and we watched as it easily cleared the centre of the arch. The chipping away of the edges of the masonry was even more advanced on the upstream side of the bridge.

For some reason there is a fable spread through the barging community that le Pont de Capestang is the lowest bridge on the Canal du Midi. It is common for purchasers of barges or designers of wheelhouses to base their decisions on the dimensions and profile of this bridge. Unfortunately for them, there are lower and more restrictive bridges further along the canal.

We followed the canal as it wound a crooked route along the sidehill. Several times we were able to look back at Capestang across a stream gully or from the end of a rib. The windings of the canal are such that the first nine kilometres of canal out of Capestang took us only 4.4 kilometres away from the town.

It was very pleasant motoring along all by ourselves under cloudless skies with the temperature in the mid-twenties. It was absolutely calm with our motion generating a gentle cooling breeze. Edi sat in her lounge chair on the foredeck reading or knitting and from time to time giving me an advanced look for oncoming boats around a bend or through a bridge hole.

Because we are traveling upstream, we need to give way to down-bound traffic at narrow spots. At this bridge we just made it before a large down-bound barge, which was not visible until we were within a few metres of, and committed to the hole.

We crossed several aqueducts across streams that flow down the slopes. These were a necessary part of the complex hydraulic works that were done over three centuries ago to build the canal.

At 1736 we approached the bank and dropped the spud pole just upstream of le Pont de Roubia. We had come 33.7 kilometres and we decided to stop for the day. To secure our stern, we used a pin pounded into the bank, ignoring the steel eyes that had been bolted to the tops of the infected plane tree stumps. Although mooring to trees is forbidden, it is very commonly done with no obvious policing.

Here the village of Roubia seems to encourage it by adding mooring eyes to the stumps, so that those who were accustomed to using the trees for moorage can still easily stop. It is now believed that the rapid spread of the canker stain has been exacerbated by mooring lines around infected trees picking up spores and moving them along the canal to healthy trees. We were stunned to see the practice being so openly encouraged.

Monday was again a clear, warm morning when at 1038 we raised the spud pole, recovered our mooring pin and continued along the canal. As we motored, we continued to see derelict and sunken boats.

In less than two kilometres we arrived at the lock that marks the end of the 54.2 kilometre pound and we were joined in the chamber by a British sailor in his 7-metre boat. Over the next five kilometres we passed through double locks at both Pechlaurier and Ognon and then a single lock at Homps.

At 1240 we secured to rings on the quai just upstream of the first bridge in Homps. We had come another 9.3 kilometres and had passed through 6 locks. The place looked pleasant, so we decided to call it a day. There is a small supermarket about half a kilometre through town and out on its edge on the through road. A short distance along from our moorage were the rental bases for Le Boat and Les Canalous. We were relieved to see that most of their rental boats were moored in their ports, thus greatly reducing the number of them that would be out jeopardizing safe navigation.

At 1103 on Tuesday morning we slipped and continued up the canal. Two and a half kilometres along we arrived at the next lock, écluse Jouarres, where there was a down-bound boat locking through, so we moored on the wooden waiting quai, trusting our lines to some wobbly posts sitting in the canal bank and passing as bollards.

From the top of the lock we continued along through placid water and under another graceful stone bridge.

Across an aqueduct, around a bend and across another aqueduct, we came to Épanchoire d'Argentdouble, which was built in 1693 to allow excess water to spill out of the canal. The towpath crosses the spillway on a series of stone arches. At 1222 we arrived in La Redort to find a very tranquil spot, so after only 6.4 kilometres and one lock, we stopped for the day.

On the way to the Intermarché is the mouth of a tunnel across the street from Château La Redorte. The château was built at the beginning of the 18th century and in the 1840s it was acquired by Count Mathieu de la Redorte, who restored it and enlarged its gardens and their enclosing walls. He had been Ambassador of France to the Court of Madrid and was later active in politics. He was on the wrong side during Louis-Napoléon's coup in 1851, and he was banished to his château and forbidden to set foot in his gardens. To deal with this and to comply to the letter of the law, if not its spirit, he had a tunnel built allowing him to leave the château without setting foot in its gardens.

We spent a relaxing two days in La Redorte, where in the Tourist Office we finally found a working wifi with a working connection to the Internet.

The widespread lack of connectivity in France today was in large measure caused by the country continuing to use the Minitel far beyond its usefulness. France in the 1980s and 90s was well in advance of the rest of the world with computer connectivity. With the Minitel, users could make train reservations, do online purchases, search the telephone directory, check stock prices, have a mail box and chat in ways that are now possible with the Internet. At the end of the century, forty-two percent of the population was connected by Minitel. It was not expandable; it was dead-end technology. The French held on. The service was finally retired in the middle of 2012.

Shortly past 1100 on Thursday we slipped our lines and continued up the canal. We passed a work site where the stumps and roots of cut-down plane trees were being grubbed out of the canal bank. Three kilometres along we came to écluse Puichéric, a double lock in which we could see three boats just beginning their descent. We pulled over to wait.

While waiting we walked up to the locks to watch the action. Edi stopped to talk with a British couple in a narrow boat.

When the locks were clear, we locked up and headed along the three kilometres to the next lock, écluse Aiguille, also a double one. It was closed for lunch, so we secured to the bank astern a bangy boat overflowing with a group of German men. There is a water tap symbol shown in the guides, and I had placed our bows next to it to make it easy to fill our tanks.

L'écluslei returned from lunch a comfortable time after the scheduled 1330 reopening and we headed into the lock to work our way up. A kilometre and a half further along we came to écluse St-Martin, another double one, where we waited for down-bound boats. Between the time we had first seen the Germans and the time we entered the lock, we had seen them down four rounds of steins of beer and glasses of wine. Possibly they thought the swerving from their alcohol impairment would counter their swerving from inept steering.

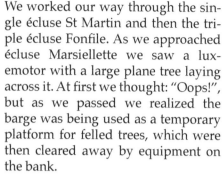

We worked our way through the single écluse St Martin and then the triple écluse Fonfile. As we approached écluse Marsiellette we saw a luxemotor with a large plane tree laying across it. At first we thought: "Oops!", but as we passed we realized the barge was being used as a temporary platform for felled trees, which were then cleared away by equipment on the bank.

We locked through the single écluse Marseillette and at the end of the tree-clearing operation we passed a very pretty skûtsje of about 12 metres length with a full sailing rig. Just beyond it at 1640 we dropped the spud pole and secured a stern line to a post in the recently denuded bank. We had come another 13.7 kilometres and had passed through ten more locks. Beside us was the road leading up into the village to the bakery.

On Friday morning We motored along the next bief past dead and dying plane trees. Then we came to a major logging operation, where an assortment of heavy equipment was on the bank cleaning-up from a very recent tree-cutting spree. Pulling up the rear was a man with a huge vacuum cleaner sucking up the wood chips and blowing them into a truck. We wondered whether the dust drifting away from the operation contained the spores of the canker stain fungus. A pair of white swans serenely surveyed their rapidly changing home.

We arrived at écluse Trèbes, a the triple lock shortly after a boat had started down the series. We knew that we would have a long wait, so we wandered up to watch the operation of the lock. Even though the locks were cycling the boats down, it was valuable to watch the workings of the multiple chambers from a totally different and detached viewpoint. We gained additional dimensions to our understanding of the system and again saw how dramatically easier it is to cycle down than it is up.

We were finally allowed in and worked our way to the top to exit past an upscale restaurant installed in the former mill house. Upstream of Trèbes we passed under another graceful old stone bridge.

Then shortly thereafter, we spotted a short concrete quay with stout bollards in a quiet rural setting. Even though we had come just 11 kilometres and had worked our way through only a triple lock, we quickly decided to stop for the day.

Up the hill from us were vineyards of the Minervois and across the canal and down the hill were planted grapes for Corbières. I checked the Minervois vines for overlooked clusters, but because they had been mechanically harvested, there was not a single remaining grape.

At 1013 on Saturday we slipped our lines and continued up canal. We moved along the two kilometres to the next lock at the canal speed limit of 8 kilometres per hour. Very soon we had a boat closing quickly from astern. I checked the GPS speedometer on my iPad to confirm I wasn't dawdling along and it confirmed we were making a point or two either side of 8. The boat continued to close rapidly at what must have been its hull speed, about double the speed limit. I mentioned the canal speed limit and bank damage to the skipper as he joined us in the next lock. He said he had no way of knowing the speed of the boat, so he just opened it up, thinking the rental company would have a speed governor on the engine.

With the bangy boat more slowly in our wake, over the next five kilometres we passed through two more single locks, then a double and another single. Then we came around a bend and through the gaps between the trees, we caught our first glimpses of La Cité, the medieval fortified city.

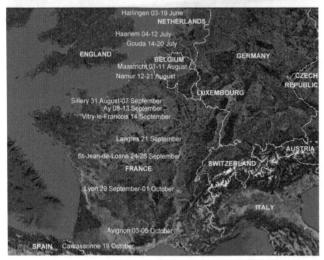

At 1245 on 19 October, four months to the day after we had left Harlingen, we arrived in le Port de Carcassonne and secured to the quai just below Pont de Marengo. Zonder Zorg had arrived in her winter home. We had come 2072 kilometres and had worked our way through 332 locks as we navigated 75 different canals, rivers and lakes and crossed three countries.

Chapter Thirty-Four

Wrapping-Up

Just forward of our tempotary moorage was Pont de Marengo, the bridge that leads from the rail station to the la Ville Basse, the main shopping district. When we were in Southern France in mid-February on our way back to Friesland from Spain, we had stopped in Carcassonne to investigate possibilities for winter moorage and we were delighted to have secured a place for Zonder Zorg here.

Our assigned moorage spot for the winter was through the bridge, up the adjacent lock and across the basin, but with a hotel barge in our spot until Monday noon, we remained on the quai below the bridge and lock. Edi hauled out the sewing machine and began assembling waterproof nylon covers to protect Zonder Zorg's lier, coo coo, fries and roer. Meanwhile, I went off into the city to scout-out the supermarkets and other shops and services.

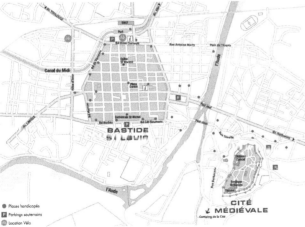

The Port is located on the north edge of Bastide St Louis or Ville Basse, which is referred to as the New Town. New because it dates only to 1247, when Louis IX founded it across the River Aude from La Cité, the fortified citadel on the hill. The first settlement in the area dates back about 5500 years, but it wasn't until about 2100 years ago that the Romans fortified the hilltop. In 462 they formally ceded the province of Septimania to the Visigoth King Theodoric II, who had

337

captured Carcassonne in 453. Through the following thousand years and more, Carcassonne was the target of attack by seemingly anyone with any aspiration to power in Western Europe. Among these were the Goths, the Franks, the Saracens, the Burgundians, the Moors, the Albigensians, and the Cathars.

Carcassonne is home to about 50,000 people. It is about mid-way along the Canal du Midi from the Mediterranean to Toulouse, and is within a few kilometre from being the most southerly part of the French canal system. A major portion of its businesses is tourism, centered around La Cité and the Canal du Midi, both of which are UNESCO World Heritage Sites. Wine growing is also a major focus here, it being in the heart of the Languedoc-Roussillon wine region, with many famous areas, such as Minervois, Corbières and Limoux nearby.

While we waited for our moorage to be freed, we were entertained by bangy boats going past us and under the rail bridge. There was no wind or current, they were not sailboats, but they appeared to be tacking down the canal. The first one made it through unscathed. But the second one decided to take an adventurous route.

It crashed into the bridge abutment, bounced off and reversed to bang its port quarter on the other abutment. With lots of engine noise and only two more bounces, it made it through the bridge hole, only to crash into the bank.

It clawed itself off the bank and crossed the canal astern of an up-bound boat and was last seen crashing into boats moored on the opposite bank.

I have from time to time through this book vented my thoughts on rental boats and the habit of the rental companies allowing people with absolutely no boating experience, knowledge or skills to rent boats up to fifteen metres in length. The companies get away with this by giving a short briefing on the operation, handling and navigation of the boat. In a few minutes, a complete novice becomes a very dangerous captain. When I rented my first boat in France in 1984,

I was shown how to start and stop the engine, how to shift to forward and astern, how to use the galley stove and how to flush the heads. With electric heads these days, the training briefing has likely been pared down.

On a more professional level, we watched as Lady Sue approached Pont de Marengo, which at 3.33 metres is the lowest bridge on the entire Canal du Midi. They gracefully glided through and into the lock with a couple of centimetres to spare above their pilothouse roof.

Écluse Carcassonne is immediately beyond the bridge and lifts the canal 3.32 metres to the basin of the port. We went through late on Monday afternoon, after the skipper of the French hotel barge had finally been convinced that he was more than five hours beyond his promised departure from our contracted mooring. Our assigned spot was across the basin from the lock on the first piece of canal bank beyond. The finger floats in the basin are meant for boats of less than fifteen metres.

After a rather grey and cool few days, Tuesday was splendidly clear and warm, with the temperature passing through 25° before midday. While Edi continued sewing covers, I worked at little jobs to prepare Zonder Zorg for wrapping-up for the winter.

We began planning our trip back to Vancouver by looking at stand-by seats on Air Canada flights from Barcelona, Paris and London, which had one, two and six daily departures respectively. We chose to fly through London, primarily because it had the most departures, but also because it was the only one with a non-stop flight to Vancouver.

Getting to London began with catching a train, so I walked up to the train station, which is directly beside the port, to look at schedules. Of the six departures listed on the board, three were late: 15 minutes, 25 minutes and 1 hour 15 minutes. We needed to leave lots of slop time in planning the first leg of the trip.

From the Capitain de Port I got the contact information for a young man who had two years previously set-up his own boat service and repair business after years doing similar work for a boat rental company. He agreed to come at 1400 on Thursday to winterize Zonder Zorg. I could have done it myself; however, clauses in most insurance policies mention denying freezing damage claims unless preventive work had been done by a licensed professional.

We spent much of Thursday morning buying train tickets to Toulouse, checking bus schedules from the Toulouse train station to the airport, booking seats to London Gatwick and printing the boarding passes, booking a taxi from Gatwick to Heathrow, reserving a room at the Ibis Heathrow and printing boarding passes from London to Vancouver. It was more complex returning to Vancouver from Carcassonne than it had been two years previously from Patagonia. In our spare time, we cleaned and packed.

Loic arrived in French fashion, half an hour late for his appointment. Two hours and €155 later, we had completed winterizing the engine, generator, furnace, hot water system, dish washer, washing machine, sinks, shower, toilet and waste sumps. Edi and I then did a final clean-up, locked-up, lashed the cover over the doors and said farewell to Zonder Zorg for a season.

We had only carry-on luggage, so the walk to the train station was pleasant. The train was on time, the bus connection was easy, as was the Easy Jet to Gatwick. Our taxi was waiting for us and the hotel reservation had worked. Friday morning the shuttle bus efficiently got us to Terminal 3, our seats were confirmed on the flight to Vancouver and it departed on time, a SkyTrain was waiting as we reached the platform in Vancouver and it wasn't raining for the block and a half walk from the station to our loft.

We had arrived in Carcassonne thirteen and a half months after we had taken possession of our skûtsje. During that time, Zonder Zorg had spent eight months in the shipyard preparing for and undergoing her refit and we had spent just over five months boating. In our boating, we travelled a total of 2370 kilometres on 102 waterways and passed through 342 locks and three countries. Among our observations are the following:

In the Netherlands:

- Pleasure boating is very common among the Dutch; there are about 150,000 cruising boats in the small nation.

- The waterways and their infrastructure are set-up to make pleasure boaters feel welcome.

- The arrangements in locks and in the waiting areas before them, appear to have been designed by people who understand the needs of the boater.

- The environment in and around the canals is pristine and well cared for.

- During our eleven weeks on the Dutch canals, we saw no broken facilities.

In France:

- Inland pleasure boating is much less common among the locals. Of the 20,000 private pleasure boats actively cruising inland in France, over fifty percent are foreign.

- The large locks on the Saône and Rhône function efficiently, and although they are very busy with huge commercial barges, they are welcoming to pleasure boaters.

- On the other hand, the Freycinet gauge locks are in poor condition. During our eight weeks on the French canals, we found over two dozen with disfunctional mechanisms that required us to wait for a roving éclusier to override or repair.

- Many bollards are missing in the locks, often in critical positions. Safety fencing has been installed to protect the public and to make it extremely difficult for lock users. In many places, sluices dump a heavy cross-current immediately before the entrance to the lock chamber.

- The entire system appears to have been designed and maintained by people with little or no knowledge of and even less concern for the needs of the pleasure boater.

- In many places, the canal banks are lined with derelict, abandoned and sunken boats and barges and except in one place, little appears to be happening to address this pollution.

- Seventy-five percent of the annual thirty to thirty-five thousand rental boat contracts are to foreigners, who need no boating qualifications or experience.

- The canal banks are being badly eroded by speeding boats, mostly rental boats, which have no speed limiters.

- Convenient and inexpensive connectivity to the Internet is sparse, but this situation is slowly improving now that the Minitel has finally been abandoned.

With all these negatives, barging in France is still a wonderful experience. If only a few of these shortcomings can be addressed and remedied, then barging on the small French canals can return to the sublime experiences I remember from previous decades. With the continued growth in pleasure boating in France, perhaps some of the revenue generated will be directed toward repairing and improving the infrastructure and making it more boater friendly. That way we'll likely dawdle a bit longer in France before heading back up to the superb boating in the Netherlands.

We have barely scratched the surface of the vast web of canals that criss-cross Europe.

CPSIA information can be obtained at www.ICGtesting.com
Printed in the USA
LVOW02s0230020114

367639LV00001B/1/P